Poverty and Social Exclusion in India

Issues and Challenges

Edited by

Aparajita Chattopadhyay

RAWAT PUBLICATIONS

Jaipur • New Delhi • Bangalore • Hyderabad • Guwahati

ISBN 978-81-316-0561-5

Published by
Prem Rawat for **Rawat Publications**
Satyam Apts, Sector 3, Jawahar Nagar, Jaipur 302 004 (India)
Phone: 0141 265 1748 / 7006 Fax: 0141 265 1748
E-mail: info@rawatbooks.com
Website: www.rawatbooks.com

New Delhi Office
4858/24, Ansari Road, Daryaganj, New Delhi 110 002
Phone: 011 2326 3290

Also at *Bangalore, Hyderabad* and *Guwahati*

Typeset by Rawat Computers, Jaipur
Printed at Nice Printing Press, New Delhi

Poverty and Social Exclusion in India

Dedicated to my

Ma

Contents

Foreword

Widespread decolonization of countries and decline in mortality are the two major achievements that the world civilization witnessed in the last century. Both ushered hope of immense increase in human welfare. The path towards progress was, however, not smooth. The decline in mortality, for example, was quite abrupt for many of the developing countries, including India, and did not accompany requisite socio-economic development. As a result, they experienced rapid population growth that tended to hamper development.

With globalization initiated towards the end of the last century, many countries, including India, witnessed unprecedented growth in their per capita GDP, particularly in the present century. This has again given rise to the fresh hope of realizing a better future for the human society, to chart a path of enormous development. There is, however, a lingering doubt about the extent of concentration of the ongoing development. Is every section of the society receiving the fruits of the development or is some getting excluded from it? It is well known that poor are particularly vulnerable towards the exclusion. It is also true that, in a male-dominated society such as India, the development might adversely affect women. To achieve an inclusive growth, there is a need to understand the different facets of the development and how it influences the diverse sections of population. This will facilitate keeping poor in proper focus while planning for development. This work is an attempt in this direction. I hope the book will be used by all those interested in understanding the nuances of the wider process of development.

T.K. Roy
Ex-Director, IIPS, Mumbai

Contributors

Abdul Shaban, Associate Professor, Centre for Development Studies, Tata Institute of Social Sciences, Mumbai.

Agnihotram V. Ramanakumar, Division of Cancer Epidemiology, Department of Oncology, McGill University, Montreal (Canada).

Ambati Nageswara Rao, Research Scholar, Tata Institute of Social Science, Mumbai.

Aparajita Chattopadhyay, Assistant Professor, Department of Development Studies, International Institute for Population Sciences, Mumbai.

Arup Ray, Research Associate, Anthropological Survey of India, Kolkata.

Ashis Sarkar, Professor and Head, Department of Geography, Presidency University, Calcutta.

Bikramaditya Kumar Choudhary, Assistant Professor, Banaras Hindu University, Varanasi.

Chandrima Chakraborty, Research Associate, Higli Inspiration, Kolkata.

D.K. Adak, Research Associate, Anthropological Survey of India, Kolkata.

D.S. Shun, Research Associate, Anthropological Survey of India, Shillong.

Dewaram A. Nagdeve, Associate Professor, International Institute for Population Sciences, Mumbai.

Gautam Kumar Mallik, Research Associate, Anthropological Survey of India, Kolkata.

Kavita Jaijan, Research Scholar, Banaras Hindu University, Varanasi.

Mohd. Sanjeer Alam, Research Associate, Centre for the Study of Developing Societies, New Delhi.

Mohammad Taghi Sheykhi, Associate Professor, Department of Social Science, Al-Zahra University, Tehran (Iran).

Nidhi Jain, Research Scholar, International Institute for Population Sciences, Mumbai.

P. Bharati, Professor and Head, Biological Anthropology Unit, Indian Statistical Institute, Kolkata

Ravi S. Singh, Associate Professor, Banaras Hindu University, Varanasi.

R.K. Sinha, Professor, International Institute for Population Sciences, Mumbai.

Sandip Anand, Assistant Professor, Xavier Institute of Management, Bhubaneswar.

Sarfaraz Alam, Assistant Professor, Banaras Hindu University, Varanasi.

Sanjay K. Mohanty, Associate Professor, International Institute for Population Sciences, Mumbai.

S. Gunasekaran, Associate Professor, Department of Applied Research, Gandhigram Rural University, Gandhigram, Tamil Nadu.

S. Tharageswari, Research Officer, International Institute for Population Sciences, Mumbai.

Swati S. Nanda, Assistant Professor, Department of Political Science, DAV PG College, Varanasi.

Syam Prasad, Research Scholar, Centre for Development Studies, Prasanth Nagar, Ulloor, Trivandrum.

Vijaya S. Durdhawale, Research Scholar, Tata Institute of Social Science, Mumbai.

Introduction

Understanding people who are living in poverty is a demanding task for Indian population planners and demographers. The book contains essays, written by eminent academics and population experts, which are carefully selected for an overview of poverty and social exclusion issues in India. There are several causes of poverty in India and these are diverse across the states. The dynamics of people living in poverty are sufficiently described to address socio-demographic-geographic aspects. About a third of the world's poor reside in India. That is the basic reason for framing the objectives of the book with a focus on poor people and its issues in the backdrop of the 8 per cent annual growth of India. The book is divided into three broad parts: Part I *Poverty and Social Exclusion* entails the outlook of reputed scholars working on poverty and social exclusion issues. Part II *National and Regional Perspectives* is mainly based on the analysis of secondary data. The papers included are broad-based and deal with national and regional issues of importance. It begins with the perspectives of countrywide issues on poor people by linking development paradigms with poverty and poverty alleviation programmes in India. It has touched upon regional development and fallacies, gender and poverty linkages, environmental dynamism and poverty, and elderly poor in India. Part III deals with case studies of local perspectives on poverty. Although Indian economy has grown steadily over the past few decades, its growth has been uneven and across the social and economic groups, geographic regions, and rural and urban areas. It includes case studies on rural development in Uttar Pradesh with special reference to Ambedkar Gram Vikas Yojana, changing perspective of poverty in Northeast India, case studies of slums and villages in West Bengal with qualitative insights and narratives, poverty alleviation strategies and their assessment in Tamil Nadu, women in unorganized sector and their struggle, education of the poor tribals in Maharashtra, and some health-related issues. Thus, most of the papers included in this volume contribute to a good discussion on emerging issues and challenges. The overview of the issues involved is given as follows:

I
Poverty and Social Exclusion: The Outlook

'Understanding Social Exclusion' by Mohd. Sanjeer Alam, the first paper of this book, is a comprehensive outlook on the whole paradigm of evolving the concept, context and problems associated with the term 'social exclusion'. This paper discusses the complex debates on social exclusion so as to understand what it means and what conceptual contribution it can make in understanding and addressing various forms of social disadvantages in varying contexts. 'Social exclusion' has been defined variously, reflecting diverse theoretical, ideological and political perspectives. It also elaborates whether and how far social exclusion relates to other concepts conventionally employed to capture various forms of disadvantages such as poverty and deprivation. Poverty may be both the cause and the consequence of social exclusion. However, people may become socially excluded even without being poor. Deprivation is a multidimensional concept involving not only lack of income and wealth but also social inferiority, disability, powerlessness, and physical and social isolation. As the idea of social exclusion is essentially Eurocentric, it is altogether an exotic concept in the context of developing countries including India. Its transplantation in Indian conditions is, therefore, fraught with problems and this paper discusses such difficulties/problems in Indian context.

The next paper by Sanjay K. Mohanty talks about the advantages and weaknesses in doing research on the multidimensionality of poverty. The objective of this paper is to outline the theoretical and methodological challenges in undertaking research on the multidimensional poverty. It critically examines two of the pioneering works of UNDP, namely, the Human Poverty Index 1 (HPI-1) and the Multidimensional Poverty Index (MPI) introduced in 2011. The suitability of both the indices in Indian context has been examined. The author suggests focusing research on missing dimension of work and employment which should be integrated into the multidimensional poverty measurement.

'Development, Poverty and Social Exclusion' by Bikramaditya Kumar Choudhary is a thought-provoking paper wherein he expresses his views on the regional inequality of poverty. Economists are always of the opinion that development will take care of all kinds of problems including social, political and ecological. On the other side, the reality is that the so-called development is the reason for all kinds of human problems. This paper links poverty, development and social exclusion in a regional perspective. There have been studies which relate development of few with poverty for many, but exclusion-related studies so far have tried to dilute the relationship between poverty and exclusion by adding non-poor also as excluded groups. It is true that process of exclusion is not confined to poor only, but the fact remains that poor are more vulnerable than others to be excluded. There has not been a clear perspective or a convincing analysis that shows how poverty and social exclusion are related under present-day conditions. Why these phenomena have become important in prosperous society and are going unchecked in poor economies and why free market policy or regulated policy has not been able to tackle it. This paper tries to explore what India can learn, if any, from these experiences to understand the process of social exclusion and aggravating regional concentration and exclusion.

II
National and Regional Perspectives

'Poverty and Poverty Alleviation Strategies in India: Trends, Dimensions and Lessons Learnt' by Abdul Shaban is the first paper of the second part of the book. It encompasses the levels, trends of poverty, and varying programmes adopted to alleviate poverty in India. India houses the largest number of the poor on this planet, and it is also an irony that India is one of the ten major economies in the world. There has been enormous shift in the share of sectoral contribution of income and the rate of growth of national income has been near two digits. However, the growth and change in the structure of the economy have not been able to benefit all the sections of the society and regions of the country. Large proportion of the population which lives in poverty in India has hardly seen any significant change in their fortune and in fact for many the livelihood opportunities have become more elusive due to pervasive market forces. This paper attempts to find out the dimensions and trends of poverty in India, examines the poverty alleviation strategies initiated by Indian government and their impact, and finds out the causes as to why high economic growth in recent years has not been able to make expected dent on poverty. The lesson learnt from Indian experience is that growth must be broad-based to make significant impression on poverty and the narrow sectoral growth may widen the personal and regional income inequality. In recent years, the rise of civil society has given a voice to the marginalized sections of society.

'Changing Perspective of Poverty in Northeast India: A Situation Analysis' by D.K. Adak, D.S. Shun and P. Bharati talks about poverty situation in the Northeast India. Northeast India is considered as one of the poor regions in India. This region is also the homeland of a large number of scheduled tribes and scheduled castes who differ from one another in terms of language, cultural set-ups and ethnicity. In this study, a situation analysis has been done to find out the changes in the level of poverty over the period of time in different states of Northeast India. The entire analysis has been based on the data collected from different secondary sources. On the basis of position of different indicators, it reveals from the study that the states of Northeast India are mostly poverty-stricken. However, Mizoram emerges as an exceptional case. As each state in the region is characterized by their own particular problems, the region cannot be treated as single homogenous unit. Thus, for a better policy for poverty alleviation in this region, emphasis should be laid to achieve development from below. The developmental policies should be on the direction to benefit the poor people that will help attain the national goal of poverty alleviation.

The third paper of this section 'Rural Development in Perspective: Theoretical Frameworks' by Mohammad Taghi Sheykhi explores the qualities of rural development as essential means to generate development in general, and thereby to lower or eradicate poverty with special reference to India. It also examines and reviews the relevant literature and theories in order to reflect a perspective on rural development. Appropriate technology package and provision of adequate financial assets play crucial role in poverty alleviation process. This paper also argues on how population growth rate plays role in rural development success. The author reflects a comparative perspective of the quality of poverty in India, China and Vietnam with statistical evidence during the past half century. This paper weighs how rural households in the developing world are marginalized, have insufficient income, and have no pensions, no social security and the like to depend on. Under such circumstances, vicious circle of poverty continues. Hence, human resource development largely contributes to alleviate poverty with special reference to the developing world. It also reviews the literature in an attempt to draw together the factors thought to influence the nature, rate, and extent of absorption of new technology and the policy measures that might affect these factors. It is expected that the current advocacy of policies based on 'appropriate technology' will be placed in a more useful perspective.

'Linking Gender and Poverty: Evidences from Indian Agriculture' by Swati S. Nanda and Sarfaraz Alam is a comprehensive study, which tries to link the overall poverty and gender with special emphasis on Indian agriculture. Though poverty is a universal phenomenon, its occurrence and implications for people situated in different socio-economic and spatial contexts vary considerably. This is particularly true in the case of gender, where power imbalance between the sexes renders women more vulnerable to the cycle of poverty. The link between gender inequality and overall human poverty at aggregate level was also indicated in the Human Development Report of 1997. Ever since, the major foci of studies on feminization of poverty have been as follows: First, women as a class tend to experience higher incidence of poverty than men. Second, the severity of women's poverty is more acute than that of men. Third, female-headed households are far more vulnerable to situations of poverty than the male-headed households. Finally, higher gender disparity implies higher incidence of poverty among women. The paper intends to look into the above hypotheses by focusing on gender basis of variations in incidence, magnitude, and growth of poverty in Indian agriculture and their correlates. It begins by making connections between gender and poverty, and then proceeds to look into the conceptual issues linking women and agriculture. Next, it focuses specifically on women and agriculture in India by examining available literature and data on the theme. The final section concentrates on required policy changes.

In the next paper titled 'Caste/Tribe Inequalities in Selected Development Indicators in India' by Nidhi Jain and Aparajita Chattopadhyay, the situation of four social groups in India is analysed from development perspectives. This paper, using NFHS-III data, assesses the extent of inequalities of selected development parameters in 10 states of India with special emphasis on caste/tribe groups. The condition of the scheduled caste population in Maharashtra, Andhra Pradesh, Karnataka and Gujarat is often better than the situation of the other backward castes in Rajasthan, Madhya Pradesh and Uttar Pradesh and the former are at par with the 'other' category of less developed states. Perhaps, unanimous reservation policy for caste groups needs to be re-looked in the context of varying level of development of these groups. Though in West Bengal, inequality is low in basic facilities as well as in social development and health care utilization, yet its performance in terms of equality is awful in nutritional status. Very high level of inequality among social groups is persisting in Rajasthan, Madhya Pradesh, Uttar Pradesh and Orissa, which could be due to the fact that at the initial stage of development, the forward class cherishes the benefits of progress the most and it tends to enhance the disparity. Tribal population needs urgent attention as they are facing inequality of opportunity in many development parameters. While the bigger states of the north and central India must take into consideration the wide disparity existing within states.

'Poverty, Disability and Social Exclusion in India' by Ambati Nageswara Rao deals with disabled people and their marginalization in India. Disabled people are estimated to make up approximately 10 per cent of world population. There has recently been a call for more information relating to disability and poverty. This is due to the realization that disabled people are disproportionately among the poorest of the poor in all parts of the world, and that international development targets are unlikely to be met without including disabled people. The basic cause of the poverty is exclusion: exclusion from social, economic and political life. In this respect, this study aims to gain deeper understanding of the relationship between poverty and disability. It is based on the review of the existing literature. First, it summarizes the current state of knowledge about disability and poverty in India. Second, it explains the reasons behind the lack of reliable information on disability and its impact. Third, it discusses the factors that leads to poverty and vice versa. Finally, it describes the efforts that are presently being made to shaping the policies to end miseries of disabled people at international and national levels. Evidence from the study confirms that disability as a cause and consequence of poverty now needs to be brought to centre stage and the development community needs to reorder its priorities to put disability in the mainstream. It also argues that disabled people are not only among the poorest of the poor in the country, but that they remain poor for very long periods of time, from generation to generation.

Changing age structure is one of the structural changes that has been witnessed in the last century. Population ageing is one of its consequences, which emerges as a global phenomenon in the present time. The Indian elderly population is currently the second largest in the world to that of China with 100 million. The absolute number of the 60-plus population in India will increase from 77 million in 2001 to 137 million by 2021. The paper 'Poverty among Elderly in India: Estimates and Determinants' by Syam Prasad looks into the living condition of the elderly in terms of poverty among the elderly. Income is included as the indicator of well-being and income poverty is measured among elderly with adjustment of size and composition of the household. The author tried to estimate the poverty among the elderly with economies of scale within the household given as 0.6 as estimated by Deaton as ideal for India. It is found that elements of social and demographic transformation act as a major determinant of poverty among the elderly.

Rapid population growth and poverty in a country deplete its natural resources and degrade the environment. 'Population, Poverty, and Environment Dynamics in India' by Dewaram A. Nagdeve is an attempt to study the changes in population and poverty in India and its states and also to highlight the environmental degradation in India. The data from various secondary sources have been analysed to study the changes and trends from 1971 to 2001. The analysis reveals that poverty and rapid population growth are found to coexist and seems to reinforce each other. The effects of population growth and poverty on environmental problems are associated with changing consumption pattern, rising demand for energy, pressure on land and deforestation. This paper highlights the linkages between population, poverty and environment and concludes with some population policy reflections and emphasizes the potential importance of natural resources for sustainable development. Population and development policy aimed at overall development should certainly include efforts to control population and poverty, and conservation and protection of natural resources for sustainable development and for better health of present and future generations.

III

Local Perspectives: Case Studies

The word 'rural' continues to catch our attention as more than 70 per cent population of India and 79 per cent population of Uttar Pradesh still live in rural areas. To solve the problem of rural areas after independence, governments introduced different developmental programmes. These developmental programmes are directly or indirectly affected by the concept of rural development which is changing in nature. 'Thinking about the Rural Poor: A Brief Appraisal of Rural Development Programmes in India with Special Reference to Ambedkar Gram Vikas Yojana' by Ravi S. Singh and Kavita Jaijan attempts to appraise various rural development programmes in India. Unfortunately, despite all good intentions, they have failed to be inclusive in nature. The marginal sections of the rural community have generally not been able to get benefits of the rural development programmes owing to a variety of traditional handicaps related to continuing exploitative nature of socio-cultural and economic relations in village society. Implementation part in case of most of the programmes launched has been considerably poor. Rural development programmes are not exception to it; rather in some cases it has been reportedly negative.

'Poverty Alleviation Programmes in Tamil Nadu' by S. Gunasekaran, based on the data collected from 900 women beneficiaries of various poverty alleviation programmes (PAPs) implemented in Tamil Nadu, focuses on the extent of human rights approach adopted in the implementation process of the PAPs in Tamil Nadu. The main PAPs considered in the study are Swarnajayanti Gram Swarozgar Yojana (SGSY), Sampoorna Grameen Rozgar Yojana (SGRY), Indira Awas Yojana (IAY) and Public Distribution System (PDS). The level of adoption of human rights approach was measured based on a three-point scale on various indicators of human rights developed for each of the selected programmes. The results showed that the extent of adoption of human rights approach was 66 per cent of the total expected score for SGSY, 37 per cent for SGRY, 65 per cent for IAY, and 93 per cent for PDS. Thus, the extent of adoption of human rights approach in PAPs in Tamil Nadu was extremely good for PDS, moderate for SGSY and IAY, and poor for SGRY. Lack of accountability on the part of government agencies was the most important lacuna in the implementation of PAPs and hence there is a need to sensitize the government officials on the importance of integrating human rights approach in poverty alleviation programmes for their success.

Discrimination between men and women is one of the most crucial disparities in many societies, particularly in India. Indian women have travelled a long way through the process of development experience of the country. A rigid and highly stratified male-dominated society left little scope for independence and autonomy of women who were subjected to many forms of discrimination, oppression and exploitation. Viewing the situation of women in India, one is compelled to admit that even after six decades of planning and development, insufficient attention has been given for proper development of women power. 'Gender Perspective on Economic Status of Women in Unorganized Sector: A Study in Tamil Nadu' by S. Tharageswari has made an attempt to formulate a theoretical review of the role of women in development, the participation of women in economic and income-generating activities, and gender perspective on economic status of women in unorganized sector. It examines the problems of women in unorganized sector in respect of opportunities for continuous employment, socio-economic improvement, and expansion, and to identify the influence on the unorganized sector in the generation of income, consumption, savings and investment. Exploratory-cum-descriptive design is used for the study. Chennai is chosen as the study area. The study underlines the necessity of bringing the unorganized sector into the ambit of national policy, which recognizes their contribution to economic processes, and protects their legal status. Particularly in the context of globalization, it is important to pay attention as to how women in this sector can benefit in the process of growth.

'A Tale of Two Villages of West Bengal' by Ashis Sarkar talks about the socio-economic aspects of West Bengal's two villages. Apparently, geography of a region seems to contribute more towards livelihood and poverty – a hypothesis tested in the present discourse with data gathered through in-depth field study. The area belongs to the *jangalmahals*, inhabited mainly by the tribals, where the so-called Maoists have been very active these days. Despite planning endeavours, areas mostly on the western fringe of *rarh* often suffer from aridity, deforestation, soil erosion, flash flood, poor economic opportunities, poverty, food inadequacy and hunger.

'Case Study of Slum/Pavement Dwellers in Kolkata' by Arup Ray, Gautam Kumar Mallik and Chandrima Chakraborty is dealt with the varied spectrum and causes of poverty along with the reasoning, which differs from one area to another. The study is an approach to find out the preliminary aspects of socio-economic condition from a social anthropological outlook. Authors have selected four places – Narkeldanga, Chetla, Dattabad and Behala in Kolkata where a large number of pavement/slum dwellers reside. The data are collected based on random sampling with main emphasis on demographic aspects and very brief outline on their socio-economic condition. The adjustment crisis, the economic insecurity, and the absence of social recognition of the pavement/slum dwellers evolve many socio-economic problems. This crisis compelled the kinship system, marriage pattern, and the social values to become incapable for proper functioning. This paper offers two propositions based on bipolar concepts – 'culture of abundance' and 'culture of scarcity' – which are built on historical and ecological dictates.

'Primary Schooling in a Tribal District of India' by Vijaya S. Durdhawale is based on qualitative assessment of primary schooling in selected tribal villages of rural Maharashtra. Poor infrastructure, transportation bottleneck, high pupil-teacher ratios, unnecessary burden on teachers for clerical works, poor quality of teaching, poor attendance, and high dropouts especially for girls along with problem in language of instruction and economic constraints are the major reasons of poor literacy in these villages. Family size in many cases is very large and for feeding family members, it becomes compulsory for children to go to work. It makes sense to have teachers from the same community or at least people communicating the same language as instructors, as language is one of the major barriers of tribal literacy. The tribal children would only feel a sense of oneness in their study and get interested in the school if their cultural aspects are embedded in the school curriculum. Economic uncertainty and financial hardship are the contributing factors for the age-old disinterest in education among the tribes. Thus, increasing the sources of income is the base to encourage willing participation in basic education.

In the next paper by Sandip Anand and R.K. Sinha, an attempt is made to understand and describe the meta-organizational issues related to public–private partnerships. This paper is based upon qualitative study of selected cases and related stakeholders. In India, interviews of twelve representatives from Janani, five from Constella Futures, two from World Bank Institute, one from Packard Foundation Programme in Jharkhand state, and five government representatives have been conducted. The research also incorporates the views of poor clients and highlights their demands. In-depth interviews of only five poor clients were conducted for this purpose. This paper is based on the content analysis of qualitative data. Post-content analysis, the content, or text has been analysed with the help of tools of semiotic analysis.

The last paper 'Assessment of Cervical Cancer Prevention and Treatment Strategies in Low-Resource Countries: Challenges and Revelations' by Agnihotram V. Ramanakumar talks about one of the most common forms of cancer and its prevention channels in the context of developing countries. Cervical cancer can be prevented by timely screening and suitable treatment. Low-resource settings take more than two-thirds of the world's cervical cancer burden: sparse investments in screening, diagnosis and treatment are the main reasons. Recent studies by the World Health Organization (WHO) have acknowledged the merit of low-cost detection techniques such as Cytology, HPV testing, and visual inspection with acetic acid (VIA) or Lugol's iodine (VILI). Large-scale cohorts or randomized clinical trials from Africa, Asia and Latin America have also documented these techniques as accurate and effective methods to detect/prevent cervical cancer and could contribute to a reduction in the burden. Human papillomavirus (HPV) is the single most necessary cause of cervical cancer and its prevalence varies between 7 per cent and 15 per cent, depending on population and age group. Understanding the dynamics of the natural history of the infection such as acquisition, clearance and persistence of infection is important in detecting cervical cancer in its early stages of progression. With the absence of systematic screening policies, developing countries are almost five decades behind the Western world (in terms of incidence rates). Recent HPV vaccination provides confidence in the future. However, several misconceptions and barriers such as cost and low public and political awareness, rivalry between pharmaceutical companies, and the possibility of type-replacement or other dominant types delay the distribution of HPV vaccines in these countries. There are other opportunities for reducing the burden of cancer by using new diagnostic tools such as type-specific serology testing, HPV viral load measurements, and by geno-typing various genetic and biological markers. Strategies such as detecting and treating the disease in the same visit may have several ethical allegations. In conclusion, most of the challenges encountered by the Third World might have answers from the experiences of the Western world, where morbidity as well as mortality have dropped rapidly in the past four decades. This paper advocates the most appropriative mix of all available information to showcase some possible solutions for eliminating cervical cancer.

Part I

Poverty and Social Exclusion: The Outlook

1

Understanding Social Exclusion

MOHD. SANJEER ALAM

The concept of 'social exclusion' is of recent origin. It has, however, very quickly acquired widespread currency in developmental literature and political and public policy discussions. Even as the concept has become widely popular, it remains a hotly contested notion; too vague a concept to fully comprehend. Not only does it lack, as critics have pointed out, theoretical underpinnings and analytical clarity, issues with regard to operationalization and measurements also remain far from settled. Questions are raised as to if social exclusion is a free-standing, novel, and distinctive concept or it is just another term saying/describing same things as does an array of concepts such as poverty, inequality, deprivation, vulnerability, and so on. Doubts are also expressed with regard to its application and suitability beyond industrialized societies where the idea of social exclusion was originally developed. Against this backdrop, the objective of this essay is to get into complex debates on social exclusion so as to understand what it means and what conceptual contribution it can make in understanding and addressing various forms of social disadvantages in varying contexts.

Historical Background

The idea of 'social exclusion' was conceived in Western Europe to capture different forms of disadvantages that had resulted from economic restructuring in 1970s. It was, however, first popularized by Rene Lenoir in France. In 1974, he estimated 'the excluded' about one-tenth of French population, a social category not protected under social insurance principles at that time (Silver, 1995: 63). It quickly spread throughout the European Union (EU) as a contagious concept and occupied the centre stage of political and public policy discourses by 1980s. In the Treaty of Amsterdam (1997), the EU declared reduction of social exclusion as its one of the main objectives. In the Lisbon Summit held in 2000, the EU reiterated and reaffirmed combating social exclusion as a major goal of its social and economic policy.

The discourse on social exclusion is, nonetheless, far wider and deeper in the United Kingdom compared to other member countries of EU. With the incoming of Labour Party to power in United Kingdom in 1997, social exclusion became a key policy issue. The new Labour government set up a 'Social Exclusion Unit' in order to provide a cross-departmental approach to complex problems of specific group. In May 2006, the issue of social exclusion was given cabinet-level priority with the appointment of Minister of Social Exclusion.

Outside EU, the discourse on social exclusion is in vogue in Canada and Australia. The United States is a notable exception among industrialized countries where social exclusion as an analytical concept did not attract much attention. Although there are considerable overlaps between the concepts of 'underclass' and social exclusion, the debates on underclass in the United States are, nonetheless, different. Here, disadvantages or exclusion of underclass are understood as an outcome of 'personal deficits' (personal characteristics and lifestyles) rather than something systemic.[1]

Of late, the concept of social exclusion has been transported to developing countries by different agencies of the United Nations Organization (UNO). International Labour Organization (ILO) has, however, taken the lead to transplant the concept into developing countries.[2] While debates rage over if at all the concept can be applied in the context of developing countries, social exclusion is increasingly being used to describe various forms of disadvantages.

Meaning, Scope and Approaches

'Social exclusion' has been defined variously, reflecting diverse theoretical, ideological, and political perspectives. In the widest and broadest sense, social exclusion means persistence of complex and multiple disadvantages. In the process of its evolution, social exclusion has been conceptualized as both 'process' and 'outcome'. As a *process*, social exclusion examines the way individuals or groups become excluded in the society in which they live. As a *state* or *condition* or an *outcome*, it identifies the most disadvantaged people or social groups who could be labelled as 'excluded' from larger social system and relationship. In brief, the concept captures both 'becoming' and 'being' excluded.

Debates have also raged over whether social exclusion refers merely to inability to *participate* in the activities of wider society or it also refers to lack of access to *rights/entitlements*. In most definitions, emphasis is laid on participation. As Burchardt et al. (2002: 30) put it cogently: 'an individual is socially excluded if he or she is geographically resident in a society but for reasons beyond his/her control, he or she cannot *participate* in the normal activities of citizens in that society, he or she would like to so participate' (emphasis added). Levitas et al. (2007: 25) combined 'rights' with 'participation'. In this formulation, social exclusion is a complex and multidimensional process involving the lack or denial of resources, rights, goods, and services and inability to participate in the normal relationships and activities available to majority of people in a society, whether in economic, social, cultural, or political arenas.

In the West, debates on social exclusion have given rise to various perspectives and approaches. Beall (2002) mentioned three approaches to social exclusion. They are *neo-liberal, re-labelling of poverty* and *transformationalist*. The *neo-liberal approach* holds social exclusion as unfortunate but inevitable side effects of global economic realignment. Simply put, the emergence of free trade and a single global market has resulted in exclusion of workers from the benefits of trade barriers and social and employment protection. The second approach (*re-labelling of poverty*) argues that social exclusion is a smoke screen, representing little more than unhelpful re-labelling of poverty. It is rather a tool used to shift the spotlight away from inequality caused by (mal)functioning of the economic system. The *transformationalist approach* focuses attention on social relations embedded in formal and informal institutions, and 'signals the use of the social exclusion framework to analyse international processes and institutional relationships associated with rapid social and economic global change and local impacts and responses'.

In the context of Britain, three key intellectual discourses can be identified that inform shifts in government's policy approach to social exclusion over time (Levitas et al., 2007). First is the *redistributive discourse* that emphasizes low income as the root cause of exclusion. It recognizes the excluded as 'deserving poor'. In other words, the problems of the poor should be addressed through benefit systems. This was the traditional social democratic approach to social policy in 1960s and 1970s. Second is the *social integration discourse* that holds unemployment as the principal cause of exclusion and views the poor as potential workers to be reintegrated in overall social order. Third is the *moral underclass/dependency discourse* that views culture as the principal reason of poverty or exclusion and regards the excluded as undeserving, implying that 'the excluded' themselves should bear the responsibility of improving their lot. This discourse was much in vogue and had influenced the government policy during the Thatcher regime.

Even as there are diverse perspectives and concerns defining social exclusion, there are certain features that encompass various definitions or perspectives on social exclusion. These common features or grounds are *multidimensionality, relativity, agency* and *dynamics*. These key attributes not only offer insights into the causes and consequences of multiple disadvantages but also underline the conceptual contribution that social exclusion can make in understanding and addressing them.

In general, the theorists of social exclusion seem to stand in agreement that social exclusion is a *multidimensional* phenomenon. It is a condition of disadvantages resulting from a complex web of social, economic, spatial, and political processes. Individuals or groups may experience social exclusion because of disadvantages and vulnerabilities that may arise from iniquitous processes of development and/or from ethnic, cultural, social, and political factors in a complex and interwoven manner (Atkinson, 1998; Turok et al., 1999; Levitas et al., 2007; Room, 1995).

The expression *relativity* implies that people get excluded because of events elsewhere in society. Whether a group or an individual is excluded cannot be decided without taking into account the conditions of others – the reference group. It is essential because people's subjective views of their own conditions are influenced by comparing their conditions with those of others, which have adverse social, psychological, and health consequences (Atkinson, 1998; Sen, 2000).

The notion of *agency* implies that exclusion can be external. If there are 'excluded' there are 'excluders' too. In other words, one group in society may effectively deny other group access to various opportunities available within the legal system (Buvinic, 2005). For example, in many industrialized countries, social gate keeping agencies make it virtually impossible for members of ethnic minorities often labelled as 'Other' to find housing accommodation in the neighbourhood lived by the majority community (Wacquant, 1993, 1996; Micheli, 1996; Tosi, 1996; Marcuse, 1997), leading to formation of ghettos of ethnic minorities. Certain group of people may also be excluded in the labour market by employers through recruitment practices, leading to unemployment or concentration of the excluded groups in inferior jobs (Turok et al., 1999). In Indian context, Dalits (ex-untouchables) are often denied legitimate social space causing social segregation and ghettoization.[3]

Prevalence of discrimination in the labour market has placed them at the bottom end of it (Thorat and Newman, 2007).

The concept of *dynamics* suggests that social exclusion is a condition of deprivation persistent overtime. Therefore, not only does it relate to current situation of say 'joblessness' or 'low income' but also to future prospect. Long-term unemployment or recurring poverty is likely to influence people's expectation of progress and in turn likely to affect their morale, self-esteem, and their attitude towards the larger society. In brief, an assessment of the extent of social exclusion has to go beyond current status (Atkinson, 1998) and, therefore, time should be an important variable to measure it.

The phenomenon of social exclusion may exist in various forms and intensity. Miliband (2006) suggested three forms: (a) wide exclusion, (b) concentrated exclusion, and (c) deep exclusion. *Wide exclusion* refers to those deprived on a single or smaller indicator(s). *Concentrated exclusion* refers to spatial exclusion, that is, concentration of the problem in particular geographical areas. *Deep exclusion* refers to those who are deprived on multiple counts. To be brief, deep exclusion is the worst kind of exclusion.

In terms of constitutive processes underlying exclusion, Sen (2000) suggested two types of exclusion – active exclusion and passive exclusion. *Active exclusion* is when there is a deliberate policy to exclude or keep particular group of people out. Such policies are often directed against immigrants, racial, ethnic, or religious minority groups. *Passive exclusion* is not brought through intended policy mechanism; it is rather an unintended outcome of social processes.

Some Proximate Concepts: Poverty and Deprivation

One of the focal points in the debates of social exclusion is whether and how far social exclusion relates to other concepts conventionally employed to capture various forms of disadvantages. Is social exclusion synonymous with the notions of poverty, deprivation, marginality, and so on? Or does it go beyond them and signal a conceptual shift in understanding complex system of disadvantages?

At the most fundamental level, social exclusion draws heavily upon the theories of poverty. Poverty remains at the heart of social exclusion. It may be both the cause and the consequence of social exclusion. However, people may become socially excluded even without being poor. In what ways then are the two concepts different? The reasons why poverty is not social exclusion and vice versa basically stems from the way the two concepts are conceptualized. Poverty has long been conceptualized as income deficits or lack of material possessions and understood in absolute terms, especially in terms of a minimum consumption basket to meet basic needs of an individual. In this formulation, poverty is a one-dimensional (material dimension) concept as against social exclusion being multidimensional.

In recent years, the concept of poverty has, however, undergone re-conceptualization to broaden its scope. 'To be poor' as Toynbee (2006) argued, 'is to fall far behind what most ordinary people have in their own society'. The capability framework as developed by Amartya Sen views poverty as capability deprivation, implying inability to do things what one has reasons to want to do. The connection between low income and poor human capital and denial of access to various opportunities and entitlements in the given society has been well established in the literature. In brief, poverty too carries the connotations of multidimensionality and relativity as does social exclusion. Of course, the elements of multidimensionality and relativity bring poverty closer to social exclusion, and yet latter is much wider a concept than former. For one thing, unlike poverty, social exclusion is a *dynamic* concept. Unlike poverty, social exclusion is not only a condition of disadvantages but it also examines the processes through which people become excluded.

The concept of deprivation also stands closer to social exclusion because both share the elements of multidimensionality and relativity. Deprivation is a multidimensional concept involving not only lack of income and wealth but also social inferiority, disability, powerlessness, and physical and social isolation (Chambers, 1997). The magnitude of a relative deprivation is the extent of the difference between the desired situation and that of the person desiring it. To put differently, one's feeling of deprivation arises out of comparing his/her situation with those who are better off. However, unlike social exclusion, deprivation is treated as a static concept. A person becomes socially excluded if his/her condition of deprivation is persistent overtime.

Two conclusions emerge out from the above discussion. One, both poverty and deprivation are integral to social exclusion. Poverty and social exclusion are both the cause and the consequence of social exclusion. Second, despite overlapping of conceptual boundaries between social exclusion and poverty/deprivation, social exclusion is much more than poverty or deprivation. Barnes (2005) presents a useful schema of distinction between social exclusion, poverty, and deprivation (Table 1).

Table 1

Poverty, Deprivation and Social Exclusion: A Comparison

Poverty	*Deprivation*	*Social exclusion*
One-dimensional	Multidimensional	Multidimensional
Physical needs	Physical needs Material needs	Physical needs Material needs Societal participation
Distributional	Distributional	Distributional Relational
Static	Static	Dynamic
Individual	Individual	Individual
Household	Household	Household Community

Source: Barnes (2005).

Issues in Measurement

A concept remains at best abstract or devoid of empirical and practical relevance unless it allows quantification by empirically identifiable indicators. Is the idea of social exclusion amenable to quantification? If yes, how to measure social exclusion in quantitative terms in order to be able to identify socially excluded? These questions have been in the forefront of the debates on social exclusion. There is, of course, broader consensus on multidimensionality of social exclusion, but greater disagreement exists on the dimensions on which individuals or groups could be identified as excluded. There are still less shared views on precise quantifiable indicators within the identified dimensions. Burchardt et al. (1999: 229) identified four dimensions on which participation is considered more important – consumption, production, political engagement, and social interactions. Barnes (2005) suggested seven dimensions across which socially excluded people could be identified: (a) financial situation; (b) ownership of durable goods; (c) quality of housing; (d) neighbourhood perceptions; (e) personal social relationship; (f) physical health, and (g) psychological well-being. Levitas et al. (2007) identified three main dimensions, each with multiple domains, sub-domains, and indicators. The three domains are: (a) resource, (b) participation, and (c) quality of life.

The problem of measurement does not end here. Even if one identifies a set of quantifiable indicators, there is the question of relative importance of indicators chosen. It can be reasonably argued that one indicator may be far important than other in terms of constitutive processes of exclusion. The problem becomes even more complicated in a socially heterogeneous society where the nature and causes of exclusion among different social groups vary a great deal. Obviously, the chosen indicators would be differentially important for different social groups. This problem can be resolved by assigning weights to indicators in order of their importance. But it is quite difficult to arrive at what indicator is of greater or lesser significance for the entire population or for a specific social group. Unless this issue is settled, there is a danger of having diverse and arbitrary set of indicators, largely depending on subjective judgement of the researcher.

Application of Social Exclusion in India: Problems and Prospects

As already discussed, the idea of social exclusion is essentially Eurocentric. It is altogether an exotic concept in the context of developing countries including India. Its transplantation in Indian conditions is, therefore, fraught with problems. What are the difficulties/problems?

One of the difficulties underlying application of the idea of social exclusion in the context of developing countries arises out of vastly different social, economic, and cultural conditions. Social exclusion in developed countries arose out of rapid economic changes and resultant social transformations. But in developing countries, social exclusion is largely embedded in the normative systems that assign roles and resources to individuals and group. In Indian context, the historically embedded normative systems continue to influence distribution of resources, power, and privilege to individuals and groups.

Second, the idea of social exclusion in the West is conceptualized in its labour market framework and welfare systems. In the West, those fallen employed received social benefits and yet considered as excluded. Loss of employment was seen not just as loss of income but also in terms of implications for social networks/bonding and sense of self-worth. But to use the unemployment criterion to identify the excluded is problematic in the context of developing countries including India, for labour markets in developing countries consist of vast informal sectors where formal employment relations do not exist. In India, for example, over 80 per cent of workers work in informal/unorganized sectors (Sinha et al., 1999; Sengupta et al., 2008), more often as casual workers. Going by western standard, casual/seasonal workers could be classified as unemployed or underemployed. Given that unemployment in the West is seen as one of the major causes of social exclusion, if western criterion of employment is employed to identify the excluded in Indian context, vast majority of population would qualify for it. By contrast, those socially excluded in the West are minorities.

Third, social exclusion in the West is intrinsically linked to strong governance and comprehensive social security system to protect people from the vagaries of labour market. In India, even the barest minimum social security measures remain unavailable to the masses of people (Bardhan, 2011). If the provision of income support of the kind given through social security system in the west is attempted in India, majority of the population would qualify for it as compared to 10–15 per cent of population in the former (Saith, 2001).

Clearly, application of the idea social exclusion in developing nations is fraught with problems. One can discover many theoretical and conceptual holes. But can the concept at all be applied to enrich understanding various forms of disadvantages in developing countries? It must be noted that at the heart of the idea of social exclusion is to understand multiple disadvantages resulting from the processes rooted in diverse domains. The sources, processes, and underlying factors of exclusion may be different in specific socio-economic and cultural contexts but the concept can be fruitfully employed to understand multiple disadvantages and deprivations and associated risk factors. If the concept of social exclusion is conceptualized in this general framework, it can be effectively used to capture the social relations, processes, and practices that cause and reinforce multiple disadvantages and deprivations. In India, for example, it may help capture interaction between multiple exclusionary processes operating across systems of gender, caste, tribe, religion, and social class and so on (De Haan, 1999).

So far, the concept of social exclusion in India is used loosely to describe one or the other form of exclusionary processes. Nor are there serious attempts to standardize as well as fine tune the concept in Indian context. For instance, Appasamy et al. (1996) conceptualized social exclusion as the denial of the basic welfare rights which provide citizens positive freedom to participate in the social and economic contexts. In a World Bank Study, Mearns and Sinha (1999) have tried to explore social exclusion with reference to access of poor and women to land. A few studies have tried to connect caste and exclusionary processes. What is common in these studies is that all of them look at exclusion from one thing or the other. It must be noted that social exclusion is not about merely looking at the dimensions individually but also about looking at complex relationship between them (Clert, 1999).

The Upshot

The concept of social exclusion originated in specific social, economic, and political contexts of Europe. Even as it has become central to academic, political, and public policy discussions in the West, the concept lacks theoretical clarity and precise meaning, largely because of diverse ideological, political, and personal perspectives involved in defining it. In broader sense, social exclusion examines complex relationship between various forms of disadvantages and deprivations. Although the idea of social exclusion at the most fundamental level draws on the theories of poverty, inequality, deprivations, and so on, it goes beyond them as an analytical concept.

In recent years, the concept has attracted widespread attention in developing countries including India but it remains far from adequately conceptualized and operationalized. As a result, the usage of the concept carries more ambiguities than in industrialized countries. Given that the concept of social exclusion evolved in a particular setting, its universal application is problematic. In order to be applicable in different settings, it needs to be contextually embedded. So far, no systematic efforts have appeared to conceptualize social exclusion framework in Indian context. However, given the pace at which social exclusion is gaining popularity as an analytical concept, an acceptable framework that may enrich our understanding to exclusionary processes or complex system of disadvantages and deprivation specific to Indian context will be put in place sooner than later.

Notes

1. The notion that people are poor or stand disadvantaged because of choices they make permeates through much of the underclass debate in the United States. The 'blame the victim' approach to deprivation actually draws upon the thesis of 'culture of poverty' propounded by Oscar Lewis (1959). Lewis in his thesis of 'culture of poverty' argued that those stand as poor share behavioural patterns which on the one hand allow them to cope with poverty, but on the other hand reproduce their disadvantages – for example, sceptical attitude towards education that is passed on to children. However, the position of conservative wing of scholars has been challenged by many. For a critical account see Byrne (2005).
2. See Rodgers et al. (1995) for a collection of studies on social exclusion in developing countries.
3. Lately, Muslim minorities have been shown to be discriminated against in housing, credit lending, and employment opportunities. Also see, Sachar Committee Report (2006), Thorat and Newman (2007), and Sanjeer (2010).

References

Appasamy, P., Guhan, S., and Hema R. (1996). *Social Exclusion from a Welfare Rights Perspective in India*. International Institute for Labour Studies and United Nations Development Programme, Research Series, 106. Geneva: ILO Publications.

Atkinson, A.B. (1998). 'Social exclusion, poverty and unemployment'. CASE Paper 4. In Atkinson, A.B., and Hills, J. (eds.): *Exclusion, Employment and Opportunity* (pp. 1–20). London: Centre for Analysis of Social Exclusion, London School of Economics.

Auletta, K. (1982). *The Underclass*. New York: Random House.

Bardhan, P. (2011). 'Challenges for a minimum social democracy in India', *Economic and Political Weekly*, 46(10), 39–46.

Barnes, M. (2005). *Social Exclusion in Great Britain: An Empirical Investigation and Comparison with the EU*. Aldershot: Ashgate.

Beall, J. (2002). 'Globalization and social exclusion in cities: Framing the debate with lessons from Africa and Asia', *Environment & Urbanization*, 14(1), 41–51.

Burchardt, T., Le Grand, J., and Piachaud, C. (1999). 'Social exclusion in Britain 1991–1995', *Social Policy and Administration*, 33(3), 227–244.

Burchardt, T., Le Grand, J., and Piachaud, C. (2002). 'Degrees of exclusion: Developing a dynamic, multidimensional measure'. In Hills, J., Le Grand, J., and Buvinic, M. (2005). 'Social inclusion in Latin America'. In Buvinic, M., and Mazza, J. (eds.): *Social Exclusion and Economic Development* (pp. 3–32). Baltimore, MD: Johns Hopkins University Press.

Byrne, D. (2005). *Social Exclusion*. Delhi: Rawat.

Chambers, R. (1997). *Whose Reality Counts? Putting the First Last*. London: ITDG Publishing.

Clert, C. (1999). 'Evaluating the concept of social exclusion in development discourse', *European Journal of Development Research*, 11(2), 176–199.

De Haan, A. (1999). *Social Exclusion: Towards a Holistic Understanding of Deprivation.* Social Development Department, Dissemination Note No. 2. London: Department for International Development.

Levitas, R., Pantazis, C., Fahmy, E., Gordon, D., Lloyd, E., and Patsios, D. (2007). *The Multi-dimensional Analysis of Social Exclusion*. Bristol: Bristol Institute for Public Affairs, University of Bristol.

Lewis, Oscar (1959). *Five Families: Mexican Case Studies in the Culture of Poverty*, New York: Basic Books.

Marcuse, P. (1997). 'The enclave, the citadel and the ghetto: What has changed in the post-fordist US city', *Urban Affairs Review*, 33 (November), 228–264.

Mearns, R., and Sinha, S. (1999). *Social Exclusion and Land Administration in Orissa, India*. Policy Research Working Papers, 2124. Washington, DC: World Bank, South Asia Regional Office. Rural Development Sector Unit.

Micheli, G.A. (1996). 'Downdrift: Provoking agents and symptom formation factors in the process of impoverishment'. In Mingione, E (ed.): *Urban Poverty and the Underclass: A Reader* (pp. 41–63). Oxford: Blackwell.

Miliband, D. (2006). *Social exclusion: The Next Steps Forward*. Wetherby: Office of the Deputy Prime Minister Publications.

Rodgers, G., Gore, C.G., and Figueiredo, J.B. (1995). *Social Exclusion: Rhetoric, Reality, Response*. Geneva: ILO.

Room, G. (1995). *Beyond the Threshold: The Measurement and Analysis of Social Exclusion*. Bristol: Policy Press.

Sachar Committee Report (2006), Government of India.

Saith, R. (2001). *Social Exclusion: The Concept and Application to Developing*. Discussion Paper, DIW Berlin.

Sanjeer, A.M. (2010). 'Social exclusion of Muslims in India and deficient debates about affirmative action: Suggestions for a new approach', *South Asia Research*, 30(1), 43–65.

Sen, A. (2000). *Social Exclusion: Concept, Application, and Scrutiny*. Working Paper, Social Development Paper No 1. Asian Development Bank, Bangkok, June.

Sengupta, A.K., Kannan, K.P., and Raveendran, G. (2008). 'India's common people: Who are they, how many are they and how do they live?', *Economic and Political Weekly*, 43(11), 49–63.

Silver, H. (1995). 'Reconceptualizing social disadvantage: Three paradigms of social exclusion'. In Rodgers, G., Gore, C., and Figueiredo, J.B. (eds.): *Social Exclusion: Rhetoric, Reality, Responses*. Geneva: ILO.

Sinha, A., Sangeeta, N., and Siddiqui, K.A. (1999). *The Impact of Alternative Policies on the Economy with Special Reference to the Informal Sector*. Delhi: National Council for Applied Economic Research.

Thorat, S., and Newman, K.S. (2007). 'Caste and economic discrimination: Causes, consequences and remedies', *Economic and Political Weekly*, 42(41), 4121–4124.

Tosi, A. (1996). 'The excluded and the homeless: The social construction of the fight against poverty in Europe'. In Mingione, E. (ed.): *Urban Poverty and the Underclass: A Reader* (pp. 83–104). Oxford: Blackwell.

Toynbee, P. (2006). *The Guardian*, 23 November.

Turok, I., Kearns, A. and Goodlad, R. (1999). 'Social exclusion: In what sense a planning problem?' *The Town Planning Review*, 70(3), 363–384.

Wacquant, L.J.D. (1993). 'Urban outcasts – Stigma and division in the Black American ghetto and the French urban periphery', *International Journal of Urban and Regional Research*, 17 (September), 366–383.

Wacquant, L.J.D. (1996). 'The rise of advanced marginality: Notes on its nature and implications', *Acta Sociologica*, 39, 121–139.

2

Doing Research on Multidimensional Poverty

SANJAY K. MOHANTY

The multidimensional poverty is a fascinating area of research cutting across the disciplines among economists, sociologists, demographers, public health professionals, and development practitioners. The central idea of multidimensional poverty is to account the multiple deprivations of human beings ranging from ill-health, illiteracy, lack of purchasing power, unemployment, etc. The concept, evolved within the human development framework, has ample research and policy relevance. The national and international developmental agenda in the last two decades including the Millennium Development Goals (MDGs) had developed strategies to mitigate the multidimensional poverty so as to increase human welfare. A series of writings on measurement, application, and limitations of multidimensional poverty appeared in the last two decades (Sahn and Stifel, 2000; Bourguignon and Chakravarty, 2003; Booysen et al., 2008; Calvo 2008; Srinivasan and Mohanty, 2008; Alkire and Foster, 2009; Mohanty, 2010).

Though multidimensional poverty is a priority area of research, it is constrained by a number of theoretical and methodological issues. The objective of this paper is to highlight the theoretical and methodological issues in contextualizing the multidimensional poverty in Indian context and motivate readers to carry out research in this direction. The discussions are presented in two sections. Section I discusses the dimensions and indicators used in defining the multidimensional poverty and section II discusses the methodology of measuring multidimensional poverty. I confined the discussion to the UNDP work on multidimensional poverty and specifically to the variables and methodology used in the Human Poverty Index 1 (introduced in Human Development Report, 1997) and the Multidimensional Poverty Index (MPI), recently disseminated by UNDP in the Human Development Report, 2010.

I
Multidimensional Poverty: Multiple Dimensions

Prior to 1990 the concept of poverty was confined to money metric poverty with a focus of income or consumption. In money metric poverty, a person was defined as poor if his/her income or expenditure falls below the minimum level, defined as poverty line. With the shift in development paradigm (human development approach) in 1990, the concept of multidimensional poverty evolved. It is built in the human development framework and intended to address the multiple failures in human capability such as ill-health, illiteracy, and undernutrition. Hence, poverty is multidimensional and the dimensions are interlinked. The issues on the conceptualization of dimensions and the relevant indicators are central to the multidimensional poverty research. Ideally, the multidimensional poverty should cover failures on all dimension on which the success is measured. Hence, the dimensions are broad and comprehensive and include the dimensions of health, education, income, work and employment, empowerment, environment, social relationship, and safety and security.

The UNDP research on multidimensional poverty focused on three key dimensions of human development, namely, health, knowledge, and income. We discuss the dimensions and indicators used in HPI-1 and the Multiple Poverty Index (MPI), developed by UNDP. The HPI-1 was introduced in 1997 and supplemented by MPI in 2010. Both the measures used the dimensions of health, knowledge, and income. While the HPI-1 is computed at the national/sub-national level, the MPI is said to capture poverty using the unit data at household level. A detailed comparison of variables used and the methodology of computing the HPI-1 and MPI are given in Table 1.

In Indian context, several organizations and researchers have dealt with the estimation of multidimensional poverty in one form or other. The three rounds of below poverty line surveys carried out by the Ministry of Rural Development used the concept of multidimensional poverty (Sundaram, 2003). Srinivasan and Mohanty (2008) using the simple measures estimated the deprivations by caste and religion in Indian states. Mohanty (2010) using the third round of the National Family and Health Survey (NFHS) estimated the multidimensional poverty in India. Malik and Mohanty (2010) using field based data linked multidimensional poverty with child schooling. Most of the studies in multidimensional poverty focussed on education, health, and income and few studies have included subjective well-being such as fear to face hardship (Calvo, 2008) in defining multidimensional poverty. Alkire (2007) outlined informal employment, empowerment, safety

Table 1

A Comparison of Variables and Methodology Used in HPI-1 and MPI

Dimensions/ variables/ methodology	*Human Poverty Index 1 (HPI-1)*	*Multidimensional Poverty Index (MPI)*
Variables used in health dimension	Probability of not surviving till age 40 (P1)	At least one member is malnourished One or more children died in the household.
Variables used in knowledge dimension	Adult illiteracy rate (P2)	No one has completed five years of schooling At least one school-age child not enrolled in school
Variables used in income dimension	Unweighted average of percentage of population without access to improved water sources Underweight children under age 5 (P3)	No electricity No access to adequate sanitation House has dirt floor Household uses dirty cooking fuel (dung, firewood, and charcoal) Household has no car and owns at most one of bicycle, motorcycle, radio, refrigerator, telephone, or television
Methodology	$HPI-1 =$ $[1/3(P_1^{\alpha}+P_3^{\alpha})]^{1/\alpha}$ $\alpha = 3$	MPI = The multidimensional headcount ratio (H) × Intensity (or breadth of poverty) (A) where H= q/n, where q is the number of people who are multidimensionally poor and n is the total population A = Proportion of weighted components indicator, d, in which on average poor people are deprived. For poor households only, the deprivation scores are summed and divided by the total number of indicators and by the total number of poor persons $A = \frac{\sum_1^q c}{qd}$ C = Number of weighted deprivation the poor experience and d is the total component indicators considered (10)
Estimates	Macro	Micro and Micro

Source: UNDP Human Development Report 1997 and 2010.

from violence, the ability to go about without shame, and psychological and subjective well-being as missing dimensions in multidimensional poverty. These dimensions are often excluded on the ground of non-availability of data and comparability across the countries.

Dimension of Health

There is some degree of satisfaction in the inclusion of health dimension in the measurement of multidimensional poverty, though there is discontent on the indicator used to measure the health domain. The health indicators used to quantify the ill health are: the probability of not surviving till certain age (say 40 years), the infant mortality rate (IMR), the under-five mortality rate (U5MR), and the maternal mortality ratio (MMR). The prevalence of underweight children and the body mass index of adult members (nutrition indicators) are also included to reflect the dimensions of ill-health.

While the HPI-1 was using the probability of not surviving till age 40 (for developing countries), the MPI used the variables such as death of one or more children in the household and at least one malnourished member in the household. The probability of not surviving till age 40 can only be computed at national and sub-national level and cannot be practised at micro-level research. On the other hand, the indicators used in the MPI, the death of one or more children in the family do not reflect the current mortality scenario in the country. For example, suppose a woman who is 49 years now experienced child loss soon after marriage (say when she was 18 years old) has passed 31 years of reproductive period since the death of her child and there has been lot of improvement in mortality situation in the last 31 years. Hence, this variable is not a good variable to capture the recent changes in mortality. It would have been better to consider child loss in the last five years so as to capture child mortality in recent years. Also, the child death does not capture the maternal deaths and adult deaths which are also critical component of life. Second, the variable 'at least one malnourished member in the household' is not uniformly collected in the three rounds of NFHS. Only in NFHS-III, information on men in the age group 15–54 years was incorporated (IIPS and Macro International, 2007). Also, there is a need to discuss the feasibility of incorporation of any underweight child in the household as about half of the children in the country are underweight. Hence, selection of indicators should be carefully done.

We feel that death of any usual member in the household below a certain age (say 65 years) in a reference period (1 or 2 years) may be helpful to capture the dimension of ill health. This can also be supplemented by the cause of death that will enhance the scope of research. It will incorporate the infant and child mortality, maternal mortality as well as the rising adult mortality. The prevalence of chronic disease and self-rated health may also be helpful to assess the ill-health of the population. With respect to nutrition measures, we recommend to use underweight children under age 5 rather than using any malnourished member in the household. We believe that if selections of indicators are not dealt carefully, it is likely to provide estimates that have limited practical reliability.

Dimensions of Knowledge

From 1990 to 2009, the knowledge dimension in human development index was represented by adult literacy and gross enrolment. The corresponding indicator used in HPI-1 was adult illiteracy rate. While adult illiteracy measures the basic literacy status of the population, it does not broadly capture the knowledge domain. The MPI in 2010 introduced two indicators, namely, any member who has less than five years of schooling and at least one school-age child not enrolled in school. But, a large proportion of children are not interested in study or parents are not interested to send children to school and so they are out of school. I recommend two refined indicators to be considered in this regard: the presence of any adult illiterate member in the household and the out of school children in the primary school age (6–10 years).

Dimension of Income

In income dimension, the HPI-1 used unweighted average of two indicators, the percentage of population not using the improved water and the percentage of children underweight for age. The definition of improved water is used differently in Indian context. While the Census of India used well water as unsafe, it is used differently in other surveys. Similarly, the underweight children under five years are good indicator but its relevance as proxy of income or consumption poverty is questionable. A large proportion of richer households have underweight children and so such indicator needs to be carefully contextualized.

The MPI used six indicators, namely, electricity, access to drinking water, access to sanitation, dirt floor, use dirty cooking fuel, and household has no car and owns bicycle, motorcycle, radio, refrigerator, telephone, and television. These indicators do not truly reflect the income dimension of poverty. While electricity is a community variable, a large proportion of rural households (rich and poor farmers) use firewood and dung for cooking as those are by product of cultivation. In the era of globalized economy, the possession of a few consumer durables does not truly reflect the economic status of the household. A large proportion of households in slums of Mumbai own all these assets/amenities and many of these are often essential for life. The correlation of economic proxies and consumption expenditure is weak in India and hence may not truly reflect the economic condition of the household (Srivastava and Mohanty, 2010). The definition of poverty is amply clear when we closely look at the experience of poor and under-privileged people. One such example from field study as documented by the World Bank group reveals: *"We eat when we have, we sleep when we do not"* (The World Bank Group, 2001). Though this refers to extreme case of starvation, there is increasing case of quiet and hidden starvation in the country.

We suggest incorporating few of the indicators such as not getting sufficient food in a reference period (any month or a year), daily purchase of staple food, and monthly per capita consumption expenditure so as to reflect the income dimension in multidimensional poverty. These indicators are robust in measuring the multidimensional poverty (Malik and Mohanty, 2010). Also, the addition of an abridged version of consumption expenditure in the much used NFHS schedule will be useful.

Mission Dimensions: Work and Employment

The missing dimensions in the multidimensional poverty research are work and employment, environment, empowerment, security, psychological and social well-being, etc. We understand the limitations of many of these dimensions but suggest incorporating at least work and employment in the multidimensional poverty research. We believe that this is a critical dimension of multidimensional poverty, though often neglected. One variable that is very powerful to capture the overall well-being of the household is the type of work. This is relatively easy to canvass and it really captures the multidimensionality of poverty. We have put forward two such indicators as an illustration, one for rural and one for urban. In rural areas, a large proportion of households work as agricultural labourer (daily wage earner) and by any means they are the poorest section of the society. In urban area, a large proportion of women work as household maid. All of us agree that these are the poorer section of the society irrespective of caste, creed, and religion and need social protection. My point is that these indicators are easy to collect in survey or census, are not complicated like income or consumption or wealth, and yet can measure the multidimensionality of poverty. Also, an assessment by the survey team member on the economic status can validate such measures.

Besides, unemployment should find a place in the multidimensionality of poverty. The unemployment rate among young people is quite high in both developing and developed countries (IIPS and Population Council, 2010). About two hundred applications are usually received for a one Group 'C' post in Mumbai; many of them are overqualified. Many countries do collect national representative survey data on work and employment and these are not used much. In Indian context, the National Sample Survey Organization (NSSO) is collecting periodic data on employment and unemployment but these data are hardly analysed. Hence, we urge researchers to incorporate work and employment which are equally critical such as health, knowledge, and income. The instability in job and underemployment is pushing many families to poverty trap. Thus, to capture the multidimensionality of poverty, we should incorporate the work and employment domain in multidimensional poverty research.

II
Methodological Issues

Multidimensional Poverty: Methodology

I begin the discussion on the methodological issues that broadly focus the quantification and aggregation of multidimensional poverty. The methodological issues in multidimensional poverty research are equally challenging. These are grouped as (a) fixing of the cut-off point for the poor and non-poor, (b) the aggregation of multiple dimensions into a single index, (c) weighting of dimensions, and (d) the unit of analyses. The methodology used in defining the HPI-1 and the MPI are shown in Table 1.

Fixing of the Cut-off Point of Each Dimension

The identification of the poor and the aggregation of the characteristics of the poor to an overall indicator are two critical measurement issues in poverty (Sen, 1976). The poor in each of the dimensions are defined as shortfalls of basic needs from a pre-specified minimum level. For example, in the health domain, the HPI-1 takes a minimum cut-off point of 40 years, while the MPI takes death of any child in the household. The education domain in MPI uses five years of education as one of the indicator. There is no hard and fast rule to fix the cut-off point and these depend on the context of research. But, the essence is that each dimension should have segregation of poor and non-poor.

Aggregation of Multiple Dimensions

The second step in quantifying the multidimensional poverty is the aggregation of multiple dimensions into a single index. In literature, three distinct approaches, namely, the union approach, the intersection approach, and relative approach are used. The union approach defines a person as poor if he/she is poor in any one dimension, while the intersection approach defines a person as poor if he/she is poor in all dimensions. The relative approach uses some predefined cut-off point such as quintile or quartile in defining the poverty line. While the union approach tends to overestimate poverty, the intersection approach tends to underestimate poverty. For example, a person who may be healthy but lives in hunger will be excluded by the intersection approach. The approach to be adapted depends on the context.

Weighting of Dimensions

The next question comes is the weighting of dimensions as well as indicators. In the dimension index on income in HPI-1, equal weight is assigned to the proportion of underweight children and the percentage of population without access to improved water but the dimensions are weighted unequally. A value of 3 is recommended to penalize the inequality. The rationale is to give higher weight in the dimension where deprivation is more. On the other hand, the MPI used a set of 10 indicators in the dimensions of education, health and living standard, assigned equal weight to each dimension, and equal weight to the variables within the dimension. There is no fixed set of rules in assigning weight to the dimensions and weights may be derived using statistical method.

Unit of Analyses

The indicators used in the calculation of MPI are both at household level and at individual level. Hence, the estimates are needed to be carefully interpreted. If all the variables are at household level, then result may be interpreted at household-level estimates. If the household estimates are weighted by household size, then the estimates may be said to be at population level. Ideally, the poverty estimates need to be at individual level such as percentage of population multidimensionally poor.

Conclusion

Because of these limitations, the estimates of multidimensional poverty by HDR 2010 were 70 per cent for the country. Such estimates have little practical utility for poverty eradication programme. Given the limitations of the variable, the MPI needs to be contextualized and the indicators need to be chosen carefully. At the outset, the multidimensional poverty should be context specific. There are dimensions and indicators that measured best in one context but do not suit in other. The indicators within each dimension should be carefully selected to truly reflect the multidimensionality of poverty. It will be rewarding to address the missing dimensions by undertaking field study and linking with the variables of interest.

References

Alkire, S., and Foster, J. (2009). *Counting and Multidimensional Poverty Measures*. Oxford Poverty & Human Development Initiative (OPHI) Working Paper 7.5. Oxford: Department of International Development, University of Oxford.

Alkire, S. (2007). 'The missing dimensions of poverty data: Introduction to the special issue', *Oxford Development Studies*, 35(4), 347–359.

Booysen, F., Von Maltitz, M., and Du Rand, G. (2008). 'Using an asset index to assess trends in poverty in seven Sub-Saharan African Countries', *World Development*, 36(6), 1113–1130.

Bourguignon, F., and Chakravarty, S.R. (2003). 'The measurement of multidimensional poverty', *Journal of Economic Inequality*, 1(1), 25–49.

Calvo, C. (2008). 'Vulnerability to multidimensional poverty: Peru, 1998–2002', *World Development,* 6(6), 1011–1020.

International Institute for Population Sciences (IIPS) and Macro International (2007). *National Family Health Survey (NFHS 3), 2005–06; India: Volume I*. Mumbai: IIPS.

International Institute for Population Sciences (IIPS) and Population Council (2010). *Youth in India: Situation and Needs 2006–2007*. Mumbai: IIPS.

Malik, B.K., and Mohanty, S.K. (2010). 'Rural poverty and child schooling: A case study of Balasore district, Orissa', *Journal of Educational Planning and Administration*, XXIII(3), 257–281.

Mohanty, S.K. (2010). *Multidimensional Poverty and the State of Child Health in India*. Asia Research Centre Working Paper No 30.London: London School of Economics and Political Science. Available online at: http: //www2.lse.ac.uk/asiaResearchCentre/_files/ARCWP30-Mohanty.pdf.

Sahn, D.E., and Stifel, D.C. (2000). 'Poverty comparison over-time and across countries in Africa', *World Development*, 28(12), 2123–2155.

Sen, A. (1976). 'An Ordinal Approach to Measurement', *Econometric*, 44, 219–31.

Srinivasan, K., and Mohanty, S.K. (2008). 'Household deprivation and its linkages with reproductive and child health care and health outcome', *Economic Political Weekly*, 43(48), 67–76.

Srivastava, A., and Mohanty, S.K. (2010). 'Economic proxies, consumption expenditure and health estimates', *Economic Political Weekly*, 45(16), 55–63.

Sundaram, K. (2003). 'On identification of households below poverty line: Some comments on the proposed methodology', *Economic and Political Weekly*, XXXVIII(9), 896–902.

The World Bank Group (2001). *Poverty Reduction and Economic Management/ Human Development/Development Economics*. Washington, DC: World Bank.

UNDP (1997). *Human Development Report*. New York: Oxford University Press. Table 1.

UNDP (2010). *Human Development Report 2010*. New York: Palgrave Macmillan.

3

Development, Poverty and Social Exclusion

A Regional Perspective

BIKRAMADITYA KUMAR CHOUDHARY

Development is said to be the remedy for all the problems that the world is facing today. The statement becomes more dogmatic when applied to the Third World countries. Economists are always of the opinion that development will take care of all kinds of problems including social, political, and ecological. On the other side of the coin, the reality is that development is the reason for all kinds of conflicts, displacements, deaths, and suicides. Noted jurist Iyer (1998) has highlighted several disadvantages of ongoing developmental process, saying as:

> India today is the victim of development, ask Medha Patkar or Sundarlal Bahguna about the victim of development ... the perilous process of environmental injuries, the polluted rivers, the disappearing mountains, the depleting mineral resources, the uprooted tribals, the submerged mother earth, and the vast multitude of marginalised human beings who are appalled by the terrorism of development and await their turn to be sacrificed at the inexorably market hungry, alter of poignant irrecoverable 'blood and iron' development manias. (Iyer, 1998: 45)

The aim of this paper is not to adopt or confront either of these two positions. Rather, the paper would develop a link between poverty, development, and social exclusion in a regional perspective. There have been studies which relate development of few with poverty for many, but exclusion-related studies so far have tried to dilute the relationship between poverty and exclusion by adding non-poor also as excluded groups. It is true that process of exclusion is not confined to poor only but the fact remain that poor are more vulnerable than others to be excluded. There has not been a clear perspective or a convincing analysis that show how poverty and social exclusion are related under present-day condition. Why these phenomena have become important in prosperous society and are going unchecked in poor economies and why free-market policy of the United States or regulated policy of Europe has not been able to tackle it. This paper tries to explore what India can learn, if any, from these experiences to understand the process of social exclusion and aggravating regional concentration and exclusion.

This paper is divided into five sections. It begins with a conceptual note on exclusion and social exclusion. Next section traces the existing link between development and exclusion and also elaborates upon the processes that bring exclusion. The third section details about the new dynamics of poverty and exclusion. The importance of a regional perspective in the study of poverty and exclusion is developed in fourth section where certain examples from India are presented to support the case for a regional perspective. The last section tries to formulate an approach that can be taken up for further study.

Exclusion/Social Exclusion: A Conceptual Note

Exclusion, in the sense of its origin as a concept, is seen as a cumulative process of deprivation up to a point where society is polarized into a majority of insiders and an increasingly walled-off minorities of outcastes – *les exclues* or the underclass (Woodward and Kohli, 2001). In Third World countries such as India, situation is quite contrary. Here majority have been excluded from participation in social, political, and economic processes for long. In India, there is very sporadic writing on exclusion/social exclusion. Though the UGC has directed or to say has been instrumental in opening up of Centre for Social Exclusion at different universities and institutes, the concept is in its formative stage. Lots of grey areas are encountered while listening to the debates/presentations which are going on to formulate courses. On one hand, it is linked to the idea of alienation, marginalization, and deprivation, while on the other hand it is confined to caste and community. The new beginning is somehow centred on caste, community, gender, and minorities, as Thorat (2006) noted that in India exclusion involves social processes that exclude, discriminate, isolate and deprive some groups on the basis of caste, ethnicity and religion. These excluded groups include former untouchables (or dalits), adivasis and some religious minorities.

Exclusion is a process whereby certain individuals are pushed to the edge of society and prevented from participating fully by virtue of their poverty, or lack of basic competencies and lifelong learning opportunities, or as a result of discrimination. This distances them from job, income and education, and training opportunities, as well as social and community networks and activities. They have little access to power and decision making bodies and thus feel powerless and unable to take control over the decisions that affect their day to day lives (European Commission, 2004). In view of British government, social exclusion happens when people or places suffer from a series of problems such as unemployment, discrimination, poor skills, low incomes, poor housing, high crime, ill health and family breakdown. When such problems combine they can create a vicious cycle. Social exclusion can happen as a result of problems that face one person in their life. But it can also start from birth. Being born into poverty or to parents with low skills has a major influence on future life chances (Government of United Kingdom, 2006). These two definitions brings individual in the centre of the conception of exclusion and somehow linked the concept with that of poverty, unemployment, ill-health, and so on, quite contrary to the view expressed by Thorat (2006), who considers caste, gender, and religion as the main determinant of the excluded groups.

Invention of the term 'social exclusion' in 1974 is attributed to Rene Lenior, then secretary in Chirac government in France, who included a variety of people such as the poor, handicapped, suicidal people, aged, abused children, substance abusers, and so on. Since then the term 'social exclusion' has attracted much attention in France, Britain, and elsewhere in the Western world; still it is noted that 'reading numerous enquiries and reports on exclusion reveals a profound confusion among experts' (Ruano-Borbalan, 1993, quoted in Atkinson, 1998). Origin of the term 'exclusion', nevertheless, is traced to Weber who identified exclusion as one from of social closure that is an intended attempt of one group to secure privileged position at the expense of other groups through process of subordination (Burchardt et al., 2002). This kind of exclusion that Jordan (1996) calls active exclusion is voluntary by including certain specific type of people through subtle membership such as 'gated communities' in cities, or network of elite educational institutions for top jobs, or a club. In this form, there is a doubt about exclusion always being negative and inclusion always being positive attribute in the society. This also draws our attention to two binaries about the form of exclusion, viz., 'active' versus 'passive' exclusion and 'voluntary' versus 'imposed' exclusion.

There have been arguments that voluntary exclusion is not bad especially taking example from certain community outside who want to retain their identity. Imposed exclusion or passive exclusion that generates due to exclusionary processes is almost unquestionably accepted as undesirable. However, voluntary exclusion is also in most cases have negative impact on society in more than one ways. I take two examples: one, if an individual leaves a job that is a voluntary exclusion of himself from the employment; the reason of resignation is because he wants to switch to higher wage job and the exclusion is not negative for him. Another condition could be that he resigns because of fear of being fired, then exclusion though seems voluntary does have a negative impact on the well-being of the individual. Second example is a set of practices in India where voluntary exclusion exist: bureaucrats are trained to exclude themselves with the dictum 'you are not the mass', this exclusion gives an elated feeling of Weberian kind; second case would be if a person from north-eastern part of the country does exclude himself/herself due to embarrassing exclamatory mark such as '*chinki*', or a person from rural Gangetic plain exclude himself/herself due to being dubbed as '*gawar*'.

Another example could be of health care service in India, where two groups are seen excluded: one who does not know about it or cannot access it due to various reasons such as distance, time, perceived discrimination, and so on and another are those who do not need it as they can afford services available outside public health care system either through insurance or can pay by themselves. The outcome is negative in both the cases; as entire health care system becomes non-friendly and more often discriminatory to the larger group.

These are different kinds of exclusions and the behavioural condition of individual or group seems important prima facie. However, the social, political, and economic processes lay the foundation of these forms of exclusions. There can be several such examples which suggest exclusion – voluntary or involuntary both have negative impact on social solidarity in post-industrialist capitalist world. Increasing securitization also symbolizes exclusion of another kind, as vast majority is excluded. Gate in this sense has become symbol of exclusion at least for neighbourhood exclusion, where outside the gate all are excluded. In these cases, minority excludes majority, quite contrary to the French conception of exclusion of minority from the mainstream.

Another related concept is of social isolation where individual or group isolates itself from larger society. The voluntary separation like that of bureaucrats can be put in the category of social isolation. In country such as India, more often social isolation leads to social exclusion, especially on the lower threshold. It has already been analysed that in India society exclusion is on two thresholds: one is the upper circuit of the society that isolates or excludes itself as they can afford to; second is the lower circuit that cannot participate in the social processes. Isolation when turned to exclusion and even isolation in itself has negative impact on society at least in two counts: social solidarity and social justice. When people do not participate, there will be lesser extent of social solidarity and if certain individuals or groups remain in social closure, there will be absence of equal opportunity.

The idea of social exclusion is considered 'a necessary and inherent characteristic of unequal post-industrial capitalism founded around a flexible labour market' (Byrne, 1999: 128). Since mid-1970s, labour flexibility has increased systematically and deregulation and fierce competition among labour has become new reality in place of Marxist conception of 'reserve army of labour'. Low-skilled workers have suffered worst due to the technological development and growing international competition since mid-1970s. Even public sector in many countries has started practicing an 'eviction of lower skilled' (Schokkaert and Sweeney, 1999). These developments have created heart of the problem of social exclusion in middle-class societies.

Existing exclusion in India cannot be sufficiently explained by existing paradigms of social exclusion. It will be better understood if all three paradigms are incorporated in one framework. In India, we do witness, the Weberian framework of exclusion where certain groups especially upper caste in dominant religious communities (including Islam and Sikh) have developed social closure and have systematically excluded vast majority of masses from goods and services. Here Sen's (2000) understanding of exclusion is also important to bring in, where he defines exclusion in terms of capabilities and not in terms of commodities. He accepts social exclusion framework as it focuses on relational root of deprivation and reinforces the understanding of poverty as capability deprivation. Indian society that is passing a transitory phase – a shift from feudal (caste hierarchy) economy to corporate economy; Marxist conception is more relevant that 'having decided being' at least in the cities of India. Even in rural India, large mass is fighting absolute poverty and consequent deprivation in all basic fields including health and education. Thus, poverty remains embedded in the conception of exclusion in India. Solidarity paradigm based on Rousseau's conception can be understood in India linking it with the question of security, physical, economic, social, and so on. Applying Hobbes' idea of liberalism, exclusion in India is certainly based on discrimination, however the causes of discrimination are not invisible rather they are explicit in terms of absence of land rights, hierarchical educational system based on income availability, unavailability of employment opportunities, and so on. In India, we need to understand the complexity of the process that creates exclusion and sites of exclusion that are products of differential processes.

Development: The Process that Brings Exclusion

It is very important to understand why certain individuals or certain groups or certain regions are poor compared to others. The reason for existing low levels of economic performance and lower level of standard of life is often advanced as complimentary to each other what Myrdal (1957) has summed up as 'poor are poor as they are poor'; later on explained as vicious cycle of poverty. The existing gaps are the result of market-oriented policy of the governments across the world. The evidence from China reveals that before implementing open-door policy, the coefficient of variation across provinces was lower compared to the scenario after adopting the open-door policy favouring the coastal areas compared to rest of the country (Demurger et al., 2004). In India, similar conclusions are drawn by Suryanarayan (2008), when he noted that, tentative estimates, if valid, indicates that the growth process between 1993–94 and 2004–05 has bypassed the majority and was not inclusive.

Development brings disparity. Its scale and nature could be different. The understanding of development depends on the way it is defined and Crush (1995) has correctly formulated in the introduction of the book *Power of Development* that development depends on who defines for whom. As its origin lay in the western world, it remained Eurocentric for a considerable period and emphasized on the 'capitalist form of growth', or in the 'growth of national income'. The Third World countries adopted the term in specific forms such as 'championing economic growth', 'catching up', 'providing governable subjects', and so on. Economic developments do provide a paradigm that can be used to help the understanding of the development of better living standard. Of course, the importance of individual level of satisfaction, personal freedom, and well-being cannot be denied while defining development. These aspects of development are equally important while understanding the process of social exclusion. However, such incorporation gives the freedom to scholars to perceive development in different ways in different cultures. Amidst the talk about alternative definition of development (Nash, 1963; Tulpule, 1996), it is necessary to stick to the mainstream classical conception of development, while explaining poverty and exclusion, as in a country such as India variables are available only for these aspects. It is not to suggest that other aspect cannot be explained, rather the process that creates this kind of poverty is responsible for related kind of deprivations that accumulate in exclusion in Indian society.

Development in contemporary world that is dominated by neo-liberal states that promote decentralization, deregulation, liberalization, and a virtual global economy, where more and more people and regions are getting excluded from the process of development. Major concern in development economies is to find a satisfactory answer to a basic question as to why different regions (countries/states/districts) grow differently leading to different degrees of income and expenditure inequalities and poverty. There cannot be single answer to this question, as there could be country-specific/region-specific factors such as governance, institution, culture, the way of intervention, and so on that play a dominant role in determining growth path (Hayami, 1997). The great inequality among nations and in between regions of nations in terms of economic performance and the distribution of benefits of such economic development is an undisputed reality. There are glaring examples of various kinds of disparities at international, interstate, and interregional levels. The concentration of development in terms of accumulation and affluence in a few parts of the world or in different parts of a nation continues to remain the law of nature across the globe. Even in the most developed countries such as the United States or the industrial countries of Western Europe, the same scenario has been observed a few decades ago and once again regional inequality is on increase in these countries (Ullman, 1964; Brenner, 1997; Mackay, 2003; Wang and Arnold, 2008). It is also true that in the poor countries or poor regions such disparities are larger and in the beginning of developmental process, these inequalities are supposed to be larger (Myrdal, 1957). The reasons advanced for such inequality have been multifarious, ranging from racial explanation to environmental determinism to resource endowment and in economic terms comparative advantage and in more docile form of racism as 'zeal to achieve' (Rees, 1989; Hilhorst, 1998; Mackay, 2003; Chakravorty, 2005).

The process of development is said to begin with the creation of external demand and certain kind of surplus and having a comparative advantage. These are pre-condition for a classical as well as neo-classical conception of development. In this scenario, relative deprivation of a region is bound to increase, and it has been suggested time and again that if state intervenes or at the later stage of development process, when decentralization begins, these disparities are liable to decrease. This has been clearly shown by the famous U-shape model of Williamson. However, the problem begins at the conception that whether the state intervene to improve the health of the deprived region and if there are economic and political compulsions for not to intervene what would be the later stage of (capitalist) development. Once again, I site example from United Kingdom, where up to the mid-1970s, there was a trend towards greater regional equality in the distribution of income and wealth in the country, but after that for next 25 years regional inequalities increased along with other forms of inequalities (Mackay, 2003). Similar situation has been reported from the United States where income inequality and concentrated disadvantage have been on the rise since the 1960s as the affluent and poor are becoming more concentrated than ever (Wang and Arnold, 2008: 259). Most of the Third World countries started development with foreign aid that had the noble intension of helping developing countries to provide their people with the material opportunities for using their talents, of living a full and happy life, and of steadily improving their lot. However, the result of such activity was emergence of more accentuated form of colonial structure of dual economy. Schumacher (1973: 135) wrote it quite clearly:

> One of the unhealthy and disruptive tendencies in virtually all the developing countries is the emergence, in an even more accentuated form, of the 'dual economy', in which there are two different patterns as widely separated from each other as two different worlds. It is not a matter of some people being rich and others being poor, both being united by a common way of life: it is a matter of two ways of life existing side by side … .

In India, the conditions after independence have been similar to what these lines read. In India, the idea of development was based on the Nehruvian conception of modernity that was based on technological advancement and industrialization. In India, lack of profitability of public sector industries has been partly due to a low rate of capacity utilization (Bhilai – 65%; Rourkela – 48%; Durgapur – 30% in 1970s). It was the government's inability to maintain a high rate of public investment and its tendency to shift its pattern of expenditure away from development-oriented projects that has had adverse effect on profitability of these industries (Kalirajan and Atika, 2003: 167). This resulted in new form of concentration of industries in different parts of the country and these regions where such industries were located become deprived regions having lots of unemployed or retrenched labour force with old technical know-how, unsuitable for employment in new industries. Limitation of technological change, missing link between production of raw materials and assembly of final product along with imbalance in industrial development has led to concentration of production and trading activities in states which have traditionally developed infrastructural facilities for large-scale production, manpower training, and financial transaction (Elizondo and Krugman, 1992, quoted in Kalirajan and Atika, 2003).

Poverty and Exclusion: New Dynamics

Inequality of life and expectation were built into the system. The elite view of society has been that since success was due to personal merit, failure was also due to personal lack of merit. The traditional bourgeois ethics, puritan, or secular had ascribed this process to moral or spiritual feebleness than lack of intellect (Hobsbawm, 1975: 246). There has been similarity in terms of conception of poverty and poor in Britain (19th century) and in India (20th century) where victim was to be blamed for their incapability to find work or to generate profit from agriculture as Government of India Report of 1928 noted, 'all the heart of the problem lies the development of the desire for a higher standard of living … the dominant feature in rural India in present days is that the will to live better is not a force to be recknowed with' (GoI, 1928: 499, quoted in Beck, 1994).

Poverty has been a reality of all 'modern' societies and so has been the attempt to protect poor with whatever intention. Brauedel (1981) wrote that the problem was to place poor in a position where they could do no harm as the bourgeois was afraid that 'sedition' might be spread among the poor inside the town or in the surrounding countryside. Brauedel was writing about the condition of 16th– and 17th century Europe. We hardly see any change in the basic consideration of the bourgeois towards poor as Jordan (1996) mentioned Gingrich (1994) saying that in USA the poor have become a target for demoralisation through coercion, it is good populist politics to recommend "orphanages" for the children of "welfare mothers" so that the mothers can be set to work for their keep.

Poverty has been often understood as social exclusion, since the term was used. Many more dimensions were added to the concept of exclusion but along with poverty and not away from poverty. In countries such as United States, United Kingdom, France, and other European countries where certain kinds of participation at various levels exist, it is a different matter to measure exclusion and poverty. Notion of vulnerability is closer to exclusion; vulnerability is not a syndrome of poverty (de Haan, 2008). Poverty means lack of want and is usually measured in terms of consumption, vulnerability means insecurity, defencelessness, and exposure to risks and shocks. In developing country such as India, insecurity is directly linked with accessibility to resources, availability of employment, provision of social security network, and so on; poor are also most vulnerable. The difference between poverty and exclusion is highlighted as where poverty counts the poor, exclusion refers to the processes that create poverty.

Most poverty analysis in the last two to three decades do study correlates of poverty such as lack of education, inaccessibility to resources, and labour market status, location. This brings us closer to a multidimensional notion of social exclusion. Destremau (2001) while presenting a case study of Morocco presented three approaches, viz., 'income poverty', 'social poverty', and 'social exclusion'. There have been different debates surrounding conception of poverty and its measurement such as absolute poverty or relative poverty; urban poverty or rural poverty; income poverty or consumption poverty; individual drift or chronic group; interpersonal poverty or inter-regional poverty; and so on. These binaries have influenced the conceptual debates and measurement processes over long time and in India another binary exists that is poverty as caste versus class. It is clear that there is sufficient amount of uncertainty about the understanding of poverty in the world and so is its relation with social exclusion.

Social exclusion is the outcome of accumulation of various deprivations that originate in poverty. In India, it is persistent in several pockets of towns and cities and most of the villages. Striking feature of accumulated effect of poverty in India begins since the childhood. There are exclusive schools for upper threshold and public schooling system for common people and there exists lower strata which remain out of school. Those who are in school, the difference are much wider. Entry to schools is based on economic capability. The schooling system in India is marked by high-fee charging profit-making ventures (often intervened by judiciary to maintain certain level of fee), unaffordable for larger section of the society. The gap continues in higher education. There are too many for few jobs and too many jobs are available for very few. This creates a vicious cycle that is becoming more and more urban-centred phenomena. Difference between towns and villages are increasing. There have been efforts to bring certain section of society into educational fold. This inclusion also results in exclusion. There has been inclusion of students from deprived section of society. But those who are included, exclude others and larger section of society remains excluded.

There have been related terms such as deprivation, marginalization, and underdevelopment having similar connotation with that of poverty at least in regional term. Poor region are often referred to as deprived region, backward region, or underdeveloped region. Most of the problem of underdevelopment is considered as local and it is argued that the local population generally does not show much concern for the macro affluence or macro-level economic crisis. Chakravorty (2005) noted that relative deprivation is a local issue; an unskilled factory worker in Calcutta is rarely concerned about the profit of industrialists in Bombay, just as a landless labourer in any district of Bihar or Orissa is unlikely to care about the income level of landlords in a district of Maharashtra. However, this fact is correct only in a situation when mobility, physical and virtual, is restricted. With mobility, the population gets exposed to the larger reality and also shows concerns, as after globalization even the person on the margin of the economy and society gets affected with the decisions that are taken at the global level.

Why Regional Perspective?

Relationship between developmental process and spatial locations has been in debate during most of the developmental history. Developmental history, as defined in the mainstream discourse, started since human has learnt about accumulation. This history traces back to the beginning of agriculture when it became possible to store the output and use it later. The sense of space, initially as a physical entity and later as cultural landscape remained attached with the process of development. The initiation of industrialization and its reliance on fund resources made the case for space more distinctive and scholars started becoming dogmatic about the spatial characteristics. The loosely understood space got more precisely defined in the late 19th and early 20th century when theories of development came into existence with the conception of external demand and comparative advantage.

It is shown by various studies that poor are concentrated in backward and slow-growing regions and therefore it is not irrelevant to go for an analysis of interstate disparities that leads to poverty and social exclusion for large majority. It has been noticed that economic liberalization has resulted in enhanced inter-state competition for instituting new industries and the race is often won by leading economies as they already have needed and sufficient infrastructure in place. Tables 1–3 show what India has achieved over the period of time and why still regional perspective is more important.

Table 1

Median per Capita Consumption (₹ per 30 days)

States/India	*Rural*	*Urban*	*States*	*Rural*	*Urban*
India	455.75	792.17	Kerala	744.58	903.12
Andhra Pradesh	488.88	748.35	Madhya Pradesh	377.33	641.9
Assam	514.71	899.4	Maharashtra	459.08	863.9
Bihar	379.75	541.75	Orissa	335.25	579.5
Chhattisgarh	345.33	698.25	Punjab	693.42	929.3
Gujarat	508.67	932.88	Rajasthan	515.14	708.21
Haryana	673.71	871.4	Tamil Nadu	469.33	819.37
Jharkhand	378.5		Uttar Pradesh	437	636.5
Karnataka	425.55	763.68	West Bengal	475	833.25

Source: Suryanarayan (2008) calculated from NSSO.

Initiatives in India for regional development started with a vision document of National Planning Commission chaired by Jawaharlal Nehru, who later became first prime minister of the country. The need to develop the poor regions and weaker sections of the society was identified. This realization was tried to translate into action during Third Plan period (1962–1967) in independent India. The efforts in India remain confined to the decentralization of industries to the industrially backward regions. It was broadly accepted that a country or region can develop only if there is sufficient scale of industrialization. However, the problem with the conception remained that industries did got established in the region but the population of the region remain broadly untouched with that, as there was not sufficient effort for skill formation to the people that was required for securing a participation in the then set-up industries. Further, no efforts were made to identify the critical aspects of people's life in these backward regions where intervention was needed either in terms of skill formation or in terms of provision of technology so that the people can improve their capabilities to harness the potentials. The Twelfth Plan, also reflects that the state is committed towards poor region and poor people.

This statement makes it clear that the past efforts to ameliorate regional disparity have not succeeded due to one or the other reasons and the twelfth plan aims to achieve higher level of equity among regions. However, one needs to be careful when reading such documents. The objective of the recent plans has been outlined to achieve higher growth rate of economy. The objective to attain higher growth rate and distribution of these to poor regions have been historically proved contradictory to each other and almost all theory of regional development has shown that in the initial stage higher growth rate of economy is needed and this can be achieved when taking benefit of agglomeration effect and only in the later phase when growth rate establishes the process of decentralization began. However, in the plan document the two contradictory goals are outlined in the same sentence without resolving the conflict through suggestions or arguments at least to show how they can be complementary and not contradictory. The setting up of state-level targets in the plan has hardly shown any expected impact on reduction of disparity among the states. Another important feature is the intra-state differences in terms of quality of life and economic performance. Maharashtra, an economically developed state, also has the district of Gadchiroli; the state of Gujarat also encompasses the district of The Dangs.

Table 2

Distribution of NSDP and Population above Poverty Line across States

States/India	*NSDP*	*Population above poverty line*	*States*	*NSDP*	*Population above poverty line*
India	—	—	Kerala	18262	87.28
Andhra Pradesh	14715	84.23	Madhya Pradesh	10907	62.57
Assam	9720	63.91	Maharashtra	23398	74.98
Bihar	6328	57.4	Orissa	9162	52.82
Chhattisgarh	—	—	Punjab	23040	93.84
Gujarat	18685	85.93	Rajasthan	12533	84.72
Haryana	21551	91.26	Tamil Nadu	19141	78.88
Jharkhand			Uttar Pradesh	9764	68.85
Karnataka	16343	79.96	West Bengal	15569	72.98

Source: Tenth Five-Year Plan, Vol. III, Planning Commission, 2007.

There were allocations for certain kind to ameliorate poverty, relocate industries, and create certain kind of infrastructure and so on. As the emphasis was on the creation of industrial centres in different parts of the country, the process and technology that would have harnessed local resources for the benefit of the people of the region were largely ignored, resulting in two India side by side. There have been several writings on these lines; here two distinct India can be identified: one urban India voicing concern for clean air, less congestion open space, and so on, and the rural India that is still struggling for two squares of meal on an assured basis. The conditions became more alarming since mid-1980s and early 1990s when a paradigm shift was witnessed in Indian economy in tune with the U-turn in the United States and European countries when boom started (Mackey, 2003; Wang and Arnold, 2008). Regional dimension of developmental

Table 3

Distribution of Amenities across States

States/India	*Household availing banking services*	*Households having permanent houses*	*States*	*Household availing banking services*	*Household having permanent houses*
India	35.54	51.8	Kerala	51.1	68.14
Andhra Pradesh	31.04	54.72	Madhya Pradesh	27.92	41.55
Assam	20.53	19.69	Maharashtra	48.13	57.82
Bihar	21.34	40.73	Orissa	24.21	27.58
Chhattisgarh	24.12	25.4	Punjab	48.5	86.1
Gujarat	37.83	65.33	Rajasthan	28.89	64.94
Haryana	45.23	65.79	Tamil Nadu	22.82	58.52
Jharkhand	30.15	31.4	Uttar Pradesh	44.12	53.38
Karnataka	39.99	58.46	West Bengal	36.79	40.43
			Uttaranchal	59.82	86.34

Source: Tables on Houses and Household Amenities, Census of India, 2001.

activities were forgotten even in the plans, and definite outcome was almost zero allocation for depressed areas, even there was no modification or efforts to re-identify depressed region or poor regions. Arguments were that once the country achieve a 'high rate' of growth, 'all problems will be the reality of past'. As expected or say suspected by the left academicians, this did not happen. Before a steady high rate of growth could be achieved, the boom busted and all efforts are once again got diverted towards 'consolidation' of economy. The tragedy of the poor region remains that they wait endlessly for the 'spread effect' and 'trickle down' to take place but before it the crisis began. These poor regions suffer when the centre reaps the fruit of the economic development but when the crises begin these are the regions, which suffer worst. This is not by accident but this is by design, as highlighted by economists across the First World and Third World (Krugman, 2009; Patnaik, 2011).

Where We Need to Focus?

Many have tried to establish link between geographical space and economic space but are yet to consider geographical space as important factor in ameliorating persistent regional exclusion. Regional perspective to understand exclusion and development is not an approach rather it indicates towards the need of a paradigmatic change. Exclusion encompasses a paradigmatic departure from existing conceptual framework of macro perspective of development and poverty count. The paradigm shift is in two ways: one it guides to analyse the processes that produce the existing socio-spatial inequalities rather than looking at causal variations;

two it firmly makes a departure from national totalitarian framework of economy, polity, and society. Rise of regional aspirations and assertions of different kinds inside and outside nation-state is only reflection of this rising trend. We have to do away with the totalitarian rationalist framework of analysis of development and poverty. Multitude of factors such as affect and shape existing socio-spatial inequalities and the inter-relationships among them needs to be linked with the explanations of exclusion and to the proposed alternatives.

We not only need to understand trade and regional development in one framework as suggested by Krugman (1991) but also draw explanations from the existing pattern of industrial development that is necessarily uneven. Study of social exclusion needs to be based on the conception of development that brings poverty of different kinds and in the process make more and more people and region excluded from the process of development. The selected dimension for different society will be different as there are different processes that result in certain specific kind of social exclusion. However, certain dimensions such as 'basic needs fulfilment', 'having an adequate income', 'attaining a certain quality of life', 'having an adequate housing', and 'being able to find a job' are essential for all societies that are fighting social exclusion. Different regions of India have different practices of resource distribution (especially land), different forms of CPR, and different social practices that alienate and deprive certain section of society. In India, caste-based economy is at decline (Srinivas, 2003) and economy-based class-caste society is forming. In such a situation, going back to classical conception of caste-based social exclusion may not be sufficient to address the real problem of Indian society. Regional dimension is important to address specific kind of deprivation at different sites of exclusion such as at dam sites, highway sides, SEZs, and industrial sites. These are outcome of larger economic link of the region to the global economic system that excludes more and more regions.

In different parts of the country, the model of socialism, the mode of oppression, and the mechanism of marginalization and process that produce poverty and exclusion have been divergent. Relationships between resources and people have been shaped on the basis of knowledge that the communities have at their disposal. Academicians and planners need to broaden their horizon to accept traditional knowledge that has shaped the land relations and other relations for ages, if we need to explain and suggest viable alternative to excluded people. There is a need to utilize local knowledge and link local culture and practices in resource planning of a particular region rather than suggesting macro-level economic and technological prescriptions. Regional perspective in 'exclusion studies' advocates for a paradigmatic shift from totalitarian rationalist global perspective to a pluralistic, often contested local and regional solutions, incorporating traditional wisdom and knowledge in resource planning for the empowerment of masses. Thus, it would not be inappropriate to suggest evolving a regional perspective to deal with the issue of social exclusion.

References

Atkinson, A.B. (1998). *Poverty in Europe.* Oxford: Blackwell.

Beck, T. (1994). *The Experience of Poverty: Fighting for Respect and Resources in Village India.* London: Intermediate Technology Publication.

Brauedel, N. (1981). *The Structure of Everyday Life: The Limits of the Possible.* Translated by Sian Reynolds. London: Collins.

Brenner, N. (1997). 'State Territorial Restructuring and the Production of Spatial Scale: Urban and Regional Planning in the Federal Republic of Germany, 1960–1990'. *Political Geography,* 16: 273–306.

Burchardt, T., Grand, J.L. and Piachaud, D. (2002). *Understanding Social Exclusion.* London: Oxford University Press.

Byrne, D. (1999). *Social Exclusion.* Buckingham: Open University Press.

Chakravorty, S. (2005). 'The History and Geography of Regional Development Theory: A Futile Search for a Paradigm'. In N. Banerjee and S. Marjit (eds.), *Development, Displacement and Disparity* (pp. 29–52). New Delhi: Orient Longman.

Crush, J. (1995). *Power of Development.* New York: Routledge.

de Hann, A. (2008). 'Social Exclusion: Towards a Holistic Understanding of Deprivation'. In A. de Han and N. Kabeer (eds.), *Social Exclusion* (pp. 3–18). New Delhi: Critical Quest.

Demurger, S. et al. (2004). 'Geography, Economic Policy and Regional Development in China'. Discussion Paper No. 1950, Harvard Institute of Economic Research.

Destremau, B. (2001). 'Poverty, Discourse and State Power: A Case Study of Morocco'. In F. Wilson, N. Kanji and E. Braathen (eds.), *Poverty Reduction: What Role for the State in Today's Globalized Economy?* Comparative Research on Poverty (CROP) Program (pp. 129–163). London: Zed Books.

European Commission (2004). 'Joint Report on Social Inclusion'. Directorate General for Employment and Social Affairs.

Government of United Kingdom (2006). 'UK National Action Plan on Social Inclusion 2003–2005'. Department of Works and Pensions.

Hayami, Y. (1997). *Development Economics.* Oxford: Clarendon Press.

Hilhorst, J.M. (1998). 'Industrialization and Local/Regional Development Revisited'. *Development and Change,* 29: 1–26.

Hobsbawm, E. (1975). *The Age of Capital.* London: Weidenfeld & Nicholson.

Iyer, V.R. (1998). 'Marginalised Indian Humanity: Do the Bells of Constitution Toll for Them?'. *Indian Journal of Social Work*, 59(1): 44–61.

Jorden, B. (1996). *A Theory of Poverty and Social Exclusion.* Cambridge: Polity Press.

Kalirajan, K. and Atika, T. (2003). 'Income Inequality and Convergence of Income Across Indian States'. In K. Kalirajan and U. Sankar (eds.), *Economic Reforms and Liberalisation of the Indian Economy* (pp. 163–184). UK: Cheltenham.

Krugman, P. (1991). *Geography and Trade.* Leuven: Leuven University Press.

——. (2009). *The Return of Depression Economics and the Crisis of 2008.* New York: W.W. Norton and Company.

Mackay, R.R. (2003). 'Twenty-five Years of Regional Development'. *Regional Studies,* 37(3): 303–317.

Martin, R. and Sunly, P. (1996). 'Paul Krugman's Geographical Economics and Its Implications for Regional Development Theory: A Critical Assessment'. *Economic Geography,* 72(3): 259–292.

Myrdal, G. (1957). *Economic Theory and Underdevelopment Regions.* London: Duckworth.

Nash, M. (1963). 'Approaches to the Study of Economic Growth'. *Journal of Social Issues,* 19(1): 1–15.

Patnaik, P. (2011). *Re-envisioning Socialism.* New Delhi: Tulika Books.

Rees, J. (1992). 'Regional Development and Policy Under Turbulence'. *Progress in Human Geography,* 16(2): 223–231.

Schokkaert, E. and Sweeney, J. (1999). 'Social Exclusion and Ethical Responsibility: Solidarity with the Least Skilled'. *Journal of Business Ethics,* 21: 251–267.

Schumacher, E.F. (1973) (1993). *Small is Beautiful: A Study of Economics as if People Mattered.* London: Vintage.

Sen, A.K. (2000). 'Social Exclusion: Concept, Application and Scrutiny'. Social Development Paper No. 1. Asian Development Bank.

Srinivas, M.N. (2003). 'An Obituary on Caste as a System'. *Economic and Political Weekly,* 38(5): 455–459.

Suryanarayn, M.H. (2008). 'What is Exclusive about Inclusive Growth'. *Economic and Political Weekly,* 43(43): 93–101.

Thorat, S. (2006). 'Exclusion and Poverty: Need for Socially Exclusive Politics and Development Approach'. *People's Democracy,* 30(5): 1–2.

Tulpule, B. (1996). 'Redefining Development and Alternative Paradigm'. *Economic and Political Weekly,* 31(45): 2991–2996.

Ullman, E. (1964). 'Discussion on Regional Applications'. *Geographica Polonica,* 1: 193–194.

Wang, F. and Arnold, M.T. (2008). 'Localised Income Inequality, Concentrated Disadvantage and Homicide'. *Applied Geography,* 28: 259–270.

Woodward, A. and Kohli, M. (2001). *Inclusions and Exclusions in European Societies.* London: Routledge.

Part II

National and Regional Perspectives

4

Poverty and Poverty Alleviation Strategies in India

Trends, Dimensions and Lessons Learnt

ABDUL SHABAN

India has undergone a significant economic transformation since it initiated economic liberalization in 1991. There has been enormous shift in the share of sectoral contribution of income and the rate of growth of national income has been near two digits. However, the growth and change in the structure of the economy have not been able to benefit all the sections of the society and regions of the country. As large proportion of the population which lives in poverty in India has hardly seen any significant change in their fortune and in fact for many the livelihood opportunities have become more elusive due to pervasive market forces. The free operation of 'invisible hand' has seen concentration of wealth in select hands. For example, the number of Indian billionaires rose from 9 in 2004 to 40 in 2007, while more than two-fifth of the population continue to live in absolute poverty. Nearly half of the Indian children under six years suffer from underweight and malnutrition, about 80 per cent from anaemia, while some 40 per cent of Indian adults suffer from chronic energy deficit (Bhaduri, 2008). In fact, the paradox of high economic growth rate (growing richness of a few) and increasing vulnerability of masses has bewildered many development analysts, who otherwise thought of increased impact of economic growth on poverty reduction.

This paper attempts (a) to find out the dimensions and trends in poverty in India, (b) to examine the poverty alleviation strategies initiated by Indian government and their impact, and (c) to find out the causes as to why high economic growth in recent years has not been able to make expected dent on poverty. This paper has been organized in five sections. The first section deals with the dimensions and trends in poverty in India, while the next section presents the strategies initiated by the government to alleviate poverty. The third section briefly highlights the typical lessons learnt from the poverty alleviation programmes, causes behind their failures, and asks why the high aggregate economic growth rate in India in 1990s and thereafter have failed to make expected dent on poverty. The last section presents summary and conclusions.

Dimensions and Trends in Poverty

The definition and concept of poverty varies widely across nations. The concept of poverty is conditioned by the minimum of good life obtained in a society. Poverty is defined mainly in two forms: absolute and relative. *Absolute poverty* is based on the concept of basic needs for survival such as food, clothing, and shelter. In many societies, a segment of population is even unable to secure for itself the needed food/nutrition for biological survival, while in other societies the basic needs of all the citizens are largely secured but there are disparities in income, access to education, and health, etc. The poverty in the latter societies usually get defined by the *relative* income, such as the segment of population having income lower than 50 per cent of national median income, and this segment is designated as poor. In India, the poverty is defined in terms of absolute poverty (access to sufficient food energy for biological survival), while in the United States or in many developed European countries, this concept has no relevance (as all the segments of population have access to basic food energy for survival) and the poverty is defined on the basis of relative disparity. The *Indian definition of poverty* emphasizes minimum level of living rather than reasonable level of living (Ramakrishna, 2004). To find out the proportion of population living below the minimum level of living, per capita expenditures are used. The per capita expenditures are assumed to be as enabling factor for getting certain minimum level of kilocalorie consumption of food.

At the time of independence in 1947, about three-fourth of the total population in India was living below the poverty line. After independence, the Government of India initiated many poverty alleviation programmes and those have made significant dent on poverty. However, poverty in India still remains very high in comparison to other countries. In 1977–1978, 51.3 per cent of population was living *below poverty line* (BPL) which declined to 36 per cent in 1993–1994 and to 21.8 per cent in 2004–2005. As shown in Table 1, the *rural poverty* was relatively higher in 1977–1978 than *urban poverty*. However, in recent years the proportion of BPL population in both urban and rural areas has almost become equal. This is mainly due to migration of rural poor to urban areas in search of livelihood. This process has often been called as *spillover* of rural poverty. In term of absolute number of people, the poverty in India is huge; about 240 million people are still living under BPL. In fact, India is a land of contrasts: it has islands of riches in the vast sea of poverty. It is the country which has maximum number of population living in absolute poverty on this planet.

Table 1

Trend in Proportion of Population Living Below Poverty Line in India

Year	*Poverty Ratio (%)*			*Number of Poor (Millions)*		
	Rural	*Urban*	*Combined*	*Rural*	*Urban*	*Combined*
1977–78	53.1	45.2	51.3	264.3	64.4	328.9
1983	45.7	40.8	44.5	252	70.9	322.9
1987–88	39.1	38.2	38.9	231.9	75.2	307.1
1993–94	37.3	32.4	36	244	76.3	320.3
1999–2000	27.1	23.6	26.1	193.2	67.1	260.3
2004–05	21.8	21.7	21.8	170	68.2	238.5

Source: NSSO, (1977–78, 1983, 1987–88, 1993–94, 1999–00, 2004–05).

The Composition of the Poor

Table 1 shows that about 170 million people in rural areas are living under BPL in India. However, not all the segment of rural population in India has been affected equally by the poverty. The rural poverty is getting concentrated in (a) the agricultural labourer households, and (b) artisan households. These two segments of the population have become more vulnerable after the commercialization of agriculture and penetration of market into agricultural and rural sector (Planning Commission, 2006). The penetration of market and commercialization has broken the *Jajmani system,* which made these sections of the population more vulnerable.

Further, it was expected that these segments of population will move to other sectors of the economy after acquiring the required skills. However, this has hardly happened. The market has displaced them from the well-knitted system of rural economy but hardly provided any place for them in skill-intensive secondary and tertiary sectors. The government, which has become subservient to the capitalist class, has hardly done anything concrete for this class except the lip services. As shown in Table 2, agricultural labourers constituted 41 per cent of the total rural poor in the country in 1993–1994, and their share increased to 47 per cent in 1999–2000. Similarly, the share of self-employed in agriculture remained higher in the above-mentioned two benchmark years. The *casualization of labour* has got intensified since the economic reform in 1991. About 90 per cent of the Indian labour force today is engaged in unorganized sector, without any labour benefits except the wages. Similar to agricultural labourers in rural areas, the urban poverty is getting concentrated among casual labourers in urban areas. Their share in total urban poor in the country has risen from 25 per cent in 1993–1994 to 32 per cent in 1999–2000. The growing dependence on casual labour market has exposed the poor to market risks which tend to increase *transient poverty*, whereby households move in and out of poverty due to fluctuations in the labour market.

Table 2

The Share of Highly Vulnerable Groups in Total Rural and Urban Poor

Area	*Occupation*	*1993–1994*	*1999–2000*
Rural	Agricultural labour household	41%	47%
	Self-employed in agriculture	33%	28%
Urban	Casual labour	25%	32%

Source: Computed using data from NSSO, 1993–1994 and 1999–2000.

Regional Dimension of Poverty

The poverty in India is largely concentrated in eastern and northern states (Figure 1). Historically speaking, the eastern and northern states in the country were relatively developed; however, the colonial rule established new kind of economy which was largely based on the international connections/trades. Thus, agricultural sector and small-scale industries on which these states were thriving got neglected and perished due to internal and external competition with the products of mechanized and big industries. Thus, the geographical landscape of the poverty has got completely reversed in the last 100 years or so. The share of backward northern states such as Bihar, Orissa, Madhya Pradesh, and Uttar Pradesh rose from 53 per cent in 1993–1994 to 61 per cent in 1999–2000, while the share of agriculturally prosperous north-western states such as Punjab, Haryana, and Himachal Pradesh declined from 3.03 per cent to 1.26 per cent. The rural poverty in southern states (Karnataka, Andhra Pradesh, Tamil Nadu, Goa, and Kerala) also declined from 15.12 per cent to 11.23 per cent during the above-mentioned years. The urban poor are getting concentrated in Uttar Pradesh, Maharashtra, West Bengal, Madhya Pradesh, and Andhra Pradesh. The share of these states in all-India urban poverty rose from 56 per cent in 1993–1994 to 60 per cent in 1999–2000 (Planning Commission, 2006).

Social Composition of the Poor

Indian society is stratified and hierarchical, based on the concept of division of work and concept of purity and pollution. It has marked social structures/social groups. The groups are Brahmins (the highest caste), Kshatriyas (the next higher group in the caste system after Brahmins), Vaishyas (the third rank group in the social hierarchy), and the Shudras (the untouchables or outcastes). The tribal groups in India are living in marginal and hilly areas. However, in general day-to-day affairs, their social position in vertical social hierarchy is similar to the Shudras. The Government of India has prepared a schedule enlisting the most vulnerable/exploited Shudras and the tribal groups. The Shudras and tribal groups included in the list are popularly known as Scheduled Castes (SCs) and Scheduled Tribes (STs), respectively. In India, the poor and deprived are: (a) the Scheduled Tribes (Adivasi) who suffer from geographical marginality and exclusion – e.g., they are less exposed to modern education and occupation; (b) SCs (Dalit or oppressed) who suffer from social discrimination; (c) other backward castes (OBCs); and (d) Muslims who bear the brunt of discrimination on religious ground. According to 2004–2005 data, 21.8 per cent (22.7% as per Government of India, 2006) of total population of India is poor, while the proportion of population of SCs and STs under BPL is 35 per cent, among the Muslims it is 31 per cent, and among OBC, 21 per cent. In contrast, only 8.7 per cent of general category population is poor.

Food Insecurity

National Sample Survey Organization (1999–2000) data show that about 3 per cent of the households in India face acute shortage of food in some of the months of the year. As opposed to the total 3 per cent of the population, about 6 per cent of the ST households face food deficiency in some of the months. Table 3 shows that food insufficiency is more temporally spread in urban households than rural households. Whereas about 73 per cent of the rural households (out of the 3% of the total households) face food insufficiency for 2–3 months, in urban area about 45 per cent of the households face food insufficiency for 4–5 months. Although the country as a whole has become self-sufficient in food grain production, recent decline in per capita availability/production of food grain can make large section of the population vulnerable.

Table 3

Percentage of Households (out of the 3%) Having Insufficient Food by Number of Food Deficient Months, 1999–2000

Area	*Number of Food Deficient Months*			
	1	*2–3*	*4–5*	*>6*
Rural	6.02	72.66	15.95	5.37
Urban	0.37	53.82	45.11	0.71
Total	5.71	71.61	17.57	5.11

Source: NSSO, 1999–2000.

Strategies for Poverty Alleviation

Raising the standard of living of masses is one of the objectives of planning in India. It was thought that the best way to achieve this objective is through mixed economy: a mixture of socialist and capitalist principles. The central planning following the example of Soviet planning system was introduced, but majority of the economy remained out of the public sector or direct government control. The First Five-Year Plan in India was initiated in 1951, and on the birth date of Mahatma Gandhi, the Father of Nation, the Community Development Programme was launched with the objective of uprooting the poverty. Many area-specific programmes were also launched thereafter in subsequent Five-Year Plans with the basic objectives of alleviation of poverty. 'Remove Poverty' (*garibi hatao*) slogan raised during election in 1971 brought into sharp focus the problem of poverty.

In fact, since the beginning of planning era in 1951, many programmes have been launched to tackle the problem of poverty and malnutrition in India. The programmes have often not yielded expected results and so they have been modified, consolidated, expanded, and improved over time. The targeted programmes initiated in India for poverty alleviation largely fall into four broad categories (Planning Commission, 2006): (a) self-employment programmes; (b) wage employment programmes; (c) direct cash transfers to the targeted groups; and (d) public distribution system (PDS). There are numerous centrally sponsored schemes under the first three categories which are designed by the central government institutions, administered by the Ministry of Rural Development, but implemented by the states, with states generally contributing 25 per cent to their cost. In addition, some state governments also have their own poverty alleviation schemes/programmes. The PDS is a totally centrally sponsored scheme (Planning Commission, 2006). Some of the recent/current poverty alleviation programmes in this regard are discussed in the following text.

Self-Employment Programmes

Many self-employment schemes have been initiated by the central government to enable the poorer section of the society to find their own employment and overcome the penury and poverty. The Swarnajayanti Gram Swarozgar Yojana (SGSY) (Golden Jubilee Village Self-employment Programme) was initiated in April 1999 after restructuring and combining the Integrated Rural Development Programme (IRDP) with allied programmes into a single self-employment programme. The basic objective of the SGSY is to bring the assisted poor families above poverty line by providing them income-generating assets through bank credit and government subsidy (http://eastgarohills.nic.in/drda/central.htm). The approach of the SGSY is based on women's self-help groups (SHGs) that have to act as a financial intermediary and a vehicle for women's empowerment. In this programme, the non-governmental organizations (NGOs) are expected to facilitate the formation of SHGs. In contrast to the IRDP, which focused only on families, the community involvement is emphasized in this programme through SHGs (Planning Commission, 2006).

This programme has been conceived as a holistic self-employment programme and it covers all aspects of self-employment of the rural poor such as (a) organization of the poor in SHGs, (b) their capacity building, (c) selection of key activities, (d) planning of activity clusters, (e) infrastructure building, and (f) technology and market support. The programme aims at establishing a large number of micro-enterprises in rural areas based on the ability of the poor and potential of each area. Assistance under the SGSY is given in the form of subsidy by the government and in the form of credit by the banks. In fact, credit is a critical component of the SGSY. Therefore, the SGSY, in contrast to the IRDP, envisages greater involvement of banks in (a) planning and preparation of project reports, (b) identification of activity clusters, (c) choice of activities of SHGs, (d) selection of individual beneficiaries, and (e) post-credit monitoring including loan recovery. In sum, the main tenets of the SGSY are: (a) key activities, (b) cluster approach, and (c) group method (Planning Commission, 2006; Thomas, 2006).

Wage Employment Programmes

The wage employment programmes have become important instruments for alleviating poverty and smoothening consumption during critical periods including drought and flood situations. They have been perceived to be both protective (via income transfer) and promotive (via infrastructure development) forms of safety nets. Until recently, three major wage employment programmes existed (Planning Commission, 2006):

1. Employment Assurance Scheme (EAS), which guaranteed 100 days of employment to rural poor; it was a Food-for-Work (FFW) programme that provided temporary employment with food grains as wages
2. Jawahar Rozgar Yojana (JRY), (Jawahar Employment Programme), also a temporary employment programme with wages paid in cash which was later replaced by Jawahar Gram Samridhi Yojana (JGSY) (Jawahar Village Development Programme)
3. Jawahar Gram Samridhi Yojana with emphasis on the creation of rural economic infrastructure as the prime objective.

These programmes were replaced in 2001 by the Sampoorna Grameen Rozgar Yojana (SGRY) (Rural Full Employment Programme), a scheme combining the various features of EAS, JRY, and JGSY. The main aim of the SGRY remains the same as for previous employment programmes: providing wage employment in rural areas and creation of economic assets. Under the scheme, wages are paid in both cash and food grains.

In the wage employment programme, FFW programme has been of significance. The FFW programme was designed to ensure employment and food security to the rural people affected by natural disasters such as droughts and floods. The National Food for Work Programme, a-100 per cent centrally sponsored scheme, was launched in the 150 most backward districts in November 2004. It aims at generating supplementary wage employment and assurance of food security through creation of need-based economic, social, and community assets.

Incessant campaign by the civil society and NGO groups led to the creation of the National Rural Employment Guarantee Act (NREGA), which for the first time guaranteed rural families living under BPL the right to work and earn wages for 100 days in a year. The NREGA was launched on 2 February 2006 in 200 backward districts with a view to extend it to all the districts within five years. The scheme subsumes both the SGRY and the FFW in the NREGA districts. Besides providing 100 days of guaranteed employment in a financial year to every rural household whose adult members volunteer to do unskilled manual work, the scheme aims at developing rural infrastructure by undertaking generation of wage employment schemes that address the causes underlying drought, deforestation, and soil erosion (Planning Commission, 2006).

Figure 1

Regional Dimension of Poverty in India, 2004–2005

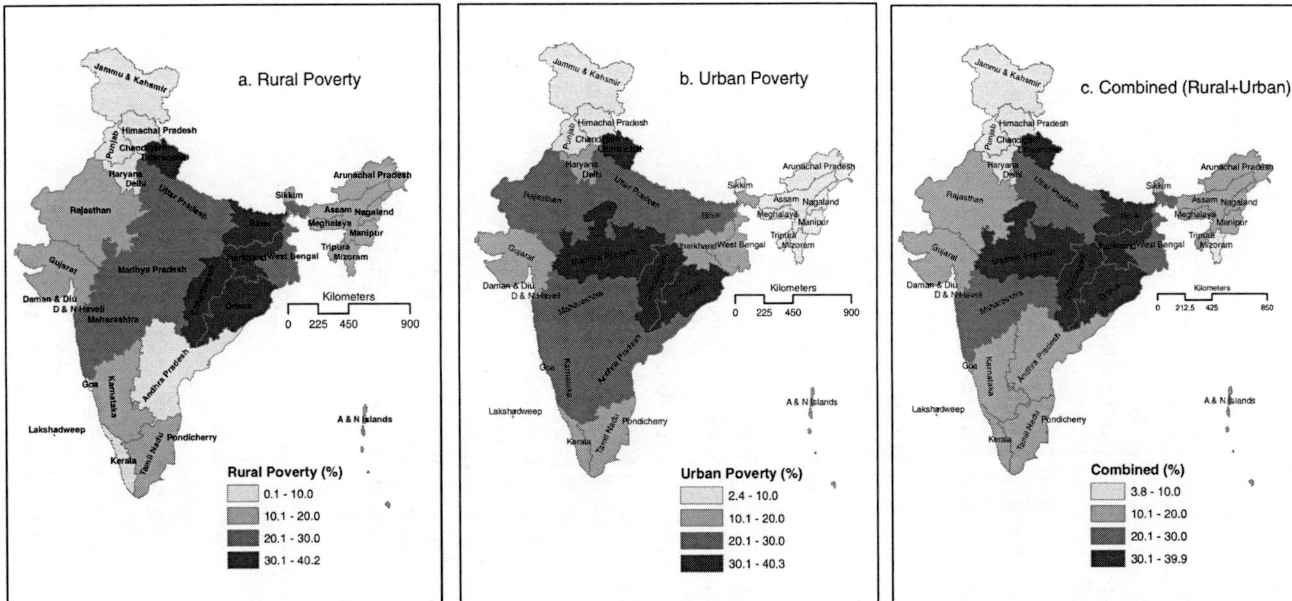

Source: Based on the data available from NSSO, 2004–2005.

Direct Transfer

Besides schemes initiated to provide employment, there are various schemes which directly transfer resources to the vulnerable groups. Such programmes have been initiated both by the central government and by the state government. Examples of such programmes such as old-age pension, unemployment bhatta (monetary compensation) for youth, special assistance for families if girl child is born,[1] and special educational assistance for the education of girl child. These provide economic security to the poor when livelihood alternatives are weak.

Public Distribution System

Through the PDS, the central government is supplying essential commodities (rice, wheat, sugar, and kerosene) at below market prices to 160 million families through 450,000 nationwide fair price shops. The access to the system was near-universal until 1997. Targeting was introduced in 1997, and now the programme is known as the Targeted Public Distribution System (TPDS). The crucial role is given to the Panchayati Raj (village self-governance) Institutions (PRIs) in the delivery of TPDS (Planning Commission, 2006).

Experiences in Poverty Alleviation: Typical Lessons Learnt

The effectiveness of poverty alleviation programmes in targeting the poor and alleviating poverty differs from state to state. Variations in effectiveness are largely due to: (a) efficiency or otherwise of the implementing machinery (i.e., the delivery system), (b) strengths of the PRIs, (c) existence or non-existence of community-based organizations of the people, and (d) initiative and innovativeness of the states in evolving approaches and institutional arrangements in harmony with the ground conditions (Planning Commission, 2006).

One of the important developments in India has been the rise of civil society which has forced both the state government and the central government to bring about many laws/acts which in turn have further deepened the democracy and given some rights in the hands of the citizens. The Right to Information (RTI) Act brought about recently has had a very wide impact. It has brought transparency in operation of the government machinery and helped in curbing the widespread corruption. However, in many of the states and districts, the act is yet to be implemented in its true spirit to bring about transparency in the many government programmes/schemes. Corruptions in many districts have been exposed in NREGA implementation due to the RTI Act. Besides the RTI, the civil society pressure on government has led to the social audit of many programmes for poverty alleviation. However, the numbers of states where social audits have been practiced are limited. Rajasthan and Maharashtra are such states where for a few programmes, social audit has been brought up. This has provided the much-needed transparency and correction in the implementation of programmes. Another important development in India has been the formidable emergence of media, both electronic and print. The rise of electronic media has been particularly emphatic since late 1980s. The media groups vie with each other and run competitive programmes to expose the real situation of poverty and penury in the country. However, the urban problems have received more attention by the media than the rural development issues.

Indian experience shows that the poverty eradication strategy necessarily has to stand on two legs: (a) a pro-poor pattern of economic growth, and (b) appropriate institutional arrangement that involves the poor themselves in the process of implementation of programmes meant for them (Planning Commission, 2006).

During the decades of 1970s and 1980s, the rate of economic growth was slow, but the pattern of growth was relatively more pro-poor. The green revolution led agricultural growth and the emphasis on community and rural development was helpful to the poor. During the decade of 1990s and after, the rate of economic growth has gone up significantly. But this growth has not generated the employment and livelihood opportunities for the poor comparable to the earlier period. As shown in Figure 2, the rate of decline in poverty has not been commensurate with higher growth (Planning Commission,

Figure 2

Poverty and GNP (Gross National Product) Growth Rate in India

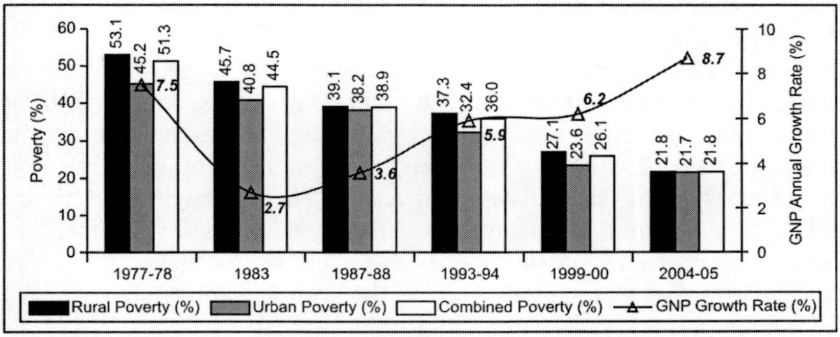

Source: Based on the data available from NSSO, (1977–78, 1983, 1987–88, 1993–94, 1999–00, 2004–05) Government of India (2007).

2006). In fact, the employment elasticity of growth declined to 0.16 in 1990s as compared to 0.52 in the 1980s. The decline in employment elasticity of agriculture was more pronounced from 0.7 in the period 1983 to 1993–94 to 0.1 during 1993–94 to 1999–2000.

Summary and Conclusions

The poverty has persisted in India in both the rural and urban areas despite a number of programmes being launched since independence in 1947. In India, the concept of poverty is based on the minimum level of living, that is the ability or capacity of a person to assure herself/himself two square meal (2,400 kcal per day in rural areas and 2,100 kcal in urban areas) a day. The data available for the year 2004–05 show that about 240 million people in the country are under BPL or they are unable to secure for themselves two square meals. India houses the largest number of the poor on this planet, and it is also an irony that India is one of 10 major economies in the world. Although during pre-economic reform period, the rate of the economic growth was relatively lower (less than 4%), it was able to make substantial dent on the poverty. In post-economic reform period, the rate of growth of national income has been near two digits (the second highest growing economy in the world after China) but the impact of the growth on poverty reduction is not as much as expected. This shows that the growth and poverty reduction may not go together, and in fact the neo-liberal regime which has brought high growth rate is based on the concentration of growth in a few technology-intensive sectors and thus is benefiting only about 10 per cent of the population. This is well reflected from the fact that number of billionaires in Indian during 2004 to 2007 have grown from 9 to 40, while much richer countries such as Japan, France, and China had number of billionaires only 24, 14, and 17, respectively, in 2007 (Bhaduri, 2008).

The lesson learnt from Indian experience is that growth must be broad based to make significant dent on poverty and the narrow sectoral growth may widen the personal and regional income inequality. In recent years, the rise of civil society has given a voice to the marginalized section of the society. Many needed laws and acts have been brought (such as the RTI Act, 72nd and 73rd Constitutional Amendments for local governance, and right to work through the NREGA) which may pave the way for the poor negotiating their shares in the economy and effective implementation of poverty alleviation programmes.

Note

1. In India, women are discriminated against within families for education, health care, employment, and in decision-making process. Dower need to be given at the time of their marriage by the families of bride. This puts women in a socially disadvantageous position and families with girl children are sucked into poverty and economic vulnerability due to the dower. Among others, these have led to the unethical and immoral practices of female infanticide and female foeticide. One of the consequences of these has been the declining sex ratio (women per 1,000 males) in India. The special assistance by the government is aimed to help the families with girl children and to assure that families do not feel that girl children are burden on them but assets.

References

Bhaduri, A. (2008). 'Predatory growth', *Economic and Political Weekly*, April 19, 10–14.

Government of India (2006). *Social, Economic and Educational Status of the Muslim Community of India – A Report*. New Delhi: Prime Minister's High Level Committee, Cabinet Secretariat.

Government of India (2007). *Economic Survey 2006–07*. New Delhi: Ministry of Finance.

NSSO (National Sample Survey Organisation). Household Consumer Expenditure in India, various rounds. Ministry of Statistics and Programme Implementation, Government of India, New Delhi.

Planning Commission (2006). *Report of the XI Plan Working Group on Poverty Elimination Programmes*. New Delhi: Government of India.

Ramakrishna, R. (2004). *Economic Reforms: Poverty and Inequality*. Paper Presented at a Workshop on 'Eradicate Poverty through Education' held at IETE. Andhra University, December 2004. Available online at: http://www.google.co.uk/search?hl=en&q=ramtej.org/ods/rrk.doc+&btnG=Google+Search&meta= (accessed on 16 January 2009).

Thomas, V. (2006). *Chronic Poverty in Rural Areas: The Role of Government Policy*. Available online at: http://www.solutionexchange-un.net.in/emp/comm_update/res-02-240306-06.doc (accessed on 16 January 2009).

5

Changing Perspective of Poverty in Northeast India

A Situation Analysis

D.K. ADAK, D.S. SHUN AND P. BHARATI

Poverty is a relative term and it is difficult to define in a simple way. In normal parlance, poverty may be defined as the inability of a person to get the minimum needs fulfilled with respect to consumption for leading a simple and healthy life. These minimum needs include food, clothing, housing, education, and basic health requirements.

Poverty in India is widespread with the nation estimated to have one of the largest concentrations of poor people in the world. The World Bank estimates that 456 million Indians (42% of the total Indian population) now live under the global poverty line of $1.25 per day (PPP). This means that a third of the global poor now reside in India. This also represents a significant decline in poverty from 60 per cent in 1981 to 42 per cent in 2005, although the rupee has decreased in value since then. Though Indian economy has grown steadily over the last two decades, its growth has been uneven when comparing different social groups, economic groups, geographic regions, and rural and urban areas. Between 1999 and 2008, the annualized growth rates for Gujarat (8.8%), Haryana (8.7%), or Delhi (7.4%) were much higher than for Bihar (5.1%), Uttar Pradesh (4.4%), or Madhya Pradesh (3.4%). Poverty rates in rural Orissa (43%) and rural Bihar (41%) are among the world's most extreme.

The Government of India recommended a requirement of 2,400 calories per person per day for rural areas and 2,100 calories for urban area two decades back. Study of per capita requirement of nutrients, however, depends upon certain diverse factors of the consuming unit, e.g., age, sex, body weight, stature, occupation, and above all the environment itself. The people living under hot humid condition of plain land certainly need different level of calorie than that the dwellers of temperate mountain region (Mukherjee and Banerjee, 2000). Side by side, measurement in terms of per capita income may not always provide satisfactory results, since such measurements may conceal the concentration of income in a few hands. Per capita consumption of some basic necessities of life, such as food, clothing, shelter even education, and health, may also prove to be unsatisfactory, in the sense of being unable to capture the essence of the real measurement of poverty. These measurements, therefore, may fail to provide any meaningful intra- or inter-regional comparison or comparisons between the two periods of time. In economies characterized by a high percentage of unemployment, it is a forgone conclusion that the capacity to spend and consume would also be much lower than in other countries, where the percentage of employment is higher. This highlights the necessity and the importance of government's spending for the maintenance of such people, since they are unable to meet the costs of the various social sectors themselves such as health sanitation at their own expense. Therefore, the lower the per capita expense on these items, higher is the level of poverty Considering all these factors, choice of indicators for measuring poverty is extremely crucial as well as difficult (Sengupta, 2000). Therefore, consumption need should also be considered while estimating poverty line. Social consumption such as primary education, health condition, sanitary situation, supply of portable water, and housing condition are needed to be computed in making such estimate.

Northeast India is considered as one of the poorer regions in our country. It was estimated in 1981 that approximately 52.63 per cent of the population in rural areas and 33.73 per cent in urban areas in Northeast India live below the poverty line. We may expect a marginal decline in the passage of time on percentage of populations in both rural and urban areas living below poverty line. A good number of special programmes and policies have been enunciated for Northeast India time to time to alleviate poverty and raise the standard of living of common people. In this study, we have made an attempt to find out the changes in the level of poverty over the period of time in Northeast India.

Data Source and Methodology

In this study, data were mainly collected from different secondary sources. For this purpose, information based on the publication of Census of India, National Family Health Survey II and III, SRS

Bulletin, Economic Survey (2001–2002) and Basic Statistics of North Eastern Region (2002) were taken into consideration. The following indicators for poverty are included in this study:

1. Poverty ratio
2. Unemployment rate
3. Literacy rate
4. Housing characteristics
5. Crude death rate (CDR) and infant mortality rate (IMR)

Poverty Ratio

Poverty ratio is derived in our country on the basis of the survey conducted by the National Sample Survey Organization (NSSO) based on household consumer expenditure. According to the 55th round results (1999–2000) of the NSSO, the poverty in our country came down from 36 per cent in 1993–1994 to 26 per cent in 1999–2000. This shows a 10 per cent decline in five years. The reform programme of the government played an important role behind this downward trend. In this backdrop, let us have a look into the scenario of northeastern states. It could be seen from Table 1 that none of the northeastern states have achieved the level of national average in terms of reduction in poverty ratio. Mizoram (6.19) has the highest level of reduction in northeast, which is followed by Arunachal Pradesh (5.88), Nagaland (5.25), and Manipur (5.24). However, Meghalaya (4.05) found to be poorest in this respect. A lower level of reduction is also noticed in the state of Assam (4.77).

Table 1

Poverty Ratios in Northeast India

States	*1993–1994*	*1999–2000*	*Reduction*
India	35.97	26.1	9.87
Arunachal Pradesh	39.35	33.47	5.88
Assam	40.86	36.09	4.77
Manipur	33.78	28.54	5.24
Meghalaya	37.92	33.87	4.05
Mizoram	25.66	19.47	6.19
Nagaland	37.92	32.67	5.25
Tripura	41.43	36.55	4.88

Source: Economic Survey: 2001–2002.

Unemployment Rate

The extent of poverty could be measured by the level of unemployment, especially in a poverty-stricken overpopulated country such as India. Higher the level of unemployment, higher is the level of poverty (Sengupta, 2000).

Table 2

Unemployment Rates in Northeast India

States	*1999–2000*				*2004–05*			
	Rural		*Urban*		*Rural*		*Urban*	
	Male	*Female*	*Male*	*Female*	*Male*	*Female*	*Male*	*Female*
India	2.1	1.5	4.8	7.1	1.6	1.8	3.8	6.9
Arunachal Pradesh	0.9	0.1	1.4	10	1.1	0.6	1.1	2.8
Assam	4.7	11.9	9.1	22.3	2.4	3.1	6.9	9.1
Manipur	2.4	2.5	7.4	10.3	1.4	0.7	5.2	6.3
Meghalaya	0.5	0.3	3.4	6.8	0.1	0.5	3.5	3.5
Mizoram	2.1	0.5	4.4	2.6	0.5	0.1	1.6	2.6
Nagaland	3	3.8	9.3	10.8	2.2	1.4	4.6	7.2
Tripura	0.8	4.6	5.5	8.8	9.6	32	16.6	56.8

Note: Unemployment rate is the percentage of unemployment with reference to labour force.

Source: Government of India, Ministry of Statistics and Programme Implementation, Central Statistical Organization (CSO), 2003.

A perusal of the changing trend of unemployment in Northeast India reveals a dismal picture (Table 2). The situation of Tripura state can be taken into consideration first in this context, where growth in unemployment rate is found to be abnormally high. While rural unemployment rate was 0.8 and 4.6 among the males and females respectively during 1999–2000 in Tripura, it increased up to 9.6 and 32 during 2004–05 among these sexes. It is interesting to note that the increase in urban sector is much more than that of the rural sector in this state. Urban unemployment rate was 5.5 and 8.8 during 1999–2000 among the males and females respectively in this state, which triggered up to 16.6 and 56.8 during 2004–05 among these sexes. The reason behind this gloomy picture is obscure. At national level, rates of unemployment, however, declined considerably from 1999–2000 to 2004–05 in rural as well as urban sector. While urban unemployment has declined considerably in Arunachal Pradesh between the two time periods, a reverse trend is perceptible in rural sector. Assam shows a sharp decline in unemployment rate among the females over the passage of time. During 1999–2000 female unemployment rate was 22.3 in this state, which declined up to 9.1 during 2004–05. In the states of Manipur, Meghalaya, Mizoram, and Nagaland, the pace of decline in unemployment rate is found to be very slow excepting, urban sector of Nagaland, where a faster decline in unemployment rate is noticed in both the sexes.

Literacy Rate

With a literacy rate of 65, we have 296 million illiterates, age 7 years and above, as per the 2001 census. Our society faces several challenges in the form of poverty, unemployment, child labour, female feticide, overpopulation, etc. But all of them evolve from illiteracy which is actually the mother of many problems. A high literacy can contribute to valuable social and economic participation by the people which will go a long way in human development and poverty eradication. Spread of education is necessary for modernization, urbanization, industrialization, communication, and commerce (Rambabu, 2001).

Table 3

Literacy Rates in Northeast India

States	*2001**	*2005–06***	*Growth in literacy rate*
India	65.38	67.6	2.22
Arunachal Pradesh	54.74	62.8	8.06
Assam	64.28	76.3	12.02
Manipur	68.87	76.5	7.63
Meghalaya	63.31	72.1	8.79
Mizoram	88.49	89.9	1.41
Nagaland	67.11	72.5	5.39
Tripura	73.66	80.2	6.54

*Census of India, 2001. **NFHS-III, 2005–06.

As can be observed in Table 3 that literacy rate has grown in Northeast India in different pace. Highest rate of growth in literacy has been observed in Assam (12.02) over the passage of time in context of Northeast India. Mizoram ranked the lowest position in this order. In this context, it can be mentioned that Mizoram attained a high level of literacy rate much before 2001 not only in the context of Northeast India but also in the context of national level. Thus, a low increase in literacy rate over time in Mizoram state (1.41) is not unexpected. States such as Meghalaya (8.79), Arunachal Pradesh (8.06), Manipur (7.63), Tripura (6.54), and Nagaland (5.39) also recorded considerably high level of growth in literacy rate over a period of five years.

Latest studies on poverty consider education to be a contributory factor towards increasing one's earning capacity and hence in determining the quality of life. Investment in educational infrastructure determines the facilities of education available (Sengupta, 2000). In Table 4, percentage of budgeted expenditure on education to total budget (revenue) is shown for Northeast India. It is surprising to note that Indian government has reduced budgetary expenditure on education in the gap of three years. While it was 21.48 during 1995–96, it came down to 13.78 during 1998–99. Thus, a reduction of 7.7 is recorded. States such as Manipur and Tripura have also followed a trend like national level, though this difference is very low in Tripura between the two periods of time. In Assam (4.02), Mizoram (3.7), and Meghalaya (3.63), considerable amount of budgetary growth is noticed in this context. However, it is interesting to note that no significant impact of growth in budgetary expenditure on education has been found on the growth of literacy in the states of Northeast India.

Table 4

Per cent of Budgeted Expenditure on Education to Total Budget (Revenue) in Northeast India (₹ in crore).

States	*1995–96*	*1998–99*	*Growth in budgetary expenditure on education*
India	21.48	13.78	–7.7
Arunachal Pradesh	15.24	16.69	1.45
Assam	27.37	31.39	4.02
Manipur	30	23.43	–6.57
Meghalaya	22.68	26.31	3.63
Mizoram	17.03	20.73	3.7
Nagaland	15.18	15.68	0.5
Tripura	21.88	20.19	–1.69

Source: NEC (2002).

Housing Characteristics

A direct fall out of poverty in our country is the poor condition of living and shortages of houses. This gives rise to slums and unhygienic living conditions, increasing the misery of poverty, which is a feature, associated more with urban poverty rather than with rural poverty (Sengupta, 2000). In this study, per cent of households living in a *pucca* house are taken into consideration for a general idea about housing characteristics in northeastern states. An inter-state comparison of percentage of households living in *pucca* house is presented in Table 5. It appears from NFHS-II results that during 1998–99, the per cent of households living in *pucca* houses were quite low in most of the north-eastern states. Except Sikkim, less than 20 per cent of the households in this region were settled in *pucca* houses. These states also stood far below the national level (32) during this period. However, though a significant increase is noticed in national level (13.9) in respect of percentage of households living in *pucca* houses in the gap of 7 years, most of the states in this region are lagging behind national level. Only exception of this is Meghalaya state, where a significant increase is noticed in growth in percentage of households (20.6) living in *pucca* house (20.6). In Sikkim, more than 50 per cent households fall in this category during 1995–96, whereas this value remains almost constant over the passage of time.

Table 5

Per cent of Households Living in a Pucca House

States	*NFHS-II* (1998–99)*	*NFHS-III* (2005–06)*	*Growth in per cent of pucca house*
India	32	45.9	13.9
Arunachal Pradesh	14.2	20.8	6.6
Assam	10.9	19.8	8.9
Manipur	7.1	10.7	3.6
Meghalaya	14.5	35.1	20.6
Mizoram	16.2	22.9	6.7
Nagaland	18.1	20.7	2.6
Sikkim	50.6	51	0.4

*In NFHS–II and NFHS–III, Sikkim is included in northeastern region in place of Tripura.

Crude Death Rate (CDR) and Infant Mortality Rate (IMR)

Rate of infant mortality is used as a reliable indicator of health status and well-being of a community or a particular geographic region. Side by side growth and development of a social group as well for a particular area depends essentially upon the level of fertility in relation to mortality. Table 6 depicts the changes in CDR and IMR in northeastern region over two periods of times.

Table 6

Crude Death Rate (CDR) and Infant Mortality Rate (IMR) in Northeastern States

States	*NFHS-II* (1998–1999)*		*NFHS-III* (2005–2006)*	
	CDR	*IMR*	*CDR***	*IMR*
India	9.7	67.6	8.4	57
Arunachal Pradesh	12.4	63.1	5.7	60.7
Assam	9.4	69.5	9.6	66.1
Manipur	9	37	5.2	29.7
Meghalaya	9.9	89	9	44.6
Mizoram	7.3	37	4.4	34.1
Nagaland	6.9	42.1	NA	38.3
Sikkim	6.3	43.9	5.1	33.7

*In NFHS–II and NFHS–III, Sikkim is included in northeastern region in place of Tripura.

***Source*: SRS Bulletin (2001).

A declining trend is perceptible in terms of CDR and IMR over time when the states of Northeast India are taken into consideration (Table 6). Though the data of CDR in this table are furnished for a short gap of time (two years), a gradual decrease is evident from the data. Only exception in this respect is the state of Assam where CDR remains almost the same, a gap of two years. However, different sources of data for CDR in this context may be a reason behind this. Some interesting feature appeared from the trend of IMR. At national level, IMR came down from 67.6 during 1998–99 to 57 during 2005–06, whereas in Meghalaya IMR came down from 89 during 1998–99 to 44.6 during 2005–06. Thus, the pace of decline in IMR in Meghalaya is much higher than our national average. Manipur also shows a considerable decline in IMR. In Arunachal Pradesh, Assam, Mizoram, Nagaland, and Sikkim, a lower level of decline is perceptible in this respect.

Conclusion

Judging from the trend from different indicators reveals that the states of Northeast India are mostly poverty stricken. However, Mizoram emerges as an exceptional state. Studies on poverty reveal education as one of the contributory factors towards increasing one's earning capacity and quality of life. Investment in educational infrastructure determines the facilities of education available. In this context, Sengupta (2000) opines that:

> it is important to highlight that educational expenditure per head as well as the literacy rate is the highest in Mizoram and the state tops the

list in terms of employment too. This prompts us to conclude that there is a positive correlation between expenditure on education, literacy rate and employment rate.

The findings of this study, however, show a different trend. It reveals that though the rate of unemployment is lowest in Mizoram, per cent of budgeted expenditure on education to total budget (revenue) in this state is comparatively lower in comparison with their sister states. But it tops the list in terms of literacy rate. A probable reason behind this may be considerably a lower percentage of budgeted expenditure on education to total budget (revenue) is enough to exert maximum impact on education.

Rele (1982) said that the survival and growth of any family or a closed social group depends intrinsically upon the level of fertility in relation to mortality. The economically advanced countries were able to reduce their death rate to less than 10 per thousand largely by providing their people with adequate and wholesome food, pure drinking water, better hospital facilities, better sewage disposal, and by taking proper measure to control various diseases (Agarwal, 1988). From this study, it reveals that Assam registers the highest death rate as well as IMR in the region. Data on per capita expenses by the government on health services reveal that health services in terms of hospitals and doctors are the poorest in Assam. Consequently, this state registers the highest death rate among seven states.

Northeast India is the homeland of a large number of scheduled tribes and scheduled castes who speak different languages, have different cultural set-ups, and are of diverse ethnic origin. Population groups differ from one another in respect of certain physical characteristics also. As each state in the region is characterized by their own peculiar problem, the northeastern region cannot be treated as single homogenous unit. Thus, whatever be the policies adopted by the planners for poverty alleviation, emphasis should be laid to achieve development from below. All developmental policies should be so geared, so as to benefit the poor people directly (Sengupta, 2000). This will help attain the national goal of poverty alleviation.

References

Agarwal, S.N. (1988). *India's Population Problems*. New Delhi: Tata McGraw Hill.

Government of India (2003) Selected Socio-economic Statistics, India, Central Statistical Organization.

Government of India (2002) Budget allocation, North-east Council.

Mukherjee, S., and Banerjee, M. (2000). 'Some indices of urban poverty in North-East India: An overview'. In Ray, B.D., Mazhari, H.K., Passah, P.M., and Pandey, M.C. (eds.): *Population, Poverty and Environment in North East India* (pp. 229–241). New Delhi: Concept Publishing Company.

Rambabu, G. (2001). 'NSSO data and poverty ratio – A needless controversy?', *Financial Daily,* The Hindu group of Publications (Internet Edition).

Rele, J.R. (1982). 'Trends and differentials in fertility'. *Population of India.* Country Monograph Series. No. 10. New York: United Nations.

Sengupta, K. (2000). 'Current status of poverty and its determinants in the north eastern region'. In Ray, B.D., Mazhari, H.K., Passah, P.M., and Pandey, M.C. (eds.): *Population, Poverty and Environment in North East India*. New Delhi: Concept Publishing Company.

6

Rural Development in Perspective

Theoretical Frameworks

MOHAMMAD TAGHI SHEYKHI

Change in agricultural technology is widely accepted and fundamental to any strategy for meaningful economic development, and thereby poverty alleviation. But, the problem of effectively harnessing new technological possibilities to meet the needs of rural development and bringing about prosperity is a highly complex one, involving far more than the provision and financing of an *appropriate* technology package. However, new technology disturbs the equilibrium of the receiving environment, and the chain of a complex technical, economic, social, cultural, and institutional effects that are neither easily predictable nor necessarily consistent with the aims of rural development. Technology change, therefore, has to be viewed more widely as the dynamic interaction between new inputs, methods, and systems (the *technology*), and the receiving environment. This suggests the need for handling technological change in developing agricultures within the context of a broadly-defined 'technology policy', with the physical technology as one instrument in a set of policy choices and intervention designed to meet well-defined objectives.

Rural Development

Globally speaking, currently above 51 per cent of world population live in rural areas (World Population, 2007), and Asia-wise, rural inhabitants in 2007 have been recorded 59 per cent of the total population of the region. Such a great number of people in rural areas need its own planning and investment in order to be able to produce its own food and secure its other necessities of life. In this chapter, various theories regarding rural development in developing world will be discussed.

By rural development, it is meant to proceed through such schemes as to alleviate poverty in different sectors in rural areas. But, the fact remains that rural area as a target group and centre of activity for employment generation for all families has to be prioritized. In the process of rural development, various income-generating and employment-oriented schemes must be initiated in the rural areas. In achieving rural development schemes, glamorization and suitable family planning must be reached and achieved with especial reference to the developing societies. In this process, reaching rural industries have to be ensured.

While talking about sustainable rural development, we may also briefly touch upon the concept of privatization (Taori, 1995). This new phenomenon may be carried out, when a multidisciplinary team takes up a holistic exercise of inducting rationale changes. The process also needs sustainable linkage-building between agriculture, rural development, and rural industrialization.

Rural development is a multidimensional process and much broader than poverty alleviation. It is implemented through socio-economic programmes and transfers. Rural development needs changing environments – enabling poor people to earn more, invest in themselves, and their communities in order to reach their key goals, and maintain the necessary infrastructures. As a global phenomenon, if rural communities are properly empowered, they can and may manage their own local development efforts. However, the existence of rural poverty provides major challenges to the governments of, and the developmental agencies in many developing societies. The failure of any rural development project even negatively affects the urban development and industrial projects.

Rural areas throughout the world tend to have similar characteristics. That is, their populations are spatially dispersed, and under such conditions they cannot have access to many services. In such rural areas, agriculture is often the dominant activity, and often other opportunities for resource mobilization are limited. Such characteristics mean that people living in rural areas face a set of factors that pose challenges to development. However, the geographical dispersion of rural populations often increases the cost and difficulty of providing rural goods and services in a satisfactory manner. That results in fewer opportunities in rural areas than in non-rural locations. Therefore, rural areas are rarely able to mobilize sufficient resources to finance their own development programmes, leaving them dependent on transfers from external resources. Moreover, rural areas in the developing societies are often politically marginalized, leaving little opportunity for the rural poor to influence government policies.

Developing countries are usually characterized by high levels of poverty within their rural areas (Chambers, 1983). In some cases such as South Africa, approximately 70 per cent of the country's poor people live in rural areas, and about 70 per cent of the rural residents are poor. In such cases, incomes are constrained since the rural economy is not sufficiently vibrant to provide them with jobs or self-employment opportunities. However, rural areas in majority of developing countries are diverse with concentrations of poverty and relative prosperity. One of the features of the rural areas in such countries is that rural housing is often substandard or non-existent, and many people are migrants, working in urban areas. As a result, the rural–urban continuum reflects as a way of life in such societies. That is to say, the population is often mobile in search of better living conditions and jobs.

Rural Population and Their Problems

High rates of population growth hinder the improvement of living standards in developing countries such as India, especially among the lower-income families. In many of the poorer countries, family-planning programmes have been adopted, but many of these have not yet succeeded in significantly reducing the rates of population increase. This situation requires further research on the determinants of fertility, and the economic costs and benefits of larger families for rural households. Knowledge of this type may be useful in shaping policies other than family planning (e.g., for education, employment, and social security), whose impact on fertility might be considered an explicit benefit.

The level of fertility in any society reflects ingrained and interrelated socio-economic factors which need to be analysed in a variety of ways – by the study of fertility differentials at one point in time, by longitudinal assessment of the impact of development projects, and as in this research, by the detailed study of small communities. In most of the developing countries, because of the prevalent poverty and vulnerability, rural families almost commonly resort to a variety of different strategies to ensure their survival. Therefore, it has become more appropriate to describe their economic activities as livelihood strategies rather than jobs or employment. The deepest poverty in rural areas belong to women, and many cases, children in such areas live in families/households with income below the minimum subsistence level. Such households usually have low levels of literacy and education, difficult and time-consuming access to water, fuel, and other services. This results in high levels of under nutrition or malnutrition, morbidity, and mortality of the children, etc. Under such conditions, there is a permanent migration of people from rural to urban areas, and not vice versa. However, internal migration is a demographic process affecting rural poverty negatively. In that, it has converted rural poverty to urban poverty (Goldstein, 1983).

Though many rural households in the developing world are totally marginalized and have no income, they do not have pensions either to depend on. Wages in the agricultural sector fall well below the minimum living level, and the seasonal workers have the added disadvantage of earning approximately less than the permanent workers.

Governments in developing countries are required to contribute towards rural development through their programmes in the following broad areas:

- Economic development
- Social investment (i.e., social infrastructure)
- Human resource development
- Natural resource-based programmes

Such programmes lead to poverty alleviation through investment in infrastructure and provision of social services. However, various such elements of rural development are required to be addressed. As a whole, rural development is understood to be multidimensional, encompassing improved provision of services, enhanced opportunities for income generation, and improved physical infrastructure, social cohesion, and physical security within rural communities. The concept of rural development places emphasis on facilitating change in rural environments to enable poor people to earn more, invest in themselves and their communities, and contribute towards maintenance of the infrastructure key to their livelihoods, in short, to identify opportunities, and to act on them. However, a successful strategy will thus make people less poor. Such specific measures assist the vulnerable and relieve the burdens of poverty.

Social sustainability is an important dimension of a successful strategy towards rural development. However, rural communities hold a wealth of social capital in the form of extended networks of mutual solidarity, shared beliefs, and traditions.

Poverty in India

India has more than 1 billion population, about two-thirds are estimated to live in rural areas. India's poverty is affecting almost 170 million of the total population. Though many of these poverty-stricken people attempt to migrate to cities, yet three out of every four continue to live in the rural areas of the country, and that helps poverty to sustain as more a rural phenomenon. Many of these poverty-stricken people are observed in areas such as Rajasthan, Orissa, Madhya Pradesh, Uttar Pradesh, and Bihar. Such region usually faces droughts and extreme water shortages too. India's elevated amount of poverty is mainly caused and appears due to the inabilities of the residents and communities to maintain essential and constant assets, and also due to shortage of financial capital. Another indicator of India's poverty reflects in illiteracy levels, insufficient health care system, and basically no capability of receiving social services. As of 2005, 85.7 per cent of India's population lives on less than US $2.5 (PPP) a day down from 92.5 per cent in 1981. This compares with both China and Vietnam making enormous progress against poverty, and the evidence suggests that rural economic growth has played a large role in this success. Using each country's own definition of poverty, with a constant real poverty line over time, China's poverty rate fell from more than 50 per cent in 1981 to about 20 per cent in 1991, and 5 per cent in 2005. In Vietnam also, poverty fell from almost 60 per cent to 20 per cent during 1993–2004 (Ravallion, 2008). However, land is the most important non-labour asset in any developing rural economy. The institutions determining how land is used are thus at the core of efforts to fight poverty. Therefore, India should also follow suit with China and Vietnam in order to lower or eradicate her poverty.

Dynamics of Growth

In rural areas, there is a dire need to revive the rural economies, and thereby to advance the engines of economic growth that would contribute towards development at national level in the developing countries. In case the direction is not so, functional and applicable strategies must be adopted. Although the specific processes vary over time and space, the general dynamics are understood in terms of sources of growth, and linkages that spread and multiply the initial impulse. Growth in agriculture, forestry, and other primary activities that bring incremental earnings into rural areas generally generates additional incomes through linkage in expenditure and employment.

It is expected that rural communities in which agriculture, forestry, tourism, and other activities are growing, such a process of growth would increase incomes, strengthen transport and communications, and thereby the 'remoteness' of rural areas is reduced. This vision is realistically attainable for rural areas in which the natural resource base supports growth in agriculture, forestry, and other such activities.

Dynamic growth will benefit many of the rural poor in the developing countries, i.e., even those who do not earn the initial incremental income. Moreover, as more active rural economies become less cut-off, they are less prone to sickness and mortality. That is, with better roads and means of communications, the chance that a sick or an injured person will get to the hospital in time increases for the prosperous and the poor, even though the chances may still not remain equal for both.

Although growth benefits many of the poor, it clearly does not benefit all. Safety nets are still needed, and the rural poor are greatly disadvantaged relative to their urban counterparts when it comes to social assistance. However, few developing countries include rural people in social security programmes, and the prevalence of self-employment means that unemployment compensation is largely irrelevant to those without work.

Human Resource Development

Rural areas in many developing countries generally suffer from capacity constraints linked to a low-skills base. What the developing countries need is the development of a separate human resource strategy, so that the skills base in rural areas is increased. Through such master plan, rural development may be pursued. To achieve such goals, transfer of personnel to rural areas, to support both hard and soft skills, is quite necessary. Where appropriate, the goodwill of experienced citizens who seek to contribute on a voluntary basis should also be utilized. However, over the intermediate to longer term, capacity constraints should be addressed through education and training. In such context, the rural development strategy must constitute deliberate and conscious choices and interventions usually through government in all spheres, after and in consultation with different targeted personalities in rural areas.

Figure 1

Rural Development Paradigm

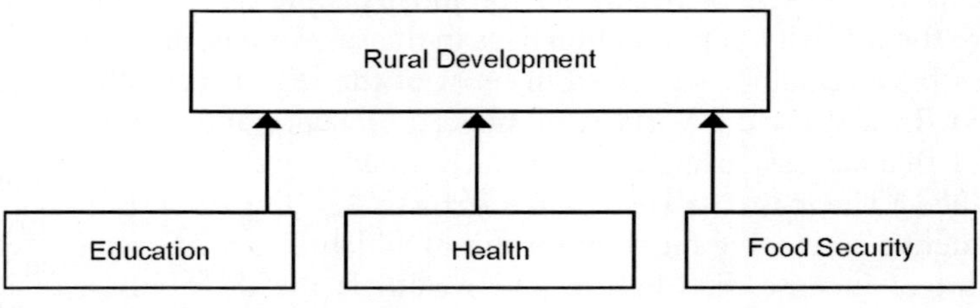

Rural Development Issues

One of the main problems of the Third World development is the struggle between the interests of the urban areas and those of the rural areas. The question is always one of either the urban areas must be developed for the best long-lasting economic results or the rural areas must receive more attention, because poverty is more visible there. First and foremost, poverty is severe in the rural areas, though it is also highly observed in urban areas.

Rural poverty is endemic among the poor households in the Third World and manifests itself in a number of ways, among others malnutrition, hunger, and disease. The groups which are affected include the landless, the near-landless, female-headed households, and children. Harrison (1993) gave a good account of the extent and magnitude of the problem. Identifying a number of causes of the problem of poverty and tackling them with a view to possible solutions will not eliminate poverty. The situation is extremely complex with many external and internal factors that exercise influences. Moreover, these factors are mutually influencing and strengthening to further complicate the situation.

Acknowledging the complexity of causes of poverty, one can accept that rural poverty is created by a number of closely linked processes that are mainly policy induced. In many developing countries, national policies and institutions have built-in biases which exclude the poor from the benefits of development. The most important of these is urban bias which pre-empts resources from rural households (Lele and Adu-Nayko, 1992).

Institutional biases are a lack of access to productive assets such as land and water. Others are families in arrangements such as lack of access to credit and inputs, and lack of grassroot institutions to encourage people's participation.

Land Issues in Development

The crisis of poverty and food production has directed attention to the question of land and land tenure issues in some developing countries. Land is the source of livelihood for most people in the Third World where the majority of population lives in the rural areas, and yet the land issues have remained unsolved in most of the region (Okoth-Ogendo, 1993). In a study on world rural poverty, Jaizairy and Stanier (1992) found that access to land, particularly arable land for the poor, had declined. The path to sustainable growth for the poor is access to productive assets, the most important of which is land. A crucial determinant of income distribution and wealth is the distribution of land rights for the poorest of the poor in the Third World. In many developing countries, landlessness has given rise to overcrowding and land degradation as people tried to make a living out of the meagre pieces on land on which they live, and this is one of the reasons land reform is about, how land is owned, and how patterns of ownership change. Land reform is said to be the only means of altering inequitable owner structures for effective development of participatory institutions, local and national (Dorner, 1972; Prosterman et al., 1990).

Integrated Rural Development

Rural problems are too many and diverse, and need more to be dealt with. That is to say, there are more that should form part of the framework for rural development in the developing world. At the same time, it is also important to identify the actors in rural development. What is often observed in the developing countries is that the elite actors' actions are more cityward; they are more involved in urban projects which are more rewarding. However, integrated rural development is highly essential in multiple dimensions in these countries.

We can therefore state that rural development is not only to provide relief to the poor, but also to eradicate poverty by inter alia, primarily addressing the following issues:

- *Equal treatment*: This covers the problem of distribution, enrichment of the elite, corruption, and empowerment of the poor.
- *Land tenure*: That includes rural development, access to land, etc.
- *Migration and population pressure*: That means, rural–urban migration is closely related to both rural and urban development. There is also integration between migration and rural production capacity.

Shift in development thinking from large-scale economic development and self-sufficient development also requires adjustments in the implementation of rural development. This does not mean that industrialization and economic development are no longer acceptable. The difference lies in the fact of a shift in emphasis in which the knowledge, abilities, needs, and interests of the poor are put first by means of a process of empowerment. This means that the people's basic needs as defined by themselves are satisfied, and that social security is provided. However, in order to ensure sustainable development, and in particular rural development, each person and community must handle its own resources and environment with the necessary care.

Conclusions

While it is acknowledged that eradicating both rural and urban poverty is a phenomenal task, it is important to realize that it is impossible to give preference to one area to the detriment of the other. This approach has led to cityward migration, which has merely transferred rural poverty to even urban areas. Apart from the fact that certain key issues such as access to land needs specific attention, it is clear that a balanced approach is needed; and more, an all-out strategy is necessary where a clear policy will enumerate agenda items for specific actors to act on. Only in this way, can the problem of rural development be tackled successfully. Luckily, as our study has shown, the poor have shown their perseverance and enterprise. They just need the vehicle of a strategy and programme for them to play a major part in the rural development.

References

Chambers, R. (1983). *Rural Development, Putting the Last First*. London: Longman.

Dorner, P. (1972). *Land Reform and Economic Development*. Harmondsworth: Penguin.

Goldstein, S. (1983). 'Migration and development'. In Goldscheider, C. (ed.): *Urban Migrants in Developing Nations: Pattern and Problems of Adjustment*. Boulder, CO: Westview Press.

Harrison, P. (1993). *Inside the Third World: The Anatomy of Poverty*. Harmondsworth: Penguin.

Jaizairy, T., and Stanier, J. (1992). *The State of World Rural Poverty: An Inquiry into its Causes and Consequences*. New York: New York University Press.

Lele, U., and Adu-Nayko, K. (1992). 'Approaches to uprooting poverty in Africa', *Food Policy*, 17(2), 95–108.

Okoth-Ogendo, H.W.O. (1993). 'Agrarian reform in Sub-Saharan Africa'. In Basset, T.J., and Crunmey, D.E. (eds.): *Land in Africa, Agrarian Systems*. Madison, WI: Madison University of Wisconsin Press.

Prosterman, R.L., Temple, M.N. and Hanstad, T.M. (1990). *Agrarian Reform and Grassroots Development*. Boulder, CO: Lynne Rienner.

Ravallion, M. (2008). Are *There Lessons for Africa from China's Success Against Poverty*? Policy Research Working Paper 4463. Washington, DC: World Bank.

Taori, K. (1995). *Rural Industrialization*. New Delhi: Vikas Publishing House.

World Population Data Sheet (2007). *Population Reference Bureau*. New York.

7

Linking Gender and Poverty

Evidences from Indian Agriculture

SWATI S. NANDA AND SARFARAZ ALAM

Though poverty is a universal phenomenon, its occurrence and implications for people situated in different socio-economic and spatial contexts vary considerably. This is particularly true in the case of gender where power imbalance between the sexes render women more vulnerable to the cycle of poverty. Like elsewhere, poverty has many faces in India. It has a regional face as some regions such as Telangana and Vidarbha are poorer than other regions of their respective states. It also has a social face as some groups such as the scheduled castes, scheduled tribes, and some of the minority groups are poorer than others on account of their being marginalized and excluded from the mainstream. It also has a gendered face. In recent years, the gendered face of poverty has attracted a lot of attention. Simply speaking, it implies that women are poorer than men. Discussions on women's poverty have drawn attention towards a number of problems including the way poverty status is conventionally analysed as well as towards the unit of analysis in poverty debates. National and international policy frameworks are increasingly acknowledging the possibilities of existence of higher poverty and related deprivations in case of women compared to that of men.

Though related discussions have been taking place since the last four decades or so, it would probably not be wrong to say that Beijing Conference 1995 with its use of the term 'feminization of poverty' made these discussions more popular in the activist and policy-making circles. As a result, one finds an enormous amount of literature focusing on women and poverty in its various facets. This paper discusses the gender basis of disparity in incidence, magnitude, and growth of poverty in Indian agriculture and their correlates. It would begin by making connections between gender and poverty, and then proceed to look into the conceptual link between women and agricultural poverty. The next part would focus specifically on women and agriculture in India by examining available literature and data on the theme. The final section would concentrate on required policy changes.

I
Gender and Poverty: Conceptual Understandings

The linkage between gender and poverty is a complex subject as it requires a reconsideration of the way poverty has been defined, conceptualized, and measured. This has to necessarily be based on an assumption that poverty has particular and unequal implications for individuals located differently. This point towards a qualitative and quantitative difference in the way poverty is experienced in regional as well as in group contexts. The significance of this assumption for gender analysis comes from the fact that women and men are situated differentially in relation to power all around the world.

It is known from United Nations documentation that women account for 70 per cent of the world's poor (UNDP, 1995: iii). Women's poverty is a direct consequence of the fact that they are paid less for their labour compared to men, have fewer resources at their disposal, and are less likely to be in a position to utilize available resources on their own favour. Recent literatures linking gender to poverty have unravelled new areas that facilitate a comprehensive understanding of issues relating to poverty. A significant linkage of gender and poverty points towards the following:

- Women having a higher incidence of poverty than men
- Women's poverty being more severe than that of men
- The existence of a trend to greater poverty among women, particularly associated with rising rates of female headship of household (*The World's Women*, 1995, and Nilofer Cagatay, 1998).

Conventional analyses on poverty have not looked at women's poverty status independently. Even a cursory look at the official statistics and academic debates, both in India and outside, is sufficient to prove this. One of the major reasons for this has been the use of the income consumption methods that attempt to define poverty according to certain absolute standards. Having enough income for a specific amount of food has been regarded as the cut-off line for poverty within a country. While this analysis successfully records absolute poverty, it fails to explain the way income is distributed among the population, and especially, among the individuals within the household.

In 1997, the United Nations Development Programme (UNDP) evolved a set of three criteria with a view to broaden the definition of poverty that would monitor and compare experiences of human poverty over time (UNDP, 1997: 17). Termed as the Human Poverty Index (HPI), these included three aspects of deprivation related to longevity, knowledge, and standard of living. This new approach looks at poverty as the absence of some basic capabilities required to live a fulfilled life. These basic capabilities have physical aspects such as being well-nourished, adequately clothed, sheltered, and avoiding preventable morbidity as well as social achievements such as partaking in the life of the community. Through this approach, an attempt is made to balance the notions of absolute and relative poverty as relative deprivations in incomes and commodities could result in an absolute deprivation in the minimum capabilities. The argument put forth by this approach is that if income is not the sum total of well-being, lack of income cannot be sum total of poverty. In this way, it seeks to broaden the scope of poverty. The new approach focuses on what people can and cannot do, and not on what people do or do not have, that is, 'whether they can live long, escape avoidable morbidity, be well nourished, be able to read and write and communicate, take part in literary and scientific pursuits, and so forth' (Sen, 1984: 497). Such a shift of focus in defining poverty along with the instructions of the Beijing Platform for Action as have led the national and international organizations to collect gender-disaggregated data on poverty.

As a consequence, women's poverty status in various aspects is being seriously taken. It has opened eyes regarding the invisibility rendered to women's work in many aspects. It has also drawn attention towards less payment and in many cases lack of payment for women's labour. Further, it has also focused on women's lack of decision-making power in various fields. The next section of the paper digs into these issues in the field of agriculture.

II
Women in Indian Agriculture

Rural communities in India, as elsewhere, are generally based on a rigid conceptualization of gender division of work space with men being regarded as belonging to public domain contributing towards economic security of the household, while women are primarily seen as contributing to household chores. However, women in real-life situations in rural India have always participated in agricultural activities in various capacities as mangers of land, farmers, and labourers. Such participation of women in the public domain in relation to agriculture is yet to be adequately acknowledged. In recent decades, however, women's visibility in agricultural field has increased owing to a trend towards gender-sensitive analysis of Indian economy in general and agriculture in particular. This has been accompanied by a general trend of increasing active participation by women in agriculture pointing towards a sort of trend towards feminization of agricultural activities. The fact that about 33 per cent of cultivators and close to 47 per cent of agricultural labourers in India are women (Vepa, 2004) has attracted a lot of attention in recent years in both the policy and academic circles. The feminization of agriculture debate centres on issues such as women's invisibility, wage, access to factors of agricultural production, and food security (Figure 1).

Figure 1
Feminization of Agriculture

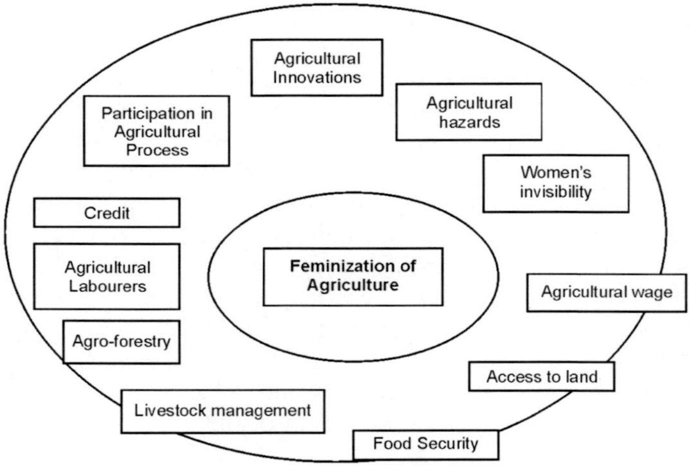

The census estimates suggest that 36.46 per cent female cultivators are found in the rural areas as compared to 42.19 per cent male cultivators (Population Census, cited in Women and Men in India, p. 41). It has also been pointed out that the number of female agricultural labour is greater in the case of both rural (43.4%) and urban (11.03%) areas compared to the male agricultural labourers in the rural (27.5%) and urban (3.4%) areas.

The role and responsibilities of women in agriculture is multidimensional. They perform household duties while contributing to agriculture at its different stages. In a typical Indian agricultural household, the man looks after the field, while the woman is responsible for cleaning, collecting fuel and water, and cooking within the house. However, a lot of work related to cultivation such as selection of seeds, storage, and transplantation are primarily performed by women. In landowning agricultural households, women's duties could be seen more as helpers of the male family members. However, it is not unusual to find women performing the duties of farmers in female-headed households. In landless agricultural households, women like their men perform the duties of labourers in others' agricultural fields with daily wage payment. The next section focuses on discussing the varied roles of Indian women in agriculture.

Women's Participation in Agriculture

Women participate in Indian agriculture both as farmers and as labourers. According to the Census of India (2001), of the total female main and marginal workers, 33 per cent are cultivators and 39 per cent are agriculture labourers. Traditionally, Indian rural households have relied on agriculture as their chief source of livelihood. Women's roles in such households are to a large extent defined by the social mores of the community. The highly complex society makes it difficult to look at women's agricultural work in terms of simple gender division of labour for the whole of India. The nature and extent of female participation also depends upon the kinds of crops cultivated and as well as the agro-production systems (HDSA, 2002). Consequently, one can see high degrees of regional variations in gender roles in agriculture. In some agro-ecological regions, women are found ploughing on the fields, while in others women's roles are found to be limited to sowing seeds and milking cows. A study, for instance, found women doing more agricultural field activities than men in Haryana (Manekar, 1990). Another study in Bhitarkanika in the state of Orissa notes caste playing an important role in determining the nature and extent of women's participation in agriculture. It suggested that women of upper castes participated less in agricultural activities compared to their lower caste counterparts owing to stricter mobility norms. The study also suggested that even lower caste women's participation was limited to boiling the rice before the drying process (Kanvinde, cited in FAO, 2009). The same pattern of inter-caste variations in women's role in agriculture is observed in the agriculturally-rich Ganga plains of North India.

However, generally speaking, in most parts of India, women in typical agricultural households are involved in main agriculture activities such as sowing, transplanting, weeding, irrigation, fertilizer application, plant protection, harvesting, winnowing, and storing, and allied activities such as cattle management, fodder collection, milking, etc., along with domestic activities such as cooking, child-rearing, water collection, fuel wood gathering, and household maintenance. In Table 1 the relative importance of female participation in specific tasks of crop production in the Kolli Hills in Tamil Nadu, as has been studied by Vedavalli (1997), is presented.

Table 1

Specific Tasks Performed by Men and Women

Activities	*Female*	*Male*
Land preparation	X	X
Ploughing	X	XX
Seed selection	XX	X
Storage	XX	X
Transplanting	XX	X
Weeding	XX	X
Applying green manure	X	X
Harvesting	X	X
Post-harvesting	X	X

Note: X/XX show relative involvement.

Source: Vedavalli (1997), cited in FAO.

Specific Roles and Responsibilities of Women

Women play varied roles in course of their participation in agricultural crop production and allied fields such as livestock production, horticulture, post-harvest operations, agro and social forestry, and fisheries. Their specific roles range from owners to landless labourers depending largely on the landowning status of farm households as well as on the social norms governing the family as well as the differences in agro-production systems. A young woman of an agricultural family, for example, might not be seen taking up the same role as an elderly woman in relation to agricultural activities. Landowning status of the family and the status of the woman in such families also contribute towards the role played by women in relation to agriculture. Women coming from landless families work in agriculture as paid labourers. Those having lesser land work as cultivators and as labourers on their own land. Elderly women with experience supervise agricultural labourers in their fields.

Researches have shown that at a very general level, weeding is typically women's responsibility, whereas harvesting and post-harvesting activities are shared between men and women (Saradamoni, 1991; Sharma et al., 1997; Vedavalli 1997; Vedavalli and Sharma 1997). Further, gender division of labour in the field of agricultural activities also depends upon women's other household responsibilities. There have been research evidences of variations in women's power to make decisions in relation to agriculture. A study concerning women in agriculture in Orissa indicates women playing a major role in the selection and storage of rice seeds for the next season (Sharma et al., 1997). This could be contrasted with studies on women in Kerala which found both women and men farmers sharing decision making on the basis of various factors such as nutritive value, taste, and size of the grain (Vedavalli 1997; Vedavalli and Sharma, 1997).

Women's Contribution to Agriculture

The real picture of women's contribution to agriculture in India, as elsewhere, remains half-drawn owing to lack of availability of data based on research and survey in the area. A survey conducted in Haryana on the farming systems found 'agricultural activities to be clearly gender tasked – pesticide dusting, spade work during field irrigation, ploughing, sowing, manure and fertilizer application, uprooting of seedlings and marketing of grains were exclusively done by men. Transplanting and storage of grains were exclusively done by women. Other farm activities such as weeding, harvesting, carrying head load, threshing and winnowing were performed jointly but predominantly by women'. These point towards substantial qualitative and quantitative contributions by women to agriculture. Such contribution, as has already been mentioned above, varies considerably across different agro-ecological systems. For example, in many Himalayan states, a pair of bullocks works 1064 hours and a man 1212 hours and a woman 3485 hours in a year on a one hectare farm, a figure which illustrates women's significant contributions to agricultural production (Shiva, 1993).

Available data collected through traditional methods have not effectively recorded the time, energy, and involvement of women in the agricultural activities. Conventional policy frameworks usually take a narrow definition of 'work' and 'economic activity' so as to define agricultural activities in terms of producing enough food, thus ignoring other important aspects such as production, processing, packaging, storage, and distribution. Such facts are, however, often overlooked by policymakers who view rural women as farmers' wives, helpers, housewives, or agricultural labourers. Also ignored is their indigenous technological knowledge of agriculture drawn from their long experience in the fields of crop storage and food processing that could otherwise be used as a valuable resource. Also important for our discussion is the way a farmer is defined in the policies and surveys conducted at the national level. The NSSO, for example, defines a farmer as one 'who operates some land (owned or taken on lease or otherwise possessed) is engaged in agricultural activities in broad sense of the term, e.g., cultivation of field crops, horticultural crops, plantation, animal husbandry, poultry, piggery, bee-keeping, vermiculture, sericulture on that land during last 365 days' (NSS, 59th Round: A-9). NSSO does not take into account activities of insignificant nature such as collecting honey from the forest, coastal fishing, and growing fruits such as coconuts, banana, guava, lemon, or papaya at a nominal scale, as agricultural activities (Census, 2001: A-10). This clearly keeps out a large number of women whose engagement in such 'insignificant' agricultural activities, in most cases, is greater than those of men. Many women who produce products in their kitchen garden that is equal in value to the paddy or wheat in the fields. In such cases, rural woman must be seen as a farmer and her contribution in terms of her productivity and her product must be measured and adequately reflected in statistics and databases.

Importance of Land to Women

Social status and socio-political power in rural India is determined by the amount of ownership of agricultural land. It has been empirically observed that those woman enjoying secure land rights are treated with greater respect and consideration than those who are landless and economically dependent. Bina Aggarwal (2003), for instance, cited the case of Maharashtra where women divorced or deserted by their husbands could be found working as agricultural labourers on the farms of their brothers who are substantial landowners. It must be noted that in the Indian context, ownership of land is associated with both economic and socio-political status of an individual. For women, land then means not only a source of security against poverty but also a source of empowerment in relation to the society. As could be seen from the Bodhgaya struggle, right to land has come to signify their right to assert themselves against and resist the violence inflicted on them by their own men (Aggarwal, 1994). This shows the significant link between women's status within the family and ownership of land. It also implies that the landowning status of a household does not necessarily make women belong to the same class, thus pointing towards the need to maintain women's land rights in economic planning.

As landownership data at the national level are seldom disaggregated by gender and are generally categorized by households (which are assumed to be headed by men), it is difficult to obtain a precise picture of the amount of land owned by women. However, field studies in Karnataka and West Bengal conducted by the Rural Development Institute (Brown et al., 2002a, 2002b) have indicated the following:

- Women comprise a disproportionate share of the landless and rarely hold legal rights to land.
- The oppressive practice of dowry is integrally linked with women's inferior access and rights to land.
- Providing women with legal rights to land will increase their status and social and economic security.

III
Women's Poverty in Indian Agriculture

From above discussion, it is clear that women play varied roles in agriculture in India. But the significance of their role is not accompanied by due recognition and necessary access to the various opportunities. The National Commission for Women (NCW) (2005, pp. 9–10) observed:

> despite their importance to agricultural production, women face severe handicaps. They are, in fact, the largest group of landless labourers, with little real security in case of the break up of the family owing to death and divorce; inheritance laws and customs discriminate against them. Land reforms and settlement programmes usually give sole title and hence the security needed for obtaining production credits to the husband. Agricultural development programmes are usually planned by men and aimed at men. Mechanization, for example, alleviates the burden of tasks that are traditionally men's responsibility, leaving women's burdens unrelieved or even increased. The excess burden of work on women also acts as a stimulus to have many children so that they can help out with chores from an early age. Extension workers, almost exclusively male, aim most their advice at men and at men's activities and crops. In some regions, this bias may depress production of subsistence food crops in favour of increased production of cash crops so that family nutrition suffers.

Thus, women's status, both as farmer or as agricultural workers, in relation to agriculture in India, is mainly inferior and they are generally poorer than men farmers and agricultural workers. They remain outside the networks of capital and credit, and have very little say in decision making related to agricultural operations. This is in spite of the fact that women's role, both as farmers and as labourers, is crucial for agricultural development in India. The higher incidence of poverty among women farmers could be explained due to lack of credit, lack of ownership to land resource, lack of innovativeness, burden of household work, lack of extension services, etc. On the other hand, higher incidence of poverty among women agricultural labourers is due to low wages earnings, low level of skills, and performance of hazardous works with higher risks to health, lack of subsidiary occupations and burden of household works (Figure 2).

Figure 2

Women's Agricultural Poverty

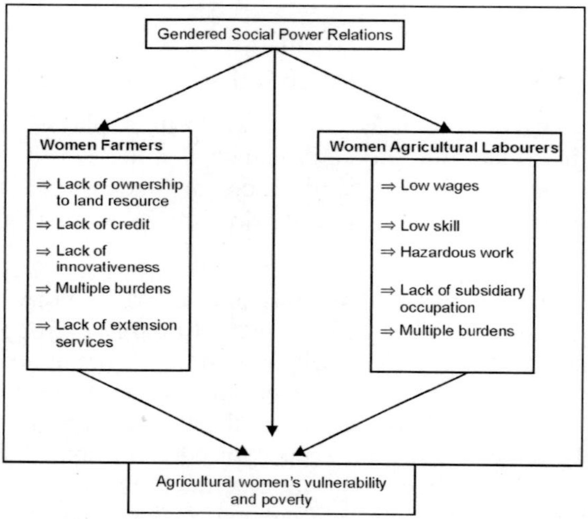

Access to and ownership of agricultural land and other productive assets are crucial in improving women's status in India. But landownership data at the national level are rarely disaggregated by gender. On the other hand, they are generally categorized by households, which are assumed to be headed by men. Because of this, it is difficult to obtain a precise picture of the amount of land owned by women. However, there have been some case studies that throw some light on the issue of women's access and ownership of land resource. Studies done by the RDI in the states of Karnataka and West Bengal pointed out that women not only comprise a disproportionate share of the landless but also rarely hold legal rights to land. These studies suggest that a number of households employed in agriculture are themselves landless and work as agricultural labourers, thus making women of those households landless (Brown et al., 2002; Brown and Chowdhury, 2002). This is compounded by the fact that government programmes, till a long time, recognized only male ownership of agricultural land. What is also true is that women in India rarely assert their ownership and control over agricultural land.

A major cause as well as consequence of women's agricultural poverty is their lack of access to credit provided by the formal financial system, thus severely constraining them to acquire the ability to own and acquire capital assets, productive resources (such as cattle, poultry, and looms), or adequate working capital. Because disbursement and repayment data are not disaggregated by gender, it is not possible to get precise national, state, or institutional estimates of women's relative access to the formal credit system. A study of credit flows by gender in a Regional Rural Banks branch and a Commercial Bank branch in a district of Andhra Pradesh suggests that outside IRDP – even in other government-sponsored credit programmes – women's access to credit is still lower. Disbursement to women ranged between 6 per cent and 12 per cent overall (World Bank, 1991).

Table 2

Male-Female Differentials in Wage Rate

District/state	*Wage rate for adult men (in ₹)*	*Wage rate for women (in ₹)*
Haryana	50–60	25–30
Saharanpur (UP)	60	35–40
North 24 Parganas (West Bengal)	40 (6 hours of work)	25 (6 hours of work)
Andhra Pradesh	40–50	25–30

Source: NCW (2005).

Though there are large number of women in agriculture and related fields (such as dairy, small animal husbandry, fisheries, social and agro forestry, *khadi* and village industry, sericulture, handlooms, and handicrafts), they still remain on the margins. Among rural women workers, 87 per cent are employed in agriculture as labourers and cultivators (Ministry of Labour, 2000–01). Though most rural women are employed as agricultural labourers and cultivators, they get paid less than their male counterparts (NCW, 2005: 17). Table 2 clearly suggests that in four states of the country (Haryana, Uttar Pradesh, West Bengal, and Andhra Pradesh) which are located in four different ecological regions (semi-dry, *terai*, alluvial plain, and plateau), the wage rate of women in agriculture is lower that that of adult men.

A survey of five districts in Andhra Pradesh by an agricultural workers union has found that more women than men were employed for cultivation of paddy, cotton, chillies, turmeric, tobacco, and flowers. Employers explained the preference for women employee in terms of their industrious nature and because they could be hired at 30–50 per cent lower wages than men (cited in UNDP, 1995: 57). According to the 'Wage Report in Rural India' for the agricultural year 2004–2005 (Ministry of Labour, Government of India), the average daily wages received by women for the period under consideration was only ₹ 44.43. Male workers were paid a much higher amount of ₹ 61.37. In yet another study, Bhalla (2007) also suggested that women get lesser wages compared to men in all the agricultural operations (Table 3).

Table 3

Gender Disparity in Average Daily Earnings of Agricultural Households 1990–2000

Activities	*Men*	*Women*
Ploughing	36.64	33.21
Sowing	38.75	28.3
Transplanting	39.53	28.95
Weeding	34.99	25.41
Harvesting	38.44	29.3
Cultivation	39.31	27.72
Forestry	46.03	33.41
Plantations	58.27	43.99
Animal Husbandry	32.25	22.68
Fisheries	54.11	34.33
Other agricultural operation	43.3	27.97

Source: Bhalla (2007: 314).

Even though women have been actively participating in large numbers, but due to prevalent unequal gender power relations, they lack participation in the household decision making. They have hardly any say in what crops to grow, what to purchase, and where to spend the savings. These facts suggest their poverty and powerlessness in household decision making. Women's position in relation to men in the field of agriculture is inferior due to lack of landownership, low wages, unemployment, and lack of access to capital and credit services, lack of knowledge of marketing strategies as well as lack of access to markets, restricted access to information, and being the inferior stakeholders in decision-making.

Another important aspect of women's agricultural status is that the women's inferior social position in power structure makes their poverty far more severe. In terms of food security, position of women is more vulnerable than men. In scarcity-ridden patriarchal society, women and girl children bear the brunt of not getting enough food to eat. Though women cook food, they are the last ones to eat. Girl children are given less food compared to boy children. As a result, women suffer more from malnutrition and are more vulnerable to disease compared to men.

Women, generally, have poor health. Their poor health is due to lack of requisite nutritional supplement and unsuitable living conditions. Women in India are responsible for cooking food using fuel wood, grasses, and animal waste that causes many kinds of respiratory diseases. Animal waste used as fuel wood generates harmful biogases affecting women. Women in some areas also perform the hazardous task of placing mixtures of mercury and oil in the grains to kill insects. The increase exposure to toxic chemicals and insecticides and pesticides, combined with water pollution, creates a number of health risks for women and their infants (UNFPA, cited in HDSA, 2002).

The rate of women's unemployment is also higher. Many studies have suggested that the technology-driven green revolution has adversely affected women's employment chances. Women as marginal workers are employed when the season demands it, are first to loose their jobs in both absolute and relative terms (cited in HDSA, 2002). In the state of Punjab, a study suggests that the decline in female labour was approximately 90 per cent following the green revolution (cited in HDSA, 2002). There are many other examples of the displacement of female labour due to introduction of technology in agriculture.

One of the reasons for severity of women's agricultural poverty is multiple burdens on them. Agricultural women, whether as farmers or as landless labourers, perform multiple tasks. They perform the duty of procreation, rearing of children, cooking, and looking after other household chores. In addition to doing household duties, which in itself is full-time job, they also participate as farmers, labourers, and agricultural helpers. This is exacerbated by the absence of economic independence. Women have less control over income generated from agriculture and allied activities. For instance, only 14 per cent of the dairy cooperative members are women, whereas the rest is controlled by men (FAO, 2002).

Again, farm women are at a higher risk of environmental degradation. Being responsible for providing water, food, fuel firewood, and fodder, women in India interact intensively with their natural surroundings. The degradation and depletion of environmental resource have inevitable direct implications for women. As a matter of fact they are the main victims of environmental degradation. Environmental degradation not only requires women to expend more energy and it may also damage their home-based enterprise (Human Development in South Asia Report, 2002). In India, many women walk miles to collect forest products such as fuel wood, fodder, honey, gum, fruits, and medicinal herbs. Although they receive little for their efforts, the decreased forests deprive them of this source of income as well (Mehta, 2000, cited in Human Development for South Asia, 2002, 2003). In Gujarat, women have been found to be walking for 4–5 hours a day gathering fuel wood (UNFPA, 2002a, cited in HDSA, 2002).

Gender biasness in extension programmes is also responsible of women's poverty. Extension services and associated benefits arising from them (such as seeds, fertilizers, and credits) accrue to men more than women, even though women's participation and role is quite prominent in agricultural development. This could be because of customs of segregation, lack of women's mobility, and predominance of male extension staffs. Extensions programmes also have a in-built gender bias by ignoring the real contribution of women and directing the main thrust of their training towards export crops, and not food crops and small livestock which usually involve women (HDSA, 2002).

Feminization of Agriculture

In recent years, the role of women in agriculture has considerably expanded both as farmers and as labourers, indicating a trend towards the 'feminization of agriculture'. As per the calculation of the M.S. Swaminathan Research Foundation (MSSRF), 28 per cent of all working women are farmers, even though not all have land titles – and 46 per cent are labourers, the remaining being in non-agricultural areas (The Hindu Business Line, 2005). In agricultural labour, 56 per cent are men and 44 per cent women. This trend, however, must be examined critically as feminization of agriculture does not necessarily point towards women's advanced status in the field. It must be noted that the above trend is also associated with the rising rates of female headships in the household.

The Human Development in South Asia Report holds three reasons responsible for this (HDSA, 2002). First, rising poverty has led to an increasing number of male migrations from rural to urban areas and to other countries, in search of better opportunities. Employment in agriculture is available for fewer days per year. In the absence of regular employment, men are forced to migrate in search of regular and better-paid work. Migration of male-specific land labourers from rural areas to urban areas has led to scarcity of labour in agriculture. As a result, more female labourers are drawn to work as underpaid agricultural workers. In many cases, women are forced to accept work in agriculture in their own village under very bad conditions as they face meagre wages, do works for long hours, hazardous work, and sexual harassment. Second, the percentage of women working in agriculture in India, especially those involved in the cultivation of high-yielding varieties increased drastically, as men moved onto non-farm employment. Within rural areas, many men have left agriculture and moved into non-farm rural activities. Third, there is a tendency towards increase in smaller land holdings in India. When land holdings are small, hiring additional workers becomes inefficient and female family members are involved to fulfil labour requirements. Women as cheap and unpaid labourers are involved.

Another reason for the increase in women labourers is the fact that farmers prefer women as agricultural workers primarily because of economic reasons. The farmer is faced with the increasing costs of production required for modern agriculture. They find that they can squeeze his labour costs by using lower-paid women workers. For example, women are preferred to men in North 24 Parganas (West Bengal) by the farm owners because they are docile, require lower wages, and are less lazy than men (ILO, 2003). In the same vein, women in agriculture families are given responsibilities related to agriculture as it saves cost of outside labour. The increase in the number of female-headed agricultural household must also be attributed to incidence such as the large-scale debt-induced suicides by farmers. In recent years, there have been many examples of suicides by male farmers due to agricultural debt. This leaves women to carry out not only the farming but also doing domestic works and repaying the loans taken by the deceased. These have only worsened the conditions of female-headed farmer's families.

While women's participation in agriculture has increased both numerically and in terms of roles in recent years, it needs to be examined more critically. As seen above, agriculture development has not resulted in alleviation of female poverty in Indian agriculture. On the contrary, it appears to have set in motion a process, which is worsening the situation of women in many regions of the country. Further, an increase in the number of women agricultural labourers may be explained in terms of the job being *the least desirable form of employment, taken up only by the poorest*, and not preferred by men because of the low payment involved (World Bank, 1991: xvii). The increase in the number of women as wage labourers could be a sign of deepening poverty forcing them 'into the labour market for family survival and an indicator that the new economic opportunities are inducing the households to move against the cultural grain to send women out to work' (World Bank, 1991: xvii). The census figures show that the processes of casualization and feminization of the workforce in rural areas are taking place simultaneously with the number of marginal women workers becoming larger and more significant, while male main workers in rural areas have declined. These facts clearly point towards some kind of casualization of women labour and increase in the incidence, severity, and trend of women poverty in agriculture.

IV
Conclusion

Agriculture is gendered, so is agricultural poverty. As has been discussed in this paper, women's poverty in relation to agriculture arises from a number of reasons. First and foremost, it has got to do with the fact that women's work and labour in the field of agriculture remains unrecognized to a great extent. Their social roles as the wife and mother of the Indian agricultural household conceal a lot of agricultural work they do along with household chores. Second, as researches have suggested, women have a long way to go as far as enjoying the same access to land rights as men is concerned. Even now, they constitute a large proportion of landless agricultural labourers, and in many cases in their own land. As a result of these, they have lower bargaining power in relation to men and remain unrecognized managers of agricultural households. The household duties ensure that they bear multiple burdens of work without even being aware of it. This lack of awareness of their own status, in turn, keeps them away from the information network of the government meant for empowerment of the agricultural workers. What also adds to the situation is the fact that most government-sponsored agricultural development and extension programmes are male oriented.

Some steps that could be taken to provide visibility, recognition, and justice to women and their work in relation to agriculture are summarized as follows:

- First and foremost, there is a need to recognize that women in agriculture are the largest landless labourer group and also that traditionally agriculture development programmes have been aimed at men.
- Poverty measuring methods must take into account women's work in all dimensions. This might mean devising newer methods to get detailed and in-depth insight into lives and works of women involved in agriculture.
- Incorporating a gender curriculum for agricultural students would go a long way in sensitizing students and researcher of the roles of women in agriculture and the problems they face.
- Policy priorities must be provided to women's rights over land. This implies the need for focus on women involved in agriculture

to have title over land. Lessons could be learnt from Bangladesh where women have taken land on lease through micro-financing institutions. Government must facilitate self-help groups of women with an aim towards this. A significant suggestion towards this has been made by the National Commission on Farmers to make the state farmlands to be made available to women SHGs (NCF, 2006). The NCF has also suggested women to be issued with 'Kisan Credit Cards speedily with joint *pattas* to house/agricultural land as collateral. Till then, indemnity bonds/guarantees should be accepted from husband, male relatives and prominent local figures' (NCF, 2006).

- The issue of women's lower rate of access to institutional credit is intimately related to title to land. The National Commission on Farmers has suggested the need for a more facilitating institutional arrangement that is sensitive towards the women in agriculture.
- Women's work must be substituted with deserving wages. What must also be considered is women's lack of power to retain their incomes. A study by the International Labour Organization (ILO) has pointed out the link between women's economic insecurity and national growth (ILO, 2004). This indicates the need to have policies and institutions that promote women's power over their own earnings.
- Technical help must be provided to women. This could be in the form of women-friendly tools, implements (NCF, 2006), as well as technical knowledge to facilitate scientific method in agriculture.
- As has been suggested by the National Commission on Farmers, local management of seeds through setting up of seed villages and community seed technology training centres with women playing a major role because of their traditional knowledge could be used in seed management (NCF, 2006).
- Government must ensure that its agricultural services and extension programmes are engendered. The Panchayats along with the SHGs could play an important role in mobilizing women in agriculture as well as in supporting the government in making its services gender-sensitive.

References

Aggarwal, Bina (2003). 'Gender and Land Rights Revisited: Exploring New Prospects via the State Family and Market', *Journal of Agrarian Change,* Vol. 3(1–2), pp. 184–224.

Bhalla, G.S. (2007). *Indian Agriculture since Independence*. New Delhi: National Book Trust.

Brown, J., Ananthpur, K., and Giovarelli, R. (2002a). *Women's Access and Rights to Land in Karnataka*. RDI Reports on Foreign Aid and Development #114. Seattle, WA: Rural Development Institute.

Brown, J., and Chowdhury, S.D. (2002b). *Women's Land Rights in West Bengal: A Field Study*. RDI Reports on Foreign Aid and Development #116. Seattle, WA: Rural Development Institute.

Cagatay, N. (1998). *Gender and Poverty*. UNDP Social Development and Poverty Elimination Division, Working Paper Series, No.5.

FAO (2002). *Fact Sheet: Women in Agriculture, Environment and Rural Production*. Available online at: www.fao.org/gender (accessed on 12 January 2010).

FAO (2009) *Asia's Women in Agriculture, Environment and Rural Production: India*. Available online at: http: //www.fao.org/sd/Wpdirect/WPre0108.htm (accessed on 21 December 2009).

Human Development in South Asia (HDSA) (2002). *Agriculture and Rural Development*. Karachi: Mahbub ul Haq Human Development Centre, OUP.

ILO (International Labour Organization) (2003). *Decent Work in Agriculture*. Labour Education 2003/2–3, No. 131–132.

ILO (2004). *Economic Security for a Better World*. Geneva: International Labour Office.

Kanvinde, H.S. (1997). 'Bhitarkanika Wildlife Sanctuary, Orissa'. *Gender Dimensions in Biodiversity Management: India* (pp. 121–126). Report submitted to FAO, RAP. Chennai: M.S. Swaminathan Research Foundation, cited in FAO Report on *Asia's Women in Agriculture, Environment and Rural Production*. Available online at: http: //www.fao.org/sd/Wpdirect/WPre0108.htm (accessed on 21 December 2009).

Manekar, K. (1990). 'Women and employment', *Employment News*, April 7–13.

Ministry of Labour (2000–2001). *Annual Report 2000–01*. New Delhi: Government of India.

National Commission for Women (2005). *Impact of WTO on Women in Agriculture.* New Delhi: National Commission for Women.

National Commission on Farmers (NCF) (2006). *Serving Farmers and Saving Farming,* Fifth and Final Report 4 October 2006, Jai Kisan: Revised Draft National Policy for Farmers. New Delhi: Ministry of Agriculture, Government of India.

Population Census (2001), cited in *Women and Men in India 2001*. New Delhi: Central Statistical Organisation, Ministry of Statistics and Programme Implementation. Government of India.

Sen, A. (1984). *Resources, Values and Development*. Cambridge, MA: Harvard University Press.

Sharma, S.D., Tripathy, S., and Gurung, P. (1997). 'Jeypore tract, Orissa'. In *Gender Dimensions in Biodiversity Management: India* (pp. 107–120). Report submitted to FAO, RAP. Chennai: M.S. Swaminathan Research Foundation.

Shiva, V. (1993). 'GATT, agriculture, and Third World women'. In Mies, M., and Shiva, V. (eds.): *Ecofeminism* (pp. 231–244). London: Zed Books.

The Hindu Business Line (2005). *Gender Issues in Agriculture*. 30 December (An interview with Mina Swaminathan of MSSRF).

UNDP (1995). *Human Development Report.* New York: New York.

UNDP (1997). *Human Development Report*. New York: UNDP.

United Nations (1995). *The World's Women 1995*. (New York: United Nations.

Vedavalli, L., and Anil Kurma N. (1997). 'Waynad, Kerala'. In *Gender Dimensions in Biodiversity Management: India* (pp. 85–94). Report submitted to FAO, RAP, Chennai: M.S. Swaminathan Research Foundation, cited in Saradamoni, K. (1991). *Filling the Rice Bowl*. Hyderabad: Sangam Books (India) Private limited.

Vedavalli, L. (1997). 'Kolli Hills, Tamil Nadu'. In *Gender Dimensions in Biodiversity Management: India* (pp. 95–106), Report submitted to FAO, RAP, Chennai: M.S. Swaminathan Research Foundation, cited in FAO, *Asia's Women in Agriculture, Environment and Rural Production: India.* Available online at: http: //www.fao.org/sd/Wpdirect/WPre0108.htm (accessed on 21 December 2009).

Vepa, S. (2004). 'Feminization of agriculture and marginalization of their economic stake', *Economic and Political Weekly*, XL, 18–24.

World Bank (1991). Gender *and Poverty in India*. Washington DC: World Bank.

8

Caste/Tribe Inequalities in Selected Development Indicators in India

NIDHI JAIN AND APARAJITA CHATTOPADHYAY

People are the real wealth of a nation and in this new millennium, nations are judged by the well-being of their people; by levels of health, nutrition, and education; by civil and political liberties enjoyed by the citizens; by the protection guaranteed to children; and by provisions made for the vulnerable and the disadvantaged (National Population Policy, 2000). India is one of the highly populated countries of the world and this huge population can be the greatest asset for the nation if they are provided with the healthy and productive lives, making education and health services widely accessible and affordable along with the stable and equitable improvements in income levels. It will not only create an environment for people to enjoy long, healthy, and creative lives, but it is also going to help in achieving the socio-demographic goals at much faster rate. But, in the long run for development, social issues are often overlooked or sometimes it is even forgotten, in the immediate concern with the economic development and improved income levels. According to Aristotle, societies cannot be judged merely by such things as income and wealth that are sought not for themselves but desired as means to other objectives (Human Development Report, 1990). Development should be related with the well-being of the people.

During the 1990s, development of people has been defined as a process of enlarging people's choices to raise their level of well-being. United Nations Development Programme (UNDP) has published a series of Human Development Reports (HDRs), which measure and rank different countries of the world on various development indicators. These reports have also shown that development of people is not only due to the economic growth, but there are many other factors behind it as well. There are many indicators to measure human well-being; UNDP has identified some of the crucial developmental parameters for cross-country comparison which includes health, mortality, education, and income to ensure 'decent' lives.

India is a signatory to the Alma-Ata Declaration (1978) which pledges 'Health for All' by 2000 AD. It has become an agreement of health throughout the world and a hope for mankind, particularly in the developing countries. But still we find India lagging far behind in context to provide healthy life to all groups of people. Policies and programmes made for the universal literacy and 'health for all' could have been successful if the utilization of the services by the disadvantaged sections of the society had not been limited due to the socio-economic constraints (Roy et al., 2004).

Socio-economic disparities put certain groups of people at disadvantage, not only economically, socially, and politically but also in terms of their possibilities to live a healthy life (Hosseinpoor et al., 2006). In India, social hierarchy plays an important role and apart from economic condition it can also act as an obstacle in utilizing available services in different sectors (Kopparty, 1994). India is a country of striking demographic diversity and substantial differences are visible between states in the achievement of basic demographic indices due to various socio-economic constraints (Drèze and Sen, 1995). Among all the socio-economic constraints, caste is one of the most pervasive forms of social stratification in India. It is often argued that disadvantaged social groups such as other backward classes (OBCs), scheduled castes (SCs), and scheduled tribes (STs) are lagging behind in the developmental process. The upward mobility of this laggard population is considered to be high-priority policy issue. In order to compensate the historical denial and have safeguards against discrimination, reservation policies are implemented in India after independence. However, caste-based reservation policies of the central government raised debates in the intellectual forefront and criticism are put forth related to such social structural adjustment policies. Reservations for the downtrodden are made to enlarge the capabilities of the backward groups and to help them to uplift their living standards and make them at par with the forwards. The Indian judiciary has upheld the compensatory reservation. The basic tenant of the reservation policy is that the previously victimized and laggard group of social disabilities is encouraged to move forward and equalize the social imbalance that is persisting for decades.

The backward class avail the reservation benefits across states with the presumptions that they all are belonging to the deprived lot. The controversy regarding this reservation policy is for two reasons: first, it considers caste as criteria when detailed statistics of castes are not available almost for a century, and second, it equates class with caste where the definition of backward class is ambiguous. Such reservations are extended to members other than Hindus (who follows caste system) who fall at par with backward class. Majority of the critics are in favour of fixing economic criteria for eliminating the better off portion from the backward class and help the genuinely poor section of the whole lot. Many members who are socio-economically poor or educationally backward are even worse than the backward class, though the former do not enjoy the reservation benefits.

In this context, this paper aims to understand the existing difference in availability of some selected development parameters to four caste groups in selected states of India. This paper is particularly focused on those development indicators that are linked with women and children as they are highly vulnerable and require 'special care and assistance' (Reed et al., 1998).

The formulation of Millennium Development Goals (MDGs) targets and indicators depict the priority and importance given to the well-being of women and child. It has also been mentioned in the World Development Indicators (2008) that prioritizing women's health will help countries meet many of the MDGs. In a country like India, the social norms, cultural traditions, and legal barriers restrict their access to resources and services available, making it even more difficult for women to seek health care for themselves or for their children. The 1987 Call to Action for Safe Motherhood explicitly framed the plight of women and children as deeply rooted in the adverse social, cultural and economic environments of society and especially the environment that societies create for women (Mahler, 1987).

The unfairness of this situation has made it obvious that the well-being of women and their children is an issue of rights. The issues related to the well-being of women and children had always been discussed and had remained an integral part of many programmes and policies, but making it as rights of women and children had been considered in the International Conference on Population and Development, held in Cairo, Egypt, in 1994. In the above context, it can be said that the progress of a society or a state or a nation can be judged by looking at the development indicators that are related to women and children. Thus, this paper aims to understand the existing inequalities in some selected developmental indicators in major states of India giving special focus on social groups. The specific objectives are to comprehend the levels of development within and across selected states by social groups, to study inequalities in comprehensive development indices within states, and to examine the effect of social groups in selected development indicators by states.

Data and Methods

This study utilizes the data obtained from the third round of National family Health Survey (NFHS-III) conducted in 2005–2006 (IIPS and Macro International, 2007). NFHS-III collected information from a nationally representative sample of 109,041 households, 124,385 women aged 15–49 across 29 states.

Tables 1 and 2 show the per cent distribution of women and per cent distribution of children aged 0–4 years and 5–17 years by caste/tribe for all the major states of India. For the analysis of this study, only those 10 states where the sample size for all four groups was found adequate have been selected. The selected states are Rajasthan, Madhya Pradesh, Uttar Pradesh, Assam, West Bengal, Orissa, Gujarat, Maharashtra, Andhra Pradesh, and Karnataka.

Table 1

Distribution of Women by Caste/Tribe in Different States, NFHS-III

(in %)

States	*SC*	*ST*	*OBC*	*Others*	*Total (N)*
India	19.2	8.4	40.5	31.9	120,604
Punjab	32.5	0.1	9.5	57.8	3077
Haryana	22.9	0.6	20.9	55.7	2311
Delhi	17.4	1.5	12.9	68.2	1466
Rajasthan	18.6	12.9	46.4	22.2	6600
Uttar Pradesh	22.5	0.8	49.8	26.9	18,945
Bihar	17	0.4	58.6	24	9483
Assam	17.1	13.5	27.9	41.6	2639
West Bengal	29.3	5.7	4.4	60.6	9163
Orissa	18.3	21.3	28.3	32.2	4756
Madhya Pradesh	17.1	21.6	39.8	21.5	7225
Gujarat	13.5	10	39.6	36.9	6153
Maharashtra	15.7	10.3	28.7	45.3	11,987
Andhra Pradesh	18.1	6.2	48.4	27.2	9553
Karnataka	16	6.8	60.4	16.8	6943
Kerala	12.3	1.7	37.8	48.2	3215
Tamil Nadu	23.1	0.9	74.2	1.8	7098

Table 2

Distribution of Children Aged 0–4 Years and 5–17 Years by Caste/Tribe in Different states, NFHS-III

(in %)

States	*0–4 Years*					*5–17 Years*				
	SC	*ST*	*OBC*	*Others*	*Total (N)*	*SC*	*ST*	*OBC*	*Others*	*Total (N)*
India	21.4	9.9	41.5	27.2	54,722	20.5	9.4	42.4	27.7	154,138
Punjab	37.6	0	9.4	53	1076	37.7	0.1	9.2	53	3389
Haryana	26.3	0.8	21.1	51.8	1029	25.7	0.2	26	48.1	3164
Delhi	22.5	1.7	15.6	60.1	519	20.6	1.5	16.2	61.7	1617
Rajasthan	22.3	14.8	45.7	17.2	3515	19.2	15.5	47	18.2	10,117
Uttar Pradesh	26	1.2	50.4	22.4	11,715	24.6	1.1	52.2	22.2	31,661
Bihar	20	0.7	58.6	20.7	6249	17.9	0.3	61.2	20.6	15,100
Assam	18.5	15.9	23.3	42.3	1022	17.4	14.9	24.3	43.3	3124
West Bengal	29.3	7.2	3.4	60.1	3490	29.5	6.7	3.9	59.9	9781
Orissa	18.6	28.4	26.9	26.2	1936	20.5	25.5	25.6	28.4	5366
Madhya Pradesh	18.6	25	40.5	15.9	3845	17.6	23.1	42	17.3	10,609
Gujarat	16.7	10.7	41.9	30.7	2587	15.6	11.3	43.6	29.5	6748
Maharashtra	16.3	12.7	26.5	44.5	4355	16.8	12.7	24.5	46	13,564
Andhra Pradesh	18.3	9.3	49.7	22.7	3141	18.6	7.4	50.7	23.3	9794
Karnataka	18.1	8.4	59.5	14.1	2565	18.9	8.3	60.8	12	7588
Kerala	11.1	2.5	36.2	50.3	893	12	2.2	37.7	48.2	2725
Tamil Nadu	27.4	0.7	70	1.8	2065	24.1	0.9	73.2	1.8	6511

To fulfil the first objective of the study, five composite indices based on selected indicators that relate to development either directly or indirectly are computed. The indicators have been grouped according to four dimensions that can be considered important from the development perspective, i.e., access to basic facilities, social development, health, and nutrition. Accordingly, we have computed basic facility index, social development index, health care index, and nutrition index, then based on all the indicators included in these four indices, we have computed an overall development index to show the overall performance in all the four dimensions. The indices constructed can be interpreted as 'higher the index value, better will be the performance'.

Brief Description and Justification for Inclusion of Variables from Policy Point of View

V_1 to V_5: Access to basic facilities, such as proper housing, safe drinking water and sanitation, electricity, and clean cooking fuel, is not only an important measure of socio-economic status of the household but also fundamental to the health of its members and, particularly, to the health of women and children. In India, water and sanitation-related infections account for between 70 per cent and 80 per cent of the burden of disease (Tenth Five-Year Plan, 2002–2007). Also, 'proportion of population with sustainable access to an improved water source and with access to improved sanitation and proportion of population using solid fuels' has been taken as indicators for monitoring progress under MDGs.

V1:	Percentage of households having electricity	**Basic Facility Index**
V2:	Percentage of households having pucca house	
V3:	Percentage of households using clean cooking fuel	
V4:	Percentage of households using improved source of drinking water	
V5:	Percentage of households having improved toilet facilities	
V6:	Female literacy	**Social Development Index**
V7:	Percentage of women working with cash	
V8:	Percentage of children aged 5–14 engaged in child work	
V9:	School attendance rate	
V10:	Percentage of women 18–29 marrying before 18 years of age	**Health Care Index**
V11:	Percentage of children aged 12–23 months who received full immunization	
V12:	Percentage of women who received recommended ANC	
V13:	Percentage of safe deliveries	
V14:	Percentage of children under age 5 who are underweight	**Nutrition Index**
V15:	Percentage of children aged 6–59 months who are anaemic	
V16:	Percentage of women who are anaemic	
V17:	Percentage of women who have low BMI.	

The overall development index has been constructed based on all the above 17 indicators.

V_6 to V_{10}: It is well-known that *female literacy* is directly related to level of social development and it is one of the key variables in the developmental process. Higher female literacy is generally associated with low fertility, and lower levels of infant and child mortality. *Also*, 'The increase in the education of women and girls contributes to greater empowerment of women, to a postponement of the age of marriage and to a reduction in the size of families. When mothers are better educated, their children's survival rate tends to increase' (Programme of Action, ICPD, 1994).

The ability of a country's economy to provide gainful employment to its population is an important aspect of country's level of development. *Paid employment of women*, in particular, has been recognized as important for achieving the goal of population stabilization in India. Women's wage work is important for economic growth and the well-being of families (World Development Indicators 2008). Women's increased earning capacity, in turn, has a positive effect on child nutrition (Dwyer and Bruce, 1988). Thus, female participation in paid labour force has a link with the development of the nation.

A child worker is defined by UNICEF as any child aged 5–11 who, in the 7 days preceding the survey, worked for someone who is not a member of the household, with or without pay, or did household chores for 28 or more hours, or engaged in any family business and any child aged 12–14 years who, in the seven days preceding the survey, worked for someone who is not a member of the household, with or without pay, for 14 or more hours, or did household chores for 28 or more hours, or engaged in any other family work for 14 or more hours. *Child work* acts as an obstacle in the development of a society and a nation. Elimination of child labour is an area of great concern and of commitment for the Government of India. Articles 24 and 39 of the Constitution provide for the protection of children from involvement in economic activities and from avocations unsuited to their age (National Report on 'A World Fit for Children', 2007).

School attendance rates for population aged 6–17 years indicate participation in schooling at any level, from primary through higher levels of education. Educational attainment is a fundamental indicator of country's level of human capital development and education system of a country is the main edifice on which the future of the nation rests. If school attendance rate continues to be low and dropouts high, country's social and economic development can be doubted in a long run. So, in National Population Policy (NPP), 2000, among 14 socio-economic goals, one goal is also to reduce the dropouts at primary and secondary school levels.

One of the goals, mentioned in NPP (2000) is to promote *delayed marriage for girls*, not earlier than age 18 and preferably after 20 years of age. The early marriage of girls generally results in a typical reproductive pattern of 'too early, too frequent and too many' that may cause higher family size, high infant and child mortality, and pregnancy complications. Adolescents' reproductive health is strongly affected by low age at marriage and such continuing practices leave long-lasting effects on women's life. Other than this, early marriage limits girl's opportunities for better education, and participation in the paid workforce. Higher value indicates that there is a need for social development and also for strict implementation of Child Marriage Restraint Act.

V_{11} to V_{13}: *Full immunization* includes BCG, measles, and three doses each of DPT and polio vaccine. Immunization of children against six vaccine-preventable diseases (namely, tuberculosis, diphtheria, whooping cough, tetanus, polio, and measles) is crucial to reduce infant and child mortality. To achieve universal immunization of children against all these six diseases is one of the goals in NPP (2000).

Important components of *antenatal care* (ANC) include three or more antenatal check-ups (with the first check-up within the first trimester of pregnancy), two or more tetanus toxoid injections, and iron and folic acid tablets or syrup for three or more months. ANC has long been recognized as a core component of maternal health services. It can help women identify potential risks and plan for a safe delivery (Millennium Development Goals Report, 2007). It is directly related to the state of reproductive and child health. Higher coverage of ANC ensures improved maternal health leading to higher child survival and lower maternal mortality.

Safe delivery means deliveries assisted by trained health personnel either at hospital or at home. Presence of a skilled health personnel is a key factor in lowering maternal mortality as nearly half of the maternal deaths in developing countries occur during labour and delivery or just after delivery (Nanda et al., 2005). Higher coverage of safe deliveries will help in attaining the goal led down by NPP (2000) of achieving 100 per cent deliveries by trained persons. It will also help, to a great extent, in achieving one of the MDGs of reducing maternal mortality which has also been specified in NPP (2000).

V_{14} to V_{17}: In developing countries, children and women are more vulnerable to malnutrition because of low dietary intakes, infectious diseases, lack of appropriate care, and inequitable distribution of food within the household. Adequate nutrition is critical to child development. Malnourished children are particularly vulnerable to growth retardation, micronutrient deficiencies, and common childhood illnesses. The *proportion of children who are underweight* is the most common indicator of malnutrition. 'Prevalence of underweight children under five years of age' is also specified as an indicator for monitoring progress of one of the MDGs. *Anaemia in young children* is a serious concern resulting in impaired cognitive performance, behavioural and motor development, coordination, language development, as well as increased morbidity from infectious diseases.

A woman's nutritional status has important implications for her health as well as the health of her children. A woman with poor nutritional status, as indicated by *low body mass index (BMI) and anaemia*, has a greater risk of obstructed labour, having adverse pregnancy outcomes, death due to postpartum haemorrhage, and illness for herself and her baby (NFHS Report). Low-birth weight, which is associated with maternal malnutrition, raises the risk of infant mortality and stunts growth in infancy and childhood (World Development Indicators, 2008).

Computation of Indices

The indicators considered in the study can be grouped as positive and negative indicators. The indicators that affect development in a positive way are categorized as positive indicators and those affecting in a negative way are categorized as negative indicators (Ram and Mohanty, 2005).

For positive indicators, the index is usually computed as:

$$\frac{V_i - V_{\min}}{V_{\max-V_{\min}}}$$

For negative indicators the index is usually computed as:

$$\frac{V_{\max-V_i}}{V_{\max-}V_{\min}}$$

where

V_i = Actual value in the series

$V_{\min}$ = Minimum value (taken as minimum value observed in the series)

$V_{\max}$ = Maximum value (taken as maximum value observed in the series).

This simply states that the state or group with a lowest value will get a score 0 and state or group with a highest value will get a score 1.

To study the extent of inequality regarding each of the above indices among social groups, we have used a simple measure 'coefficient of variation' which can be calculated as follows:

$$\text{Coefficient of variation (CV)} = \frac{\sqrt{n\Sigma X_i^2 - (\Sigma X_i)^2}}{n\overline{X}}$$

where

X_i is the value of a particular index for i-th group in a particular state.

$\overline{X}$ is the average of all the four X_i values of particular index in that state.

The calculated value of CV is generally between 0 and 1. In case of perfect equality among groups, the value of CV will be zero. However, the calculated value, if it is not zero, will show the extent of variation or inequality among social groups in that particular index within particular state. Higher the calculated value of coefficient of variation of a state, greater is the degree of inequality in that state among four social groups regarding that particular index. Accordingly, the states have been ranked in a descending order based on the value of CV. State to which Rank 1 is given is having high inequality among social groups regarding the particular index. Similar procedure is followed to examine inequality among four social groups regarding each of the five indices given earlier (Roy et al., 2004).

To examine the net effect of social groups, on different development indicators, logistic regression has been applied. Ten separate regressions have been carried out considering 10 selected development indicators as the dependent variable, while controlling for other socio-economic characteristics.

Findings

Levels of Development

Table 3 shows the basic facility index values for all the states by caste/tribe and for the states as a whole. In case of basic facilities such as electricity, improved toilet facility, improved source of drinking water, pucca house, and safe cooking fuel, Gujarat has got the first rank. Maharashtra, Andhra Pradesh, and Karnataka have also performed well. While Orissa, Assam, Madhya Pradesh, and Uttar Pradesh are lagging behind in case of basic facilities. Noteworthy here is that the states such as Gujarat, Maharashtra, Andhra Pradesh, and Karnataka have not been able to improve the conditions of STs, even after attaining the highest values of facility index, and STs here are still deprived of the basic facilities. SCs and OBCs in Gujarat, Maharashtra, Andhra Pradesh, and Karnataka are doing far better than their counterparts and in some cases they are better than the 'others' in Rajasthan, Uttar Pradesh, Assam, and Madhya Pradesh.

Table 3

Basic Facility Index (BFI)

States	*SC*	*ST*	*OBC*	*Others*	*Total*
Rajasthan	0.39	0.13	0.43	0.8	0.41
Madhya Pradesh	0.34	0.17	0.34	0.65	0.25
Uttar Pradesh	0.31	0.09	0.36	0.63	0.31
Assam	0.23	0.22	0.32	0.42	0.22
West Bengal	0.36	0.2	0.5	0.61	0.51
Orissa	0.25	0.08	0.35	0.49	0.13
Gujarat	0.66	0.36	0.61	1	0.94
Maharashtra	0.59	0.31	0.72	0.77	0.84
Andhra Pradesh	0.57	0.41	0.61	0.83	0.77
Karnataka	0.5	0.45	0.64	0.73	0.73

Note: The variables considered are: 1. percentage of households having electricity, 2. percentage of households having *pucca* houses, 3. percentage of households using clean cooking fuel, 4. percentage of households using improved source of drinking water, and 5. percentage of household having improved toilet facility.

Table 4

Social Development Index (SDI)

States	*SC*	*ST*	*OBC*	*Others*	*Total*
Rajasthan	0.32	0.24	0.36	0.58	0.17
Madhya Pradesh	0.54	0.37	0.5	0.68	0.43
Uttar Pradesh	0.37	0.34	0.39	0.59	0.28
Assam	0.65	0.63	0.76	0.63	0.8
West Bengal	0.55	0.47	0.65	0.61	0.57
Orissa	0.54	0.32	0.57	0.76	0.52
Gujarat	0.59	0.39	0.45	0.72	0.58
Maharashtra	0.72	0.55	0.79	0.75	0.9
Andhra Pradesh	0.63	0.51	0.6	0.69	0.63
Karnataka	0.62	0.45	0.68	0.81	0.76

Note: The variables considered are: 1. female literacy, 2. percentage of women working with cash, 3. percentage of children aged 5–14 years engaged in child work, 4. school attendance rate, and 5. percentage of women 18–29 years marrying before 18 years of age.

Table 4 shows the social development index values by caste/tribe and as a whole for all the states under study. This table shows that Maharashtra, Assam, Karnataka, and Andhra Pradesh are doing better than all other states in most of the social development indicators considered in the study, while Madhya Pradesh, Uttar Pradesh, and Rajasthan are having the lowest ranks in social development index. STs in all the states are not performing satisfactorily except in Assam and Maharashtra. The same is with SCs and OBCs in Uttar Pradesh and Rajasthan; they are not performing well in these two states. Interestingly, the index values of 'others' in Rajasthan, Uttar Pradesh, and West Bengal are either almost same or less than that of the OBCs and SCs of Maharashtra, Andhra Pradesh, and Karnataka.

Table 5

Health Care Index (HCI)

States	*SC*	*ST*	*OBC*	*Others*	*Total*
Rajasthan	0.31	0.12	0.32	0.53	0.18
Madhya Pradesh	0.34	0.14	0.35	0.65	0.21
Uttar Pradesh	0.14	0.02	0.21	0.34	0
Assam	0.3	0.35	0.47	0.33	0.23
West Bengal	0.55	0.48	0.76	0.63	0.63
Orissa	0.52	0.28	0.62	0.73	0.52
Gujarat	0.69	0.37	0.58	0.81	0.7
Maharashtra	0.65	0.37	0.79	0.76	0.8
Andhra Pradesh	0.7	0.39	0.69	0.92	0.82
Karnataka	0.62	0.46	0.79	0.91	0.87

Note: The variables considered are: 1. percentage of children aged 12–23 months who received full immunization, 2. percentage of women who received recommended ANC, and 3. percentage of safe deliveries.

Table 5 shows the values of health care index for all the four caste/tribe groups and also for the states as a whole. If we look at the overall performance of states in health care index, it is found that both western states, viz., Gujarat and Maharashtra, and southern states, viz., Andhra Pradesh, and Karnataka, are doing good, while Rajasthan, Madhya Pradesh, Uttar Pradesh, and Assam have a long way to go. If we concentrate on caste/tribe differentials within the states, it can easily be seen that within each state, STs are the poor performing among all four groups, while other three groups, i.e., SCs, OBCs, and 'others' are showing variations. In Andhra Pradesh, Karnataka, Gujarat, Maharashtra, and West Bengal and also in Orissa, these three groups are doing fairly well in health care utilization but in Rajasthan, Madhya

Pradesh, Uttar Pradesh, and Assam these groups are not performing well. If we see the index values of OBCs and SCs of western and southern states, they are performing even better than the 'others' of Rajasthan, Uttar Pradesh, and Assam, where 'others' are at par with STs of western and southern states.

Table 6

Nutrition Index (NI)

States	*SC*	*ST*	*OBC*	*Others*	*Total*
Rajasthan	0.49	0.34	0.59	0.63	0.58
Madhya Pradesh	0.32	0.12	0.44	0.62	0.16
Uttar Pradesh	0.44	0.42	0.54	0.64	0.57
Assam	0.35	0.57	0.56	0.52	0.54
West Bengal	0.46	0.08	0.75	0.64	0.6
Orissa	0.42	0.2	0.59	0.72	0.42
Gujarat	0.47	0.07	0.49	0.71	0.54
Maharashtra	0.57	0.38	0.69	0.71	0.81
Andhra Pradesh	0.49	0.37	0.52	0.67	0.64
Karnataka	0.49	0.37	0.6	0.69	0.68

Note: The variables considered are: 1. percentage of children under age 5 who are under weight, 2. percentage of children aged 6–59 months who are anaemic, 3. percentage of women who are anaemic, and 4. percentage of women with low BMI.

Table 7

Overall Development Index (ODI)

States	*SC*	*ST*	*OBC*	*Others*	*Total*
Rajasthan	0.38	0.21	0.43	0.65	0.34
Madhya Pradesh	0.39	0.21	0.41	0.65	0.27
Uttar Pradesh	0.33	0.23	0.38	0.57	0.31
Assam	0.39	0.45	0.53	0.49	0.47
West Bengal	0.47	0.3	0.65	0.62	0.57
Orissa	0.42	0.21	0.52	0.67	0.38
Gujarat	0.6	0.3	0.53	0.82	0.7
Maharashtra	0.63	0.41	0.75	0.75	0.84
Andhra Pradesh	0.59	0.43	0.6	0.77	0.71
Karnataka	0.55	0.43	0.67	0.78	0.75

Note: All the 17 variables that have been used for other four indices are considered.

Table 6 shows values of nutrition index for all states by caste/tribe groups and also for states as a whole. It can be seen from the table that

Maharashtra, Andhra Pradesh, Karnataka, and West Bengal are ahead in nutrition index among all the states under study. However, special attention is needed for Madhya Pradesh which is far behind in the index value from all other states. Caste/tribe-wise differential within states denote that in all the states except Assam, STs represent the poor performing group, especially in Gujarat, West Bengal, Madhya Pradesh, and Orissa. In Assam, STs are performing better than all other three groups. SCs are also not performing well in nutrition index in most of the states. But, there is a consistency in the performance of OBCs and 'others' in almost all the states.

Table 7 shows the values of all states by caste/tribe groups and also for states as a whole in the overall development index which denotes the average performance in all the development indicators used in the study. This table depicts that performance of Maharashtra, on an average, is better than all other states in all the indicators. Gujarat, Andhra Pradesh, and Karnataka have also got satisfactory values in the overall development index. The average performance of Rajasthan, Madhya Pradesh, Uttar Pradesh, Orissa, and Assam cannot be said satisfactory. If we see the caste/tribe differential within the states, it can be said that STs are not performing well in almost all the indicators among all the four groups. On comparing interstate caste/tribe differentials, it can be seen that average performances of 'others' of Rajasthan, Madhya Pradesh, Uttar Pradesh, Assam, and Orissa in all the indicators are the same as that of SCs and OBCs in western and southern states. Table 8 presents the rank of social groups combined with state in each of the indices, indicating the relative performance of groups belonging to different states. It gives a comprehensive picture of performance of four caste/tribe groups in different states.

Inequalities within States

Table 9 gives the state-wise values of coefficient of variation for each of the indices. The ranks given in the table represent the relative position of states by inequality among caste/tribe regarding each of the indices. Rank 1 shows the highest inequality and rank 10 shows the lowest inequality existing within states. In case of basic facilities, Uttar Pradesh, Rajasthan, Orissa, and Madhya Pradesh are characterized by extreme inequality among four social groups, while in Assam, Andhra Pradesh, Karnataka, and Maharashtra, there is more equality regarding access to basic facilities. Rajasthan, Orissa, Gujarat, and Uttar Pradesh are revealing high inequality with respect to social development. On the contrary, Assam, Andhra Pradesh, West Bengal, and Maharashtra are characterized by least inequality among four social groups regarding

Table 8

Ranking in Development Indices

Caste/tribe combined with state	*Rank in*				
	ODI	*BFI*	*SDI*	*HCI*	*NI*
Gujarat – Others	1	12	6	3	3.5
Karnataka – Others	2	5	1	2	5
Andhra Pradesh – Others	3	2	8	1	7
Maharashtra – Others	4.5	4	5	7	3.5
Maharashtra – OBC	4.5	6	2	5	6
Karnataka – OBC	6	9	10	4	12
Orissa – Others	7	18	4	8	2
Madhya Pradesh – Others	8	8	9	13	11
West Bengal – OBC	9	17	11	6	1
Rajasthan – Others	10	3	21	19	10
Maharashtra – SC	11	14	7	12	16
West Bengal – Others	12	13	17	14	8
Andhra Pradesh – OBC	13	11	18	10	19
Gujarat – SC	14	7	20	11	25
Andhra Pradesh – SC	15	15	13	9	23
Uttar Pradesh – Others	16	10	19	29	9
Karnataka – SC	17	16	16	16	21
Assam – OBC	18	30	3	22	17
Gujarat – OBC	19	12	31	17	24
Orissa – OBC	20	27	22	15	14
Assam – Others	21	21	15	31	20
West Bengal – SC	22	24	23	18	26
Assam – ST	23	35	14	27	15
Karnataka – ST	24	19	30	23	33
Andhra Pradesh – ST	25	22	27	24	32
Rajasthan – OBC	26	20	36	32	13
Orissa – SC	27	33	25	20	30
Uttar Pradesh – OBC	28	26	32	36	18
Maharashtra – ST	29	31	24	26	31
Assam – SC	30	34	12	34	34
Madhya Pradesh – SC	31	28	26	30	36
Madhya Pradesh – OBC	32	29	28	28	27
Rajasthan – SC	33	23	38	33	22
Uttar Pradesh – SC	34	32	35	38	28
Gujarat – ST	35	25	33	25	40
West Bengal – ST	36	36	29	21	39
Uttar Pradesh – ST	37	39	37	40	29
Madhya Pradesh – ST	38	37	34	37	38
Orissa – ST	39	40	39	35	37
Rajasthan – ST	40	38	40	39	35

social development implying that state of social development in all the four groups is more or less the same in these states. As in case of basic facilities, in health care also, Uttar Pradesh, Madhya Pradesh, Rajasthan, and Orissa are showing greater extent of inequality implying that caste/tribe is having strong influence on the receipt of health care services. West Bengal, Assam, Karnataka, and Maharashtra reveal the least inequality in this respect. It indicates that health care services in these states have been able to reach all the four groups to a great extent. Regarding nutritional status of women and child, inequality is highest in Gujarat, West Bengal, Madhya Pradesh, and Orissa. The least disparity among four groups regarding nutritional status is found in Uttar Pradesh, Assam, and Andhra Pradesh suggesting that there is not much variation in nutritional status of different caste/tribe in these states.

With respect to overall development, Rajasthan, Madhya Pradesh, Orissa, and Uttar Pradesh are showing high inequality among all the four groups. In Assam, Andhra Pradesh, Karnataka, and Maharashtra, on the other hand, the inequality is least regarding overall development. Equality in Andhra Pradesh, Karnataka, and Maharashtra can be taken as welcoming feature as all the three states have performed well in the overall development index and these states have been able to provide an overall development to all the four groups by reducing the gap between them.

Effect of Caste/Tribe on Developmental Indicators

It has already been seen that all the four social groups are not similar in their performances in various development indicators in different states. As discussed earlier, these differences among groups can be a result of other attributes that are associated with different castes/tribes. So, it is essential to adjust the effect of these other variables on different development indicators to see the effect of caste/tribe per se. Results of logistic regression are given in Tables 10–12 which show the relationship between caste/tribe and development indicators considered, after controlling the effect of other variables.

Age at Marriage

Differentials between SC women and 'other' women regarding age at marriage disappear in most of the states once we adjust the effect of other confounding variables. Differentials persist only in Rajasthan, Uttar Pradesh, Orissa, and Karnataka where SC women are more likely to get married before 18 years of age as compared to women in 'other' category. Especially in Rajasthan, it is much more likely than other states.

Differentials between ST women and 'other' women exist in Uttar Pradesh, Orissa, and Karnataka even after adjusting the effect of other socio-economic variables. In Uttar Pradesh, the odds for ST women of getting married before 18 years of age is 4.6 times ($p < 0.05$) higher as compared to women in 'other' category. The corresponding odd ratios are 2.2 and 2.6 in Orissa and Karnataka, respectively, i.e., ST women in Orissa and Karnataka are 2.2 and 2.6 times more likely to get married before 18 years of age as compared to 'other' women.

Differentials between OBC women and women in 'other' category persist in seven out of ten states even after adjusting the effect of other factors. The odds of getting married before 18 years among OBC women are almost 1.3 times ($p < 0.05$) higher in Madhya Pradesh and Andhra Pradesh as compared to women in 'other' category. The corresponding odd ratios are 1.5 and 1.8 for Uttar Pradesh and Rajasthan. The likelihood of getting married in young age (less than 18 years) is much more (almost 2.1 times) in Orissa and Karnataka for OBC women. Only in Maharashtra, OBC women are less likely to get married in young age as compared to women in 'other' category.

Table 9

Ranking of States by Extent of Inequality in Different Development Indices among Social Groups

States	*BFI*		*SDI*		*HCI*		*NI*		*ODI*	
	CV	*Rank*	*CV*	*Rank*	*CV*	*Rank*	*CV*	*Rank*	*CV*	*Rank*
Rajasthan	0.546	2	0.336	1	0.451	3	0.219	7	0.375	1
Madhya Pradesh	0.463	4	0.209	5	0.491	2	0.48	3	0.373	2
Uttar Pradesh	0.556	1	0.236	4	0.669	1	0.174	10	0.331	4
Assam	0.274	8	0.084	10	0.174	9	0.18	9	0.11	10
West Bengal	0.367	5	0.12	8	0.172	10	0.531	2	0.272	6
Orissa	0.52	3	0.285	2	0.31	4	0.408	4	0.363	3
Gujarat	0.344	6	0.239	3	0.263	6	0.535	1	0.326	5
Maharashtra	0.299	7	0.131	7	0.259	7	0.228	5	0.22	7
Andhra Pradesh	0.25	9	0.107	9	0.278	5	0.213	8	0.203	9
Karnataka	0.193	10	0.2	6	0.246	8	0.226	6	0.211	8

Child Work

Differentials between SC and 'other' category regarding child work mostly disappear after adjusting the effect of other socio-economic factors, except in Madhya Pradesh, West Bengal, and Gujarat where odds of being engaged in child work are 1.4–1.5 times higher for SC children as compared to children who belong to 'other' category.

Differentials regarding child work between ST children and 'other' children persist in six out of ten states, which are Rajasthan, Madhya Pradesh, West Bengal, Orissa, Gujarat and Andhra Pradesh after adjusting for the effect of other factors. In all these states ST children are more likely to get engaged in child work as compared to 'other' children.

Differentials between OBC and 'other' category regarding child work are striking in seven out of ten states even after controlling the effect of other confounding variables. In Madhya Pradesh, the odds for an OBC child of being engaged in work are 1.7 times higher as compared to 'other' child. In other six states, Rajasthan, Uttar Pradesh, Orissa, Gujarat, Maharashtra, and Andhra Pradesh, the corresponding odd ratios vary between 1.3 and 1.5.

Table 10

Relationship between Caste/Tribe and Social Development Indicators – Results of Logistic Analysis

States	*Age at marriage*			*Child work*			*School attendance*		
	SC	*ST*	*OBC*	*SC*	*ST*	*OBC*	*SC*	*ST*	*OBC*
Rajasthan	2.297**	1.771	1.828**	1.315	2.156**	1.394**	1.6**	1.362*	1.113
Madhya Pradesh	1.303	1.064	1.36*	1.44*	2.028**	1.693**	1.642**	2.457**	1.357**
Uttar Pradesh	1.789**	4.571*	1.585**	1.165	0.845	1.264**	1.588**	1.642**	1.263**
Assam	1.079	0.908	0.91	0.696	0.917	0.738	1.018	1.338	0.796
West Bengal	1.158	0.8	0.956	1.491*	1.867**	1.7	1.178	1.826**	0.732
Orissa	1.598*	2.242**	2.172**	1.082	1.715**	1.507*	1.461**	2.596**	1.298*
Gujarat	0.83	1.111	1.208	1.501**	2.041**	1.518**	1.175	1.674**	1.791**
Maharashtra	1.168	0.733	0.742**	1.074	1.164	1.328*	0.97	1.487**	0.899
Andhra Pradesh	1.295	0.992	1.328*	1.355	2.16**	1.479*	1.253	2.112**	1.375**
Karnataka	1.91**	2.661**	2.061**	1.101	1.414	1.095	1.289	2.184**	1.283*

*Significant at 5 per cent level of significance and 'others' who are not SC, ST or OBC is the reference category. **Significant at 1 per cent level of significance.

Notes: Age at marriage: 0 = 18 years or more, 1 = less than 18 years.
Child work: 0 = no, 1 = yes.
School attendance: 0 = attending, 1 = not attending.
Variable controlled for age at marriage: Women education, women's work status, religion, SLI, mass media exposure, place of residence.
Variable controlled for child work and school attendance: SLI, religion, place of residence, sex of child, type of family, mother's education, mother's work status.
In caste category, reference is 'others' in each regression.

School Attendance

In six out of ten states under study, the differentials between SC children and 'other' children regarding school attendance are due to differences in socio-economic conditions. Rajasthan, Madhya Pradesh, Uttar Pradesh, and Orissa are the states where, even after adjusting the effect of other socio-economic variables, SC children are 1.5–1.6 times more likely to be without attending school as compared to children in 'other' category.

As far as differential between ST and 'other' category is concerned regarding school attendance, it is quite striking that in all the states under study, except Assam, ST children are more likely not to attend school as compared to 'other' children. Especially in Madhya Pradesh and Orissa, it is much more likely than other states.

Table 11

Relationship between Caste/Tribe and health Care Indicators – Results of Logistic Analysis

States	*Full immunization*			*ANC*			*Safe delivery*		
	SC	*ST*	*OBC*	*SC*	*ST*	*OBC*	*SC*	*ST*	*OBC*
Rajasthan	0.919	11.95**	1.489	1.791	1.667	0.968	1.278	0.775	0.77
Madhya Pradesh	1.16	1.661	0.904	1.123	0.965	1.15	1.859**	2.349**	1.246
Uttar Pradesh	1.631*	1.323	1.173	1.73*	2.08	1.504*	1.573**	6.48*	1.35**
Assam	3.12	2.054	2.643	0.998	1.132	0.645	1.67*	1.201	1.286
West Bengal	0.754	0.691	0.743	1.107	0.401*	0.593	1.551**	2.473**	0.748
Orissa	0.754	0.873	0.631	1.14	0.789	1.138	1.744**	3.276**	1.013
Gujarat	0.402	0.462	0.671	1.12	2.133*	1.387	1.14	2.724**	0.99
Maharashtra	0.953	1.919	1.154	1.367	0.929	0.861	0.909	2.21**	1.174
Andhra Pradesh	1.853	2.461	2.161*	2.046**	3.751**	1.361*	1.537	5.664**	1.799*
Karnataka	1.311	1.832	1.895	1.433	0.959	0.603**	1.621*	1.942**	1.063

*Significant at 5 per cent level of significance and 'others' who are not SC, ST or OBC is the reference category. **Significant at 1 per cent level of significance.

Notes: *Full immunization*: 0 = fully immunized, 1 = not fully immunized.
ANC: 0 = received, 1 = not received.
Safe delivery: 0 = safe delivery, 1 = unsafe delivery.
Variable controlled for full immunization: Mother's education, mother's work status, mass media exposure, birth order, sex of the child, SLI, religion, place of residence.
Variable controlled for ANC and safe delivery: Women's education, women's work status, mass media exposure, SLI, religion, place of residence, partner's education.
In caste category, reference is 'others' in each regression.

Differentials in school attendance between OBC and 'other' category cannot be explained as an effect of other socio-economic variable in six states. In Gujarat, OBC children are 1.8 times more likely to be without attending the school. In the other five states, Madhya Pradesh, Uttar Pradesh, Orissa, Andhra Pradesh, and Karnataka, the corresponding odd ratios are slightly less, varying between 1.2 and 1.4.

Full Immunization

Differentials in full immunization between SC and 'others' are found in nine states due to differences in socio-economic conditions and not because of their caste affiliations. Only in case of Uttar Pradesh, differentials between SC and 'others' persist where SC children are more likely to be without full immunization ($p < 0.05$) as compared to children in 'other' category even after adjusting the effect of socio-economic variables.

The same pattern can be observed even for ST in Rajasthan and OBC in Andhra Pradesh. After adjusting the effect of socio-economic factors, ST children in Rajasthan and OBC children in Andhra Pradesh are more likely to be without full immunization as compared to 'other' category in respective states. Especially, in Rajasthan, differentials between ST and 'other' children are striking, with much higher odds of not receiving full immunization among ST children as compared to 'other children.

Antenatal Care

Differentials between SC women and 'other' women regarding ANC disappear in all the states except Uttar Pradesh and Andhra Pradesh, after adjusting the effect of socio-economic variables. In both these states, SC women in similar socio-economic situation are more likely to be without ANC as compared to 'other' women.

Disparity regarding ANC between ST and 'other' women in many of the states can be explained mostly as an effect of socio-economic factors except in West Bengal, Gujarat, and Andhra Pradesh. As compared to women in 'other' category, ST women are more likely to be without ANC in Gujarat and much more so in Andhra Pradesh, while in West Bengal, the opposite is true, i.e., ST women there are less likely to be without ANC as compared to 'other' women.

Differentials between OBC women and 'other' women in seven out of ten states are mostly due to the dissimilarity in socio-economic conditions and they disappear after adjusting the effect of these factors. Only in Uttar Pradesh, Andhra Pradesh, and Karnataka, differentials persist even after adjusting the socio-economic conditions. In Uttar Pradesh and Andhra Pradesh, the odds of not receiving ANC for OBC women are 1.4–1.5 times higher as compared to women in 'other' category. In Karnataka, however, OBC woman in the same socio-economic situation as a woman in 'other' category is less likely to be without ANC.

Safe Delivery

In six out of ten states under study, the discrepancy regarding safe delivery between SC women and 'other' women persists even after adjusting the effect of other factors. In Madhya Pradesh, odds of unsafe delivery among SC women are 1.9 times higher than women in 'other' category. The corresponding odds ratio is 1.6–1.7 in all other five states, Uttar Pradesh, Assam, West Bengal, Orissa, and Karnataka.

Differentials between ST women and 'other' women in eight out of ten states even after adjusting the effect of socio-economic factors are quite striking. In Madhya Pradesh, West Bengal, Orissa, Gujarat, Maharashtra, and Karnataka, given the same socio-economic situation, odds of unsafe delivery are two to three times higher among ST women as compared to 'other' women, while in Andhra Pradesh and Uttar Pradesh the odds for unsafe delivery are five to six times higher.

Given the same socio-economic situation, OBC women in Uttar Pradesh and Andhra Pradesh are more likely to go for a delivery not assisted by any health personnel, as compared to women in 'other' category. In all other states, differentials regarding safe delivery between OBC women and women in 'other' category are mainly due to differences in socio-economic conditions and they disappear once we adjust the socio-economic factors.

Underweight

Differentials between SC and 'other' castes regarding prevalence of malnourishment in children mostly disappear after adjusting the effect of other socio-economic factors. Only in Uttar Pradesh, Orissa, and Andhra Pradesh, as compared to children in 'other' category, SC children in similar socio-economic situation are more likely to be underweight.

As compared to children in 'other' category, ST children are more likely to be underweight in Madhya Pradesh, Uttar Pradesh, Orissa, Gujarat, and Maharashtra. Especially in Uttar Pradesh and Gujarat, it is much more likely than other states. In Assam, however, ST children if in the same socio-economic situation as children in 'other' category are less likely to be underweight.

In eight out of ten states, differentials between OBC children and 'other' children regarding malnourishment are due to the difference in socio-economic conditions and they disappear after adjusting the effect of these factors. In Uttar Pradesh, the odds of being underweight among OBC children are 1.3 times higher than 'other' children, while in West Bengal, OBC children with similar socio-economic condition as 'other' children are less likely to be underweight.

Child Anaemia

Differentials between SC children and children in 'other' category regarding prevalence of anaemia persist even after adjusting the effect of other factors, only in case of Assam where SC children are 1.7 times more likely to be anaemic than 'other' children. In all other states, differentials between SC and 'other' in prevalence of child anaemia can be explained as the difference in socio-economic conditions.

As compared to children in 'other' category, ST children are more likely to be anaemic in Madhya Pradesh, Assam, and Orissa and much more so in West Bengal and Karnataka, even after adjusting the socio-economic conditions. In all other states, differentials between ST children and 'other' children disappear, after adjusting the effect of other confounding variables.

As far as differentials regarding child anaemia are concerned between OBC and 'others', in all the states, these differentials are due to the difference in socio-economic conditions and they disappear once we adjust the effect of socio-economic factors.

Women Anaemia

Differentials regarding prevalence of anaemia between SC women and 'other' women can be described mostly as an effect of socio-economic factors except Madhya Pradesh. In case of Madhya Pradesh, the likelihood for a SC woman to be anaemic is 1.3 times higher than a woman in 'other' category.

Like child anaemia, in the case of women anaemia also, differentials between ST and 'other' are striking in seven out of ten states. In Rajasthan, Madhya Pradesh, West Bengal, Orissa, Gujarat, and Maharashtra, ST women are more likely to be anaemic as compared to the women in 'other' category. On the contrary, in Uttar Pradesh, ST women as compared to 'other' women are less likely to be anaemic.

Again, in Uttar Pradesh, OBC women are less likely to be anaemic, when we compare them with 'other' women regarding anaemia prevalence. In all other states, differentials between OBC and 'others' are due to difference in socio-economic factors that disappear once we adjust the effect of these factors.

Body Mass Index

In six out of ten states under study, the differentials between SC women and 'other' women regarding 'low BMI' disappear once the effect of socio-economic factors is adjusted. Madhya Pradesh, Uttar Pradesh, Orissa, and Gujarat are the states where SC women in the same socio-economic condition as 'other' women are more likely to have low BMI. Especially in Gujarat and Orissa, it is much more likely than other states.

Given the same socio-economic situation, in Rajasthan, Madhya Pradesh, Orissa, and Maharashtra, odds of having low BMI among ST women are 1.3–1.7 times higher as compared to 'other' women, while in Gujarat, the corresponding odds are 3.2 times higher than women in 'other' category. This is strikingly different from ST women in Assam who are less likely to have low BMI as compared to 'other' women even after adjusting for other factors.

OBC women, even in the same socio-economic condition as 'other' women, are more likely to have low BMI in Madhya Pradesh, Gujarat, and Andhra Pradesh. In the remaining states, differentials regarding 'low BMI' are due to difference in socio-economic factors and these differentials disappear when the effect of these factors is adjusted.

Conclusions

This paper assesses the extent of inequalities of selected development parameters in 10 states of India with special emphasis on caste/tribe groups. It brings out the fact that the ST population of India is the most disadvantaged group across states and they deserve reservation for socio-economic betterment. STs of Uttar Pradesh, Orissa, and Rajasthan justify attention in provision of basic facilities, social development, while in health care utilization the condition of these populations in Uttar Pradesh, Rajasthan, and Madhya Pradesh is appalling. Even in West Bengal and Gujarat, the nutritional status of the STs warrants pressing need for improvement.

Conditions of the caste groups are not similar in the selected development indicators across states. The analysis clearly reveals that the condition of the SC population of Maharashtra, Andhra Pradesh, Karnataka, and Gujarat is often better than the situation of the OBCs of Rajasthan, Madhya Pradesh, and Uttar Pradesh and the former are at par with the 'other ' category of less developed states. Perhaps, unanimous reservation policy for caste groups needs to be re-looked in the context of varying level of development of these groups in different states.

Inequality among caste groups within states is less in Assam, Karnataka, Andhra Pradesh, and Maharashtra. Though in West Bengal, inequality is low in basic facilities, social development, and health care utilization, its performance in terms of equality is awful in nutritional status where it stands in the second highest order following Gujarat in

Table 12

Relationship between Caste/Tribe and Nutrition Indicators – Results of Logistic Analysis

States	*Underweight*			*Child anaemia*			*Women anaemia*			*Low BMI*		
	SC	*ST*	*OBC*	*SC*	*ST*	*OBC*	*SC*	*ST*	*OBC*	*SC*	*ST*	*OBC*
Rajasthan	0.974	0.788	0.789	1.223	1.356	0.961	1.201	1.942**	1.128	1.16	1.665**	0.878
Madhya Pradesh	1.331	1.523*	1.071	1.328	1.645**	1.022	1.328**	2.404**	0.968	1.393**	1.459**	1.283*
Uttar Pradesh	1.411**	2.362**	1.302**	1.097	1.326	1.021	0.94	0.492*	0.836**	1.296**	1.186	1.092
Assam	1.226	0.39**	1.014	1.693*	1.893*	1.328	1.016	1.075	1.011	1.248	0.328**	0.891
West Bengal	0.781	1.549	0.41*	1.237	3.537**	1.005	1.151	1.574*	0.901	1.067	1.137	1.037
Orissa	1.488*	1.958**	1.389	0.939	2.092**	0.946	1.162	1.525**	1.124	1.881**	1.496**	1.197
Gujarat	1.08	2.294**	0.998	0.877	1.813	1.007	1.089	2.906**	1.111	2.01**	3.232**	1.774**
Maharashtra	1.336	1.671**	1.143	1.216	1.185	1.176	1.058	1.433**	1.059	1.05	1.282*	1.001
Andhra Pradesh	1.733*	1.516	1.359	1.012	1.024	1.07	1.025	0.974	1.045	1.294	1.212	1.277*
Karnataka	0.798	0.845	0.969	1.594	2.686**	1.291	0.928	1.167	1.008	1.04	1.323	1.019

Notes: *Underweight*: 0 = no, 1 = yes.
Child anaemia: 0 = not anaemic, 1 = anaemic.
Women anaemia: 0 = not anaemic, 1 = anaemic.
Low BMI: 0 = no, 1 = yes.
In caste category, reference is 'others' in each regression.

terms of inequality, mainly because of very poor condition of the tribes. The position of Assam is noticeable in this regard. There prevails unanimity among social groups. The overall development of the ST population in Assam is the highest among the tribal groups in selected states and it is even better off than many SCs and OBC population of Rajasthan, Madhya Pradesh, and Uttar Pradesh. Very high level of inequality among caste/tribe groups is persisting in Rajasthan, Madhya Pradesh, Uttar Pradesh, and Orissa which could be due to the fact that at the initial stage of development, the forward class cherishes the benefits of development the most and it tends to enhance the disparity. However, in nutrition index, Rajasthan and Uttar Pradesh reveal an appreciable performance across caste/tribe groups possibly for the well performance of the Integrated Child Development Services-III (ICDS-III) scheme which gives special emphasis on these two states (along with Kerala, Tamil Nadu, and Maharashtra) targeting the most vulnerable groups of population including children up to 6 years of age, pregnant women, and nursing mothers belonging to poorest of the poor families and living in disadvantaged areas including backward rural areas, tribal areas, and urban slums.

Looking into the differentials of selected development indicators by caste/tribe groups, after controlling the relevant socio-economic variables, it could be ascertained that in some occasions the significant difference of four subpopulation persists due to their very caste/tribe affiliation. These differentials are maximum in social development parameters such as child work and school attendance where besides tribal population, OBCs in many states along with SCs of some states are doing significantly appalling compared to the 'other' caste. Why OBCs even in the better off states are performing poorly is a matter of enquiry. Coming to health care indicators such as full immunization and ANC, except a few instances, caste/tribe differentials do not exist indicating a good programmatic effort to cater the service to all subgroups. Yet, safe delivery needs more proactive programmatic implementation and knowledge dissemination as the utility of safe delivery has perhaps not percolated well into the tribal groups as well as some SCs community in states such as Rajasthan, Madhya Pradesh, Uttar Pradesh, West Bengal, and Orissa along with Assam and Karnataka. In nutritional parameters, tribes are the most deprived lot in almost all selected states. Here also, except a few cases in point (such as caste groups of Uttar Pradesh, Madhya Pradesh, Orissa, and Gujarat in some selected nutrition indicators), the differentials by caste groups do not persist. So, a lot needs to be done to improve the condition of the disadvantaged groups in India if equity is given priority in the policy frame. Tribal population needs urgent attention as they are facing inequality of opportunity in many development parameters. While the bigger states of the north and central India must take into consideration the wide disparity among caste/tribe groups existing within states.

References

Drèze, J., and Sen, A. (1995). *India Economic Development and Social Opportunity*. Delhi: Oxford University Press.

Dwyer, D., and Bruce, J. (eds.) (1988). *A Home Divided: Women and Income in the Third World*. Stanford, CA: Stanford University Press.

Hosseinpoor, A.R., Van Doorslaer, E., Speybroeck, N., Naghavi, M., Mohammad, K., Majdzadeh, R. et al. (2006). 'Decomposing socio-economic inequalities in infant mortality in Iran', *International Journal of Epidemiology,* 35, 1211–1219.

ICPD Programme of Action. Available online at: http: //www.un.org/popin/icpd2.htm (accessed on 24 April 2010).

International Institute for Population Sciences (IIPS) and Macro International (2007). *National Family Health Survey (NFHS-3), 2005–06: India: Volume I*.

Kopparty, S.N.M. (1994). *Social Inequality and Health care*. New Delhi: Northern Book Centre.

Mahler, H. (1987). 'The safe motherhood initiative: A call to action', *Lancet*, (1), 668–670.

Nanda, G., Switlick, K., and Lule, E. (2005). *Accelerating Progress towards Achieving the MDGs to Improve Maternal Health*. World Bank. Available online at: http: //siteresources.worldbank.org/HEALTHNUTRITIONANDPOPULATION/Resources/281627-1095698140167/NandaAcceleratingProgresswithCover.pdf (accessed on 26 April 2010).

Ram, F., and Mohanty, S.K. (2005). *State of Human Development in States and Districts of India*. Mumbai: IIPS.

Reed, H.E., Koblinsky, M.A., and Mosley, W.H. (1998). *The Consequences of Maternal Morbidity and Maternal Mortality: Report of a Workshop*. Washington, DC: National Academy Press.

Roy, T.K., Kulkarni, S., and Vaidehi, Y. (2004). 'Social inequalities in health and nutrition in selected states', *Economic and Political Weekly*, 39(7), 677–683.

UN (n.d.). *Millennium Development Goals Report*, 2007. Available online at: www.un.org/millenniumgoals (accessed on 25 April 2010).

United Nations Development Programme (1990). *Human Development Report*. Delhi: Oxford University press.

World Bank (2008). *World Development Indicators 2008*. Washington, DC: World Bank.

9

Poverty, Disability and Social Exclusion in India

AMBATI NAGESWARA RAO

Disability is not a tragedy but an inconvenience. According to the United Nations (UN), the persons with disabilities (PWDs) are those who are unable to ensure, wholly or partially, the necessities of normal individuals as a result of deficiency in their physical or mental capacities.

About 600 million persons or one-tenth of the world population are estimated to be disabled in one form or another, e.g., visual, auditory, physical, speech, cognitive, and neurological. The proportion of the disability varies from country to country. It is low in developed countries and high in the developing countries. According to the UN, one person in twenty has a disability. Of those, three out of four of these live in a developing country. More often than not they are among the poorest of the poor. Recent World Bank estimates suggest that they may account for as one in five of the world's poorest. Disability limits access to education and employment and leads to economic and social exclusion. Poor people with disabilities are caught in a vicious cycle of poverty and disability, each being both a cause and a consequence of the other (Elwan, 1990).

The PWDs in India form the largest disadvantaged group like in most countries of the world. As a group, they are starved of the usual services and facilities available to the general public as they have been subjected to long history of neglect, isolation, poverty, deprivation, and at times pity as well. They yet do not have an effective economic, political, or media power in India. Society and social attitudes play an important role in determining the participation of disabled people in social and economic life. These persons frequently live in poor conditions, owing to inadequate facilities of health, hygiene, and poor means of transport and communication, thus they find it difficult to get their due share. Most of the international development organizations realized that disabled people are disproportionately among the poorest of the poor in all parts of the world, and that international development targets are unlikely to be met without including disabled people. They also recognized that the basic cause of the poverty among disabled population is due to exclusion: exclusion from social, economic, and political life.

This paper attempts to gain deeper understanding of the relationship between poverty and disability in India. This study is based on the review of the existing literature. The relationship between poverty and disability in India has been analysed with the help of socio-economic status of disabled people.

The paper has been organized into three sections for it more meaningful comprehension. The first section deals with the definitional aspects and estimates of disability, the second part deals with the analysis of poverty and disability in India with the help of socio-economic status of disabled, and the third part deals with the review of legislative acts and policies for disabled people and government initiatives for reducing poverty among the disabled people and final part consists of suggestions to alleviate poverty among the disabled people.

I

Defining Disability

Disability is a complex phenomenon to measure for a number of reasons. People's understanding of definitions of disability and the concept of disability itself vary. It is possible for one person to define themselves as disabled when another person with an identical condition would not. The most common definition and classification of disability for use by the government for all purposes was determined with the enactment of the Persons with Disabilities (Equal Opportunities, Protection of Rights and Full Participation) Act, 1995. Disability has been classified into seven classes on the basis of a medical definition. These classes include people with:

1. Blindness
2. Low vision
3. Leprosy (cured)
4. Hearing impairment

5. Locomotor disability
6. Mental retardation
7. Mental illness.

Further, in order to have the coverage under the term 'persons with disabilities', the extent of disability should not be less than 40 per cent as certified by medical authority. The legislation came into effect on 7 February 1996. There is no other definition of disability or classification of disability accepted for any purpose by the government for the entitlements of people with disabilities (Persons with Disabilities Act, 1995).

However, in the National Trust Act, 1999, another two classes have been included for the benefit under the said act. These groups have been defined in the National Trust for Welfare of Persons with Autism, Cerebral Palsy, Mental Retardation and Multiple Disability Act 1999, as follows:

(a) Autism means a condition of uneven skill development primarily affecting the communication and social abilities of a person, marked by repetitive and ritualistic behaviour.
(b) Multiple disabilities means a combination of two or more disabilities as defined in Clause (2) of the Persons with Disabilities (Equal Opportunities, Protection of Rights and Full Participation) Act 1995.

The government, both administratively and legally, accepts the respective disability definitions in the aforesaid legislation for all purposes. In order to have proper appreciation of the coverage of each of the aforesaid seven groups, the Persons with Disabilities (Equal Opportunities, Protection of Rights and Full Participation) Act 1995, has given the following respective definitions to each of them.

(a) Blindness refers to a condition where a person suffers from any of the following conditions namely:
    (i) Total absence of sight; or
    (ii) Visual acuity not exceeding 6/60 or 20/200 (Snellen test) in the better eye with correcting lenses; or
    (iii) Limitation of the field of vision subtending an angle of 20N0 [Should be '20E'] or worse.
(b) Cerebral palsy means a group of non-progressive conditions characterized by abnormal motor controlled posture resulting from brain insult or injuries occurring in the pre-natal or infant period of development. This group has been put under the category of locomotor disability for all benefits under the act.
(c) Hearing impairment means loss of 60 decibels or more in the better ear in the conversational range of frequencies.

(d) Leprosy-cured means any person who has been cured of leprosy but is suffering from:
   (i) Loss of sensation in hands or feet as well as loss of sensation and paresis in the eye and eyelid but with no manifest deformity;
   (ii) Manifest deformity and paresis but having sufficient mobility in their hands and feet to enable them to engage a normal economic activity;
   (iii) Extreme physical deformity as well as advanced age which prevents him from undertaking any gainful occupation.

(e) Locomotor disability means disability of the bones, joints, or muscles leading to substantial restriction of the movement of limbs, or any form of cerebral palsy.

(f) Mental illness means any mental disorder other than mental retardation.

(g) Mental retardation means a condition of arrested or incomplete development of the mind of a person who is specially characterized by sub-normality of intelligence.

(h) Person with low vision means a person with impairment of visual functioning, even after treatment or standard refractive correction but who uses, or is potentially capable of using, vision for the planning, or execution of a task with appropriate device.

Disability Estimates in India

The World Health Organization (WHO) estimates (2001) that 10 per cent of any given population is disabled. It is likely that Indians' disability rate is within a range of 4–9 per cent, which would be comparable with other countries. The Census of India collected information on disability since its inception in 1872. It had discontinued after 1931 due to the limitations in authenticity and quality of data collection. Since the year 1981 had been proclaimed as the 'International Year for the Disabled', it resulted in inclusion of a question on disability. However, only three broad categories of physical disabilities such as 'totally blind', 'totally dumb', and 'totally crippled' were incorporated during the House listing Operations of 1981 Census. But the question on disability was not included in the 1991 census. However, with the pressure of various NGOs, international agencies and the obligation under Persons with Disabilities (Equal Opportunities, Protection of Rights and Full Participation) Act, 1995, the disability was again incorporated in Census of India, 2001. In 2001 census, information on disability of five types (seeing, speech, hearing, movement, and mental) was collected (Naidu and Deepa, 2008).

The two main official sources of nationwide disability statistics was census and NSS (National Sample Survey). According to Census 2001, the total disabled population in India was 21,906,769 which constitute more than 2 per cent of total population. Moreover, 1 per cent of the total population was having visual disability followed by movement, speech, mental, and hearing disabilities.

Table 1

Number of Disabled Population and Types of Disability

	Population	*Percentage (%)*
Total population	1,028,610,328	100
Total disabled population	21,906,769	2.1
Disability rate (per lakh population)	2130	NA
Type of disability		
Visual impairment	10,634,881	1
Speech impairment	1,640,868	0.2
Hearing impairment	1,261,722	0.1
Movement	6,105,477	0.6
Mental	2,263,821	0.2

Source: Registrar General of India (2001), Census of India, 2001.

Table 2

Estimates of Disability in India by Census and NSSO

Disability type	*Census 2001*		*NSSO 2002*	
	Number	*Percentage (%)*	*Number*	*Percentage (%)*
Visual	10,634,881	48.55	2,826,700	15.29
Speech	1,640,868	7.49	2,154,500	11.65
Hearing	1,261,722	5.76	3,061,700	16.56
Locomotor	6,105,477	27.87	10,634,000	57.51
Mental	2,263,821	10.33	2,097,500	11.34
Total	21,906,769	100	18,491,000	100

Source: Registrar General of India (2001), Census of India, 2001 and NSS 58th Round 2002 as reported in Bhanushali (2005).

While National Sample Survey Organization (NSSO) in the year 2002 covered the seven areas of disabilities as defined under the

Persons with Disabilities Act, 1995, the census covered only five groups by merging blindness and low vision in one category. They estimated the disabled population in India as 1.85 cores which constitute 1.8 per cent of the population. The differential estimates of census and NSS is mainly because of study design effect and definitional variations. Like for wider definition, Census of India estimates people with seeing/visual disabilities more as compared to NSSO estimates (Bhanushali, 2005) (Tables 1 and 2).

Total Population and Disabled Population

The following points are worth noting while comparing the disabled population to the total population in India (Table 3). First, 2.1 per cent of the total population are disabled which could be considered as significant. Second, there exists not much difference (3.44%) between the proportion of male and female in the total population. But, in the case of disabled, males constitute 57.54 per cent and females only 42.46 per cent, a difference of 15.08 per cent. Third, with respect to place of residence of disabled persons, the difference between the rural and urban is 50 per cent, while among the total population it is 44 per cent only. Thus, disabled persons are more from rural areas.

Table 3

Total Population and Disabled Population in India

Total population		*Disabled population*	
Total	1,028,610,328 (100)	Total	21,906,769 (2.1)
Male	532,156,772 (51.7)	Male	12,605,635 (57.54)
Female	496,453,556 (48.26)	Female	9,301,134 (42.46)
Rural	742,490,639 (72.2)	Rural	16,383,382 (74.81)
Urban	286,119,689 (27.8)	Urban	5,518,387 (25.19)

Figures in parenthesis are percentages.

Source: Census of India, 2001.

Prevalence and Incidence Rate of Disabilities

In definition, the prevalence rate is the number of disabled persons per lakh of population and the incidence rate is the number of disabled persons per lakh population during the year. The NSSO report brings out the fact that there has been a significant decline in the prevalence and incidence of disability. The prevalence rate was 1.77 per cent in 2002 against 1.88 per cent in 1991 (MSJE, 2004–05, annual report). The prevalence rate for males was 2 per cent, while it was 1.49 per cent for females in 2002. Prevalence rates have shown declining trends during 1991–2002 for all disability types except for locomotor disability. Significant decline was registered for the visually impaired during the year 1991–2002 (Table 4).

Table 4

Prevalence and Incidence Rates of Disability as Per the NSSO Surveys (per one lakh person)

Types of disability	*Rural/ urban*	*1981*		*1991*		*2002*	
		Prevalence	*Incidence*	*Prevalence*	*Incidence*	*Prevalence*	*Incidence*
Locomotor	Rural	829	53	1074	53	1046	49
	Urban	679	54	962	52	901	52
Visual	Rural	553	38	525	25	296	13
	Urban	356	30	302	20	194	9
Speech	Rural	304	4	273	5	220	3
	Urban	279	5	237	5	193	3
Hearing	Rural	573	19	467	15	342	8
	Urban	390	15	339	12	254	7

Source: Published in Annual Report 2004–2005, MSJE.

II
Review of Literature

Poverty is both a cause and a consequence of disability. The literature says that poverty and disability reinforce each other, contributing to increased vulnerability and exclusion. Lwanga-Ntale's (2003) study focused on the issues of disability and poverty in Uganda. One of the conclusions of this study was that disabled people face various forms of exclusion, isolation, and neglect and this condemns them to perpetual (chronic) poverty. Another conclusion is that different categories of disabled people have different needs and are affected differently by poverty, which supports the statement that social values are very important when it comes to considering who is disabled.

Somehow, there seems to be a vicious cycle. Several articles illustrate this. One of them is about the barriers to care in (rural) Zambia. Health care is an expensive service that many people in Zambia cannot afford. Birbeck's (2000) study showed that few people who are able to pay for the transportation and medical fees (most rural economies rely on a bartering system, so the expenses exceed most people's monetary abilities) can be referred to a medical centre with imaging capabilities and neurological expertise. Most people with complaints will not immediately consult a physician, most of the times due to lack of money. For example, people with headaches caused by mass lesions are often seen by the physician when visual loss has already occurred, or seizures become manifest along with progressive neurological deficits. Delayed evaluation (in this case due to financial issues) often results in advanced disease, no longer amenable to treatment. The symptoms and consequences of neurological disease will make a person socially and economically vulnerable, which in itself limits their access to care even more. This case study shows that poverty may lead to delayed evaluation by a physician and therefore may cause disability. This disability may exclude people socially and economically, which makes them poorer and gives them even less access to care, which in turn may aggravate their disability.

Thomas' (2005) study in Cambodia showed that poor people lack access to basic health care which means that simple infections, illnesses, and injuries could result in permanent disability because they go untreated or are mistreated. All informants who became disabled later in life indicated that they became poorer after they were disabled, and most said they had become much poorer. This might be explained by the fact that disability can have an impact on a person's ability to work and earn a living. It can be illustrated by a case study about a woman who had rice fields and several animals. After carrying a heavy bag, she had a back injury; the doctor gave her an injection, which paralysed her. She was not able to carry out her work anymore, so she had to rent out her land and sell her animals. The only income she then had was by renting the land. Another reason for this woman becoming poorer is that she was not able to come out of her house to meet and see other people. Being poor is seen as a multidimensional concept.

Poverty also appears to be a high-risk factor for unintentional injuries, resulting in disability. Research conducted in Vietnam shows that poverty increases the chances of injuries at home (specifically in children and elderly people), at work (specifically in adults between 15 and 59 years), and for 'other' injuries. In this study, Thanh et al. (2005) stated that poor adults are at a greater risk of injuries at work, because people living under harsh economic conditions are willing, or forced, to accept jobs that expose them to extremely high risks or unsafe conditions. Their housing and traffic environments are also often very risky.

Poverty and Disability

The relationship between poverty and disability is dialectic. According to the World Bank estimations, one in five of the world's poorest persons has some form of disability. The UN suggests that 82 per cent of these persons live below poverty line in developing countries. However, there is still a lack of detailed research on the links between poverty and disability. The World Bank estimates that 25 per cent of the entire population in developing countries is adversely affected as a result of disabilities. Poverty is both a cause and a consequence of disability. Poverty and disability reinforce each other, contributing to increased vulnerability and exclusion. It is estimated that as many as 50 per cent disabilities are preventable and directly linked to poverty. UN statistics states that 30 per cent of all impairments are caused by malnutrition and a further 20 per cent by infectious diseases. WHO estimates that there are 1.5 million blind children, 70 per cent of blindness is either preventable or treatable. WHO estimates 50 per cent of hearing disability is also preventable (World Bank, 2008).

Poverty is about vulnerability – being exposed and powerless in the face of risks and shocks to the household. It is also caused by scarce and uncertain levels of private assets and access to services. The relationship between poverty and disability is complex and multidirectional. Poverty contributes to disability through a lack of education, malnutrition, poor health care, polluted environments, occupational and road accidents, and conflicts and disasters. The few services that are available to people with disabilities are often underfunded, poorly managed, and capacity constrained. In tandem, poverty and disability create a vicious circle. While the nexus from poverty between disability and poverty, sufficient evidence, as well as how those factors may increase impairment and disability. Poverty and hunger are almost inevitably linked to insufficient nutrition, poor housing, and inadequate health care services. These factors lead to an increased risk of impairment, which in turn may lead to disability.

Even though there are no proper research studies and data on poverty and disability and its relations in India, one can understand the link by seeing the socio-economic status of the disabled people. India is a vast country spread over diverse geographical terrain, which makes planning and implementation of various national programmes very difficult. Indian communities are heterogeneous, with wide differences in socio-economic status, educational attainment, religion, and ethnicity. This diversity can cause friction and affect services because different groups in a community have widely differing needs and priorities. Often the needs of disabled people, who are in a minority, are not considered priorities by other groups. Disabled people living in poverty have always suffered from a double disadvantage and are also at high risk of becoming even poorer. The same is true for all people living in poverty, who have a high risk of facing a disabling condition because of their limited access to basic services, including health, education, sanitation, and higher rates of exposure to hazardous working conditions.

Poor nutrition during pregnancy, genetic factors, infectious diseases, poor sanitation, and crowded living conditions together with poor food, lack of basic health and rehabilitation services, and lack of immunization against such diseases as polio and rubella are among the major causes of disability. Modernization itself is also a causal factor, as in the cases of infants born with a disability as a result of inappropriate medication used during pregnancy, traffic accidents resulting in loss of limbs and blindness, and infections as a result of pesticide and fluoride poisoning. Ageing is another major contributing factor.

Less than one-quarter of the households in the country had toilet facilities within their places of residence; the proportion was less than 10 per cent for rural households and around 64 per cent for urban households (Asian Development Bank, 2005). Access to toilet facilities for scheduled caste and scheduled tribe households was lower than that of other households in almost all states. The lack of facilities for disposal of wastewater is one of the main causes of prevailing ill health and morbidity levels in the country. At the household level in rural areas, problems related to sanitation are not caused by a shortage of resources, but essentially by a lack of awareness and education. The situation is reversed in the case of urban sanitation and solid waste management, especially sewage disposal. In urban areas, poor solid waste management practices pose a significant threat to safe drinking water. Millions of people in the country suffer from water-borne diseases because of lack of access to safe drinking water. People living in poverty suffer from a higher prevalence of such diseases.

Disability and Discrimination

PWDs face barriers ranging from discriminatory attitudes, abuse, violence, and barriers to access that lead to segregation and exclusion in the family context, at work, school, and in society especially since disability is often seen as a burden and shameful. These negative attitudes and perceptions of disability affect the self-esteem of people with disabilities. They also face barriers that prevent them from enjoying their civil, political, economic, social, cultural, religious, and development rights. This is largely due to widespread ignorance and prejudice in societies. It is also because some legislation fails to protect the rights of people with disabilities and to meet the standards and principles of international human rights instruments. They are also viewed as a burden and a curse by their families and hence regarded as 'second-class citizens'. This affects their dignity as members of the family and society as a whole.

Gender and Disability

There is a general preference for male children in India. Girls are often neglected and receive less food than boys. They are also less likely to be educated. If girls and women in general are not valued, then disabled girls and women are likely to be even less so. Women with disabilities suffer double discrimination. Recent UNESCO studies suggest that 1–2 per cent of children with disabilities receive a formal education; boys with disabilities attend school more often than girls. Studies show that women with disabilities are two to three times more likely to be victims of physical and sexual abuse than other women. It is estimated that 3–4 per cent of PWDs in developing countries have access to rehabilitation and appropriate basic services such as medical rehabilitation, orthopaedic devices (less than one person have a wheelchair; 20 million people are in need of it), pre-school education, and so on (available online at: www.unesdoc.unseco.org).

Lack of Educational Opportunities

Disabled children and youth rarely receive a formal education and it is difficult for them to gain access to vocational training. PWDs are rarely entrusted with family or community responsibilities. The situation is even worse for the disabled girl children and women, for them the fact of being female is viewed as a further social disadvantage. A survey on the 'Status of Education of Disabled Children' says that 55 per cent of the disabled people were illiterate, while only 9 per cent had completed secondary or higher level education. The total number of children with disabilities in the age group of 5–18 years was 47.24 lakhs and the enrolment ratio per 1,000 children was 450. Only 11 per cent of the children with disabilities in this age group went to special schools in urban areas, while the percentage was just one in rural areas. The study also found that 23 per cent more boys were in school as against disabled girls (Mavoothu et al., 2008). Non-inclusive nature of the country's educational institutions, the low quality of education at the specialist schools, and lack of vocational training are some of the issues to be addressed to create more talent pool of disabled.

Disability and Employment

The work activity status of disabled persons depicts that about 46 per cent of disabled populations in both rural and urban areas were without any work (Table 5). Thus, in spite of the PWD Act, 1995, employment scenario has not changed for the disabled persons. Provision of reservation of 3 per cent jobs in all government services has not changed employment scenario for disabled persons. Only 1.8 per cent and 7.3 per cent disabled persons in rural and urban areas respectively were regular employees in 2002. Even the nature of employment was only in low-level profile of jobs with low income. Although 3 per cent job reservation in all categories was stipulated in the PWD Act, 1995, yet very few attempts have been made by the state governments to identify the jobs to be reserved for A and B groups in majority of the states (Chandrasekar, 2006). A significant proportion of the disabled persons were attending domestic work, which does not generate any significant income opportunities rather majority of them are under paid or at best provided basic food requirements. Thus, employment scenario for people with disabilities is bleak and requires immediate steps from government and private sectors.

Table 5

Work Activity Status

(in %)

Work Activity Status	*Rural*	*Urban*
Self-employed in agriculture	10.6	9.4
Self-employed in non-agriculture	5.1	2.2
Regular employee	1.8	7.3
Casual employee	8.8	4.9
Attending educational institution	13.7	16
Attending domestic work	12.8	13.5
Begging	0.5	0.9
No work	46	44.5
All	14,085,000	4,406,000

Source: NSSO 58th round (July–December 2002).

III
Empowering the Disabled: Indian Perspective

India is a signatory to the proclamation of the Asian and Pacific Decade of Disabled Persons 1993 to 2002. It has taken various steps towards fulfilling the targets of the proclamation. India has taken the initiatives to integrate people with disabilities through vocational training and employment in all mainstream programmes in order to enlarge the coverage of the disabled population.

The Constitution of India

The Constitution of India refers to disabled people in two places. Article 41 of the Constitution calls upon the government at all levels to make effective provisions for securing the right to work, education, and to public assistance in cases of unemployment, old age, sickness, and disablement (Zutshi, 2004) Article 16 (3) and (4) of the Constitution encourages the state to frame any law, make provision for the reservation of appointment or posts in favour of any backward class of citizens which, in the opinion of the state, have not been represented. Other relevant articles in the Indian Constitution providing constitutional guarantees for disabled persons are as follows:

- *Article 15(1)*: It states that the government should not to discriminate against any citizen of India (including disabled) on the ground of religion, race, caste, sex, or place of birth.
- *Article 15(2)*: It states that no citizen (including the disabled) shall be subjected to any disability, liability, restriction, or condition on any of the above grounds in the matter of their access to shops, public restaurants, hotels, and places of public entertainment or in the use of wells, tanks, bathing places, roads, and places of public resort maintained wholly or partly out of government funds or dedicated to the use of the general public.
- *Article 17*: No person including the disabled irrespective of his belonging can be treated as an untouchable. It would be an offence punishable in accordance with law.
- *Article 21*: Every person including the disabled has his life and liberty guaranteed.
- *Article 23*: There can be traffic in human beings (including the disabled), and beggar and other forms of forced labour are prohibited and the same is made punishable in accordance with law.
- *Article 29 (2)*: The right to education is available to all citizens including the disabled. No citizen shall be denied admission into any educational institution maintained by the state or receiving aid out of state funds.

Despite, such a progressive constitution and judiciary, the approach to disability has been motivated by charity. The Indian society views disability as an individual issue and treats it within the means available to a family. Families in India rely on the services of charitable institutions. Similarly, the Government of India is dependent on non-governmental organizations (NGOs) to secure basic rights such as education, work, and shelter for people with disabilities.

Legislative Protection

In order to fulfil its international commitment and constitutional mandate, India has formulated policies, programmes, and enacted legislations to promote health care, education, training, employment opportunities, etc., for PWDs. Some of the important legislations holding the field of disability are as follows:

- 1992 Rehabilitation Council of India Act
- 1995 The Persons with Disabilities (Equal Opportunities, Protection of Rights and Full Participation) Act
- 1997 Mental Health Act
- 1999 National Trust for the Welfare of Persons with Autism, Cerebral Palsy, Mental Retardation and Multiple Disabilities Act
- 2006 National Policy for Persons with Disabilities Act.

The Persons with Disabilities (Equal Opportunities, Protection of Rights and Full Participation) Act of 1995 is the most significant piece of legislation that has been enacted in India. The act makes provisions for preventive and promotional aspects of rehabilitation such as education, employment and vocational training, and research and manpower development while aiding in the creation of barrier-free environments, rehabilitation of PWDs, unemployment allowances for PWDs, special insurance schemes for employees with disabilities, and the establishment of homes for persons with severe disabilities. The act is the most comprehensive legislative act enacted to ensure equal opportunities for PWDs allowing them to fully participate in nation building.

Other major legislative acts include the Mental Health Act of 1997 and the Rehabilitation Council of India Act of 1992. The Mental Health Act's purpose was to provide better social services to people with learning disabilities. It included the establishment and maintenance of hospitals and nursing homes for persons with intellectual disabilities. The Rehabilitation Council of India Act was established in order to regulate the training of professionals in the field of education for people with special needs.

In 1999, the government passed the National Trust for the Welfare of Persons with Autism, Cerebral Palsy, Mental Retardation, and Multiple Disabilities Act. The trust's objective is to enable and empower those with disability to live as independently and as fully as possible within or close to the community while stringing facilities providing support to PWDs to live within their own family structure. The trust also extends support to registered organizations to provide need-based services during periods of family crisis.

The National Policy for Persons with Disability Act, announced in February 2006, attempts to clarify the framework under which the state, civil society and private sector must operate in order to ensure a dignified life for PWD and support for their caregivers. The National Policy for Persons with Disability includes the following:

(i) Extending rehabilitation services to rural areas
(ii) Increasing trained personnel to meet needs
(iii) Emphasizing education and training
(iv) Increasing employment opportunities
(v) Focusing on gender equality
(vi) Improving access to public services
(vii) Encouraging state governments to develop a comprehensive social security policy
(viii) Ensuring equal opportunities in sports, recreation, and cultural activities
(ix) Increasing the role of civil society organizations as service providers to PWD and their families

The policy recognizes the need to replace the earlier emphasis on *medical rehabilitation* with an emphasis on social *rehabilitation*. Community-based Rehabilitation (CBR) is seen as an effective means of rehabilitation, and the policy states that CBR will be encouraged.

Role of NGOs

India is a democratic country with a very strong NGO component, especially so in the field of disabilities. Looking back at the history we find that the first facility for children with mental retardation was established by an NGO. Even before various polices, concessions, and acts came into effect, the NGOs were working for persons with mental retardation investigating their commitment and the little financial resources that they could pool together.

Today, with various schemes of benefits and concessions in order, the NGOs have been strengthened by the government. Most of the schemes by the government seen earlier such as the NHFDC, ADIP, and financial assistance for establishment of special schools/programmes (including building grants and maintenance grants) are in order to support the NGOs in the good work that they carry out for the betterment of PWDs.

There are three broad categories of voluntary organizations serving the disabled in the country. They are as follows:

1. Those organized by the disabled themselves
2. Managed by the parents/guardians of the disabled
3. Organized on humanitarian grounds.

NGOs are:

(a) Sensitive to the local needs, hopes and aspirations, working in the area, flexible, available for consultation
(b) Help in generating psychological satisfaction

(c) Honest and missionary zeal.

NGOs have the potential for execution which can be magnified by the government support. What we need is a coordinated approach projecting comprehensive goals for the rehabilitation of handicapped.

Government Initiatives to Reduce Poverty among Disabled People

While the links between disability and poverty are well known and understood, there is an absence of statistical data to determine the scale and scope of the problem. At the most basic level, there is a lack of accurate data to measure the number of PWDs in India. Although most poverty reduction programmes have a mandatory reservation of 3 per cent for the disabled in all their schemes as a result of the Persons with Disabilities Act 1995, there are no data on the numbers of disabled people who are reached through these programmes.

Despite the systemic challenges to addressing the needs of disabled people within the national poverty reduction strategy, there are a number of initiatives that are providing some measure of social security to people with disabilities.

Special Benefits: Pensions and Health Allowances

Under the country's social protection structure, persons above the age of 18 years who are more than 40 per cent disabled are entitled to a disability pension, the amount of which varies from state to state. The amount of disability pension depends on the prosperity and the commitment of the state towards disability concerns. Seven states and UTs have no disability pension programme. Only 12 states and UTs provide an unemployment allowance. Goa is the only state granting tax exemptions on purchases of equipment for self-employment for people with disabilities (Asian Development Bank, 2005).

The National Social Assistance Programme has provisions to cover disabled people who are over 45 years old and, under certain conditions, age restrictions can be relaxed by the district committee. However, not all states have such committees.

Health services are provided free of cost; hence, there is no special health allowance for PWDs or those below the poverty line. Departments of welfare in many states provide free distribution of assistive aids and appliances for PWDs, with the help of the National Ministry of Social Justice and Empowerment. Some states have also taken the initiative to conduct free surgery for correctable conditions.

Housing and Transportation

Twenty-two states and UTs provide a conveyance allowance to disabled state government employees. Bus concessions are given in 26 states and

UTs. Persons with 100 per cent visual impairment or more than 80 per cent locomotor disability are eligible for concession on air travel (Asian Development Bank, 2005).

Under the poverty reduction schemes and programmes in urban and rural areas, disabled people can access housing through Indira Awas Yojana. Some states, such as Tamil Nadu, have established proactive programmes, providing free housing sites or agricultural land to disabled people living below the poverty line.

Disabled government employees, as well as those suffering a serious illness, may receive housing within the general pool of the government's residential accommodation. A request for government housing must be made to a special recommendation committee and be approved by the urban development ministry. The fifth Central Pay Commission has recommended that a transport allowance should be given to central government employees with disabilities to compensate them for the cost of commuting between residence and place of duty.

Family Benefits

Disabled children of government employees are eligible for a family pension benefit, even if the children are born after the retirement of the employee.

Community-based Rehabilitation

In the early 1980s, CBR emerged as an important approach to addressing disability issues in the wider social context. With the realization that stand-alone medical interventions did not complete the rehabilitation process, CBR programmes gradually began to incorporate education, vocational training, social rehabilitation, and prevention. Along with this shift came the recognition that CBR needed to deal with issues related to disabled people's lives at all times and to seek to change not only the disabled individual, but also the context in which he or she lived. Addressing these contextual factors involved changing attitudes of other persons in the community to accept people with disabilities; promoting their social integration; and promoting equal opportunities in education and employment. Empowering communities to manage their programmes was another important contextual step in the CBR approach.

Lack of organizational ability and knowledge about disability on the part of community development organizations remain a major barrier to integration. Disability is seen as a 'specialist' issue; many organizations feel that they do not have the expertise to address it. Further, disabled people tend to be recognized only by their disability and not by any other parameter, such as gender, poverty level, and ethnic status. Lack of mobility, education, and skills continue to prevent disabled people from participating in development programmes as full stakeholders and equal partners.

Other Poverty Alleviation Programmes

As a part of poverty alleviation programmes both Ministries of Rural Development and Urban Affairs and Employment are running umbrella schemes for promoting wage employment among urban and rural poor respectively. These include the following:

- *Sampoorna Grameen Rozgar Yojana* (a rural wage employment scheme) administered by Ministry of Rural Development. This scheme is linked with the infrastructure development in the village and provides wage employment to the rural poor in projects such as the construction of roads (Rungta, 2004).
- *Swarnajayanti Gram Swarozgar Yojana* (SGSY) is a rural self-employment scheme run by the Ministry of Rural Development. It has a goal of improving the family incomes of the rural poor and, at the same time, providing for flexibility of design at the grassroots level to suit the local needs and resources. It aims at establishing a large number of micro-enterprises in the rural areas. The effort under SGSY is to cover 30 per cent of the poor in each block in the next five years. Care is taken to ensure that the maximum number of panchayats is covered without jeopardizing the quality of the programme. Efforts are also made to involve women members in each self-help group. At the block level, at least half of the groups are exclusively women (Rungta, 2004).
- *Swarnajayanti Shahari Rozgar Yojana* (SJSRY) (urban employment scheme) seeks to provide gainful employment for the urban unemployed or underemployed through encouraging the setting-up of self-employment ventures or provision of wage employment.

Barriers and Gaps

At present, programmes targeting poor PWDs are poorly implemented, especially with respect to decentralization. Resources allocated through urban and rural poverty alleviation departments are rarely utilized fully. For example, many seats reserved for PWDs within government-sponsored employment and vocation training programmes remain empty because programme staff do not have the relevant information or are not motivated to promote these opportunities among people with disabilities. In spite of regular government orders and office memorandums, the needs and concerns of PWDs have not been taken up as a priority by the local implementing offices. There is also a lack of knowledge and understanding of the rights of disabled people among local government personnel. However, there has been little sign of progress through the implementation of the Persons with Disabilities (Equal Opportunities, Protection of Rights and Full Participation) Act 1995, but there are some problems with the act, which are as follows:

- Though the act is in operation from February 1996, but the message of the act has not percolated at the grassroots level. All advocacy efforts such as seminars, workshops, and meetings have been largely confined to metropolitan cities, state capitals, or major towns.
- The concern for the disability sector and commitment to implement the act, in letter and spirit, in majority of implementing authorities is not visible.
- There is considerable increase in budget allocation in the Ministry of Social Justice and Empowerment and by certain state government. During the period 1996–1997, the allocation was only ₹ 650 million which was increased to ₹ 2300 million in 2000 and in 2001 it is ₹ 5500 million. The percentage share of disabilities budget has also increased from 4.8 per cent to 8 per cent. This is appreciable.
- No action plan has been made and no time frame provided for implementing various provisions of this Act by majority of Ministries and States.
- The Meetings of Coordination and Executive Committees are not held regularly. Members do not show desired knowledge and sincerity towards the cause. In a few states, committees have not been formed. In certain committees, NGOs and disable persons are not included despite provision.
- Three states have provided more than 3 per cent reservation in government jobs namely, Madhya Pradesh (6%), Karnataka (5%), and Gujarat (4%). In Meghalaya and Nagaland, no such reservation has yet been provided.
- Government of India has made 3 per cent reservation in all groups, A, B, C, and D posts, while only in Maharashtra and Mizoram reservation for all the four groups have been provided. States of Madhya Pradesh and Orissa have such reservation for groups B, C, and D posts, while all other states have made 3 per cent reservation for C and D group posts only.
- The Ministry of Rural Development, Government of India has reserved 3 per cent funds in poverty alleviation programmes for PWDs. This is a welcomed step. In 11 states, benefit of this provision has been taken.

There are also other barriers and gaps such as prevalent negative attitudes about the potential of people with disabilities as contributors and physical barriers making public buildings, facilities, and workplaces inaccessible, and inadequate educational and skill development programmes and non-inclusion and inaccessible mainstream vocational training and employment programmes. However, according to Javed Abidi, Executive Director, National Centre for Promotion of Employment of Disabled People (NCPEDP), the entire preparation process of the National Policy for Persons with Disability was a sham – no significant attempts were made to circulate the draft among PWD and NGOs for their comments, in 2005 (Info Change News, 2006). This was unlike the successful consultative process adopted prior to finalizing the 1995 PWD Act.

IV
Suggestions for Alleviating and Reducing Poverty of Disabled People

Disabled activists argue that action to alleviate and reduce the poverty of disabled people needs to be based on a social model of disability. The discussion here has already highlighted some of the implications of a social model of disability for alleviating and reducing the poverty of disabled people. It points to a number of policies. It will be helpful to examine these in more detail. They include the following:

1. *The full involvement of disabled people in the conceptualization, analysis, and discussion of poverty*: Without this involvement, disabled people's experience and the effects of institutionalized discrimination which they face are likely to be ignored or distorted. There are distinct issues around the nature and causes of disabled people's poverty which should be recognized. It is also likely to be helpful for disabled people's organizations to have discussions and develop alliances with other groups experiencing poverty, including older people, lone parents, and low-paid workers.
2. *The economic inclusion of disabled people*: At the heart of most disabled people's poverty is their restricted access to the labour market. To overcome this, a four-track approach is needed. This includes increasing education and employment training opportunities for disabled people; encouraging flexible and accessible employment; meeting the additional costs of impairment, and challenging prejudice against disabled people in employment by providing accurate information about their abilities (Beresford, 1996). In this way, disabled people will be transformed from a

group treated as dependent and a drain on societies' economies, to a group which is economically productive and can contribute socially, politically, and culturally to its fullest ability.

3. *The re-allocation of resources*: The prevailing charitable and medical response to disability has been the establishment of institutions. These are expensive, inappropriate, and ineffective and beyond the resources of poorer economies. Disability is a political, social, and economic issue, not a medical or charitable one. Resources should be shifted away from medical technologies and institutions and non-disabled 'expert' salaries, and should be directed to nutrition and support for indigenous, low-tech strategies to minimize disability and to cushion its impact.
4. *Supporting disabled people's organizations and countering their impoverishment*: Poverty and dependence prevent people having control over their lives. They make people feel bad about themselves. Poverty restricts people's access to information, education, and knowledge. Disabled people's organizations have a crucial part to play in reaching and involving disabled people, increasing their confidence and skills, and supporting them to break out of this vicious circle. As Venkatesh, Director of Action on Disability and Development (ADD) India, says, 'If people feel good about themselves, they can start to create change' (Coleridge, 1993: 17).
5. *A changed role for state and government*: In western societies, the main governmental response to disability has been the creation of social welfare policies based on income maintenance and segregated services. This has been challenged by disabled people's organizations for perpetuating poverty and dependency. Because disability is a social and not an individual issue, the state has a central role to play in recognizing and supporting the rights of disabled people. This does not mean taking on a traditional role as welfare service provider. Rather, it means providing a legal framework to support disabled people's equal rights and integrating disability into mainstream policies. Instead of seeing the rights and needs of disabled people, they should become an inherent part of all policies, including employment, land, income support, and health and child care policies.
6. *Aid, development, and disability*: There are many similarities in the way in which international aid policy and domestic charity address disability. Disabled activists argue that governments and non-government agencies should base aid policy and practice on a development, not charity model, working to involve and empower

disabled people (Coleridge, 1993). Aid policy should include specific components, identified by disabled people, addressing the rights and needs of disabled people. It is also crucial to decouple aid from the disabling arms trade.

Conclusion

The relationship between poverty and disability is a two-way one. Liisa Kauppinen in the World Summit on Social Development said, 'Disability increases poverty and poverty increases disability' (see Beresford, 1996). Disabling policies and practice generates poverty among disabled people, notably through disabled people's marginalization by and exclusion from the labour market and poverty generates ill health and impairment. This is true in both rich and poor societies. Poverty generates impairment by reducing intellectual abilities, causing immediate physical damage, and leading to early onset of frailty. Research in the United Kingdom confirms the strong link between economic inequality, ill health, and early death.

This relationship is true of inequalities both within and between societies. People in poverty in Britain are more likely to be affected by illness and disability. In one UK study of families living on income support, almost two-thirds of families reported long-term illness or disability. Malnutrition produces one in five impairments in the world today (Abberley, 1987). More than 90 per cent of infant impairments are due to social causes such as poverty and disease. 'Malnutrition, mothers weakened by frequent childbirth, inadequate immunization programmes, accidents in over-crowded homes, all contribute to an incidence of disability among the poor people that is higher than the people living in easier circumstances' (Coleridge, 1993: 64).

If they are to be effective, policies for poverty reduction and alleviation need to have a twin focus. They must be concerned with the economic inclusion and income needs of disabled people, and they must challenge the broader creation of impairment through poverty. Policy is needed to address both the rights and needs of disabled people, and the social and economic creation of impairment to break the link between poverty and disability.

People with disabilities (PWDs) tend to be among the most socially and economically marginalized populations wherever they exist. Disability and poverty tend to go hand in hand, forming a cycle of cumulative causation. Disabled people are more likely to become disabled than those who are not. In official reports, literature, and data, disability in developing countries is largely ignored. Due to lack of accurate data on disability, the needs of disabled people are often poorly served by development agencies. Disability issues are often viewed as outside the mainstream of development theories, policies, and practices. Disability is a major cause of poverty, social exclusion, and inequality throughout the world, on a part with gender discrimination and the denial of human rights. It is already known that living in poverty increases the chance of getting an impairment; disabled people generally experience higher rates of poverty as a result of being disabled and that when people living in poverty become disabled they are often more severely marginalized than that of the wealthier people. The existing legislation needs to be effectively implemented. The amendments that have been suggested to the act should be tabled and passed in the parliament. Disability should become an integral part of all national policies. Poverty reduction is never met unless PWDs are included. India and other developing countries must strive to ensure that they accept their responsibilities of the policy agenda, particularly the empowerment of the poor of which PWDs form a part.

References

Abberley, P. (1987). 'The concept of oppression and the development of a social theory of disability', *Disability, Handicap and Society*, 2, 5–20.

Asian Development Bank (2005). *Disabled People in Development, India*. Country Report, Foundational for International Training and Regional and Sustainable Development Department, ADB. Available online at: http://www.adb.org/Documents/Reports/Disabled-People-Development/India.pdf

Beresford, P. (1996). 'Poverty and disabled people: Challenging dominant debates and policies', *Disability & Society*, 11(4), 553–567. Available online at: http: //www.tandfonline.com/doi/pdf/10.1080/09687599627598.

Bhanushali, K. (2005). *Defining Disabilities: NSSO vs Census*. Available online at: www.disabilityindia.org/nsso-census.cfm.

Birbeck, G. (2000). 'Barriers to care for patients with neurologic disease in rural Zambia', *Archives of Neurology*, 57, 414–417.

Chandrasekar, M. (2006). *Persons with Disabilities in India – A Compilation*. Available online at: http: //www.geocities.ws/mahesh_mobility/pwd_india.htm.

Coleridge, P. (1993). *Disability, Liberation and Development*. Oxford: Oxfam in association with Action on Disability and Development.

Elwan A. (1990). *Poverty and Disability: A Background Paper*. World Development Report. Washington, DC: World Bank.

Info Change News (2006, August). *National Policy for the Disabled*: *No Clear Roadmap for Action*. Available online at: http://infochangeindia.org/

disabilities/features/national-policy-for-the-disabled-no-clear-roadmap-for-action.html.

Lwanga-Ntale, C. (2003). 'Chronic poverty and disability in Uganda', *Development Research & Training*, April 2003.

Mavoothu, D., Poduval, R.P., and Arunachalam, P. (2008). *HR Initiatives for Differently Abled by Indian Corporates, Rights of the Disabled*. New Delhi: Serials Publication.

MSJE (Ministry of Social Justice and Empowerment, Government of India) (2005–2006). *Annual Report 2005–06*. Available online at: www.socialjustice.nic.in.

Naidu, N., and Deepa, S. (2008). *Disability and Gender in a Socio-economic Perspective in India, Rights of the Disabled*. New Delhi: Serials Publication.

Persons with Disabilities Act (1995). *The Persons with Disabilities (Equal Opportunities, Protection of Rights and Full Participation) Act 1995 Preliminary Chapter I Section 2 (i)*. Available online at: http://socialjustice.nic.in/disabled/act.htm

Rungta, S.K. (2004). *Training and Employment of people with Disabilities: India 2002*. An Ability Asia Country Study. Bangkok: ILO.

Thanh, N.X., Hang, H.M., Chuc, N.T.K., Byass, P., and Lindholm, L. (2005). 'Does poverty lead to non-fatal unintentional injuries in rural Vietnam?', *International Journal of Injury Control and Safety Promotion*, 12(1), 31–37.

Thomas, P. (2005). *Poverty Reduction and Development in Cambodia: Enabling Disabled to Play a Role*. Disability KAR, April. DFID, UK.

World Bank (2008). *Disability and Poverty: A Survey of World Bank Poverty Assessments and Implications*. S P Discussion paper, No. 0805. Available online at: http://siteresources.worldbank.org/DISABILITY/Resources/280658-1172608138489/WBPovertyAssessments.pdf.

World Health Organization (2001). *International Classification of Functioning, Disability and Health*. Geneva: WHO.

Zutshi, B. (2004). *Disability Status in India. Case study of Delhi Metropolitan Region Development*. New Delhi: Jawaharlal, Nehru University.

10

Poverty among Elderly in India

Estimates and Determinants

SYAM PRASAD

Ageing can generally be described as the process of growing old and is an intricate part of the life cycle. Basically, it is a multidimensional process and affects almost every aspect of human life. Introduction to the study of human ageing has typically emphasized changes in demography focusing on the 'ageing of population' – a trend, which has characterized industrial societies throughout the 20th century but in recent decades, it has become a worldwide phenomenon. Ageing is basically the result of a two-dimensional demographic transformation which is explained by overall declines in mortality and fertility.

This is a dynamic process, first observed in post-industrial European societies in the 19th century. The United Nations Conference of Ageing Populations in the context of the family held in Japan in 1994 observed that in all developed countries at least one demographic issue is common: population ageing which was the inevitable consequence of fertility decline. But although fertility decline is usually the driving force behind changing population age structures, changes in mortality assume greater importance as countries reach lower levels of fertility. Ageing of the population is a major phenomenon in the present-day world as a result of the changing demographic transition. Though the phenomenon has a universal character, it occurs in various countries at different point of time. The ageing is a phenomenon already occurred in the developed countries in the later half of the 20th century. The similar situation is emerging in the developing countries in the recent periods. Although the proportion of elderly 60 and above is considered to be relatively low in the case of the developing countries such as India and China, they have a larger population base. Developed countries have aged with high social and economic development, the social and economic condition of the elderly in the developing world is a cause for concern as most of them end up in living below poverty line in old age due to inefficient social security. Here, poverty and deprivation is one of the key elements in the life of elderly where social security system is weak. Here, we look up on poverty among elderly in Indian context.

Ageing in India

Population ageing is the most significant consequence of the process known as demographic transition. Reduction in fertility leads to a decline in the proportion of young in the population. Coupled with fertility decline, reduction in mortality enhances the lifespan of individuals leading to higher life expectancy at older ages. In other words, population ageing involves a shift from high mortality/high fertility to low mortality/low fertility.

In the beginning of 20th century, the life expectancy for India was just 23 years for both sexes. In 1947, when India became independent from the British rule, life expectancy was around 32 years – added nine years during the first half of the 20th century. Improvements in public health and medical services have led to substantial control of specific infectious diseases and eradicated few more diseases, which translated into significant decreases in mortality rates among all ages. Government-sponsored sanitation and maternal and child immunization programmes have improved maternal health and reduced infant mortality. The infant mortality in 2002 for India is 63–62 for males and 65 for females (Registrar General, 2004). This has enhanced the life expectancy at birth to 61 years for males and 63 years for females – 30 years increase during the second half of the 20th century (Registrar General, 2003). The decadal growth rate among elderly population during 1991–2001 is about 40 per cent – double than the general population growth of 21 per cent. The percentage of elderly in India has increased from 5.4 per cent in 1951 to 6.4 per cent in 1981 and further to 7.4 in 2001. If the percentage of elderly population is above 7 per cent in any country, as per the UN criterion that country is ageing. In other words, India has emerged as 'ageing India' in the beginning of the 21st century. Thus, 21st century is the century of old.

Ageing and Poverty

The changing age structure of a population can have long run economic and social implications and create imbalance within the generations. The studies show that the change in the intergenerational balance can have implication on the economy and society. The lives of many older people are more frequently negatively affected by the social and economic insecurity that accompany demographic and development process (World Bank, 1994). The growth of individualism and desire of the independence and autonomy of the young generation (Serow, 2001) affect the status of the elderly. The studies show that socio-economic condition of older women is more vulnerable in the context of the demographic and socio-cultural change (Tout, 1993). The situation of the elderly poverty has been a consistent phenomenon in the Third World as the older population is deprived of the basic needs (Keyfitz and Flieger, 1990). The eight diminution of deprivation among the elderly as poverty, social inferiority, social isolation, physical weakness, vulnerability, seasonality, powerlessness, and humiliation of the aged. The poverty is sought to be a major risk of ageing in developing countries and study by the World Bank reveals that in most of the developing countries, the older people and dependent are poor and vulnerable (World Bank, 1994).

The linkage between ageing and poverty and deprivation can have three channels of relations. They interlinked through the links on production relations, health implication, and social institutions that affect different stages of life cycle.

The elderly presents make its implication on the production function within the household and thus on overall work effort that reflects in the income and production (Schwarz, 2003). In other words, in most of the case presents of elderly can create distortion in the production function as they are physically unfit to work. This can have direct effect on the well-being of the households that reflects in the poverty among aged. The inability in the initial endowment of an individual that deteriorates as they go up in the life cycle can make them more vulnerable (Zwi, 1999). There is a perceived notion that elderly presents in a household will reduce economies of scale as it increases the consumption of more private goods such as medicines that can reduce overall welfare of the households.

Physical and health risk is very high among the aged group. The precise implications of population ageing for future levels of health and health care utilization depend on whether the increases in life expectancy experienced in general are accompanied by an increase or decrease in health problems in later life (Gruenberg, 1977; Kramer, 1980; Manton, 1982). Elderly are likely to have more health concern than the rest of the population. Process of ageing is likely to be accompanied by changes in the pattern of diseases in the epidemiological tradition. In the past, Western nations have witnessed a change in the pattern of morbidity which is mainly a shift from infective to chronic and degenerative diseases with high incidence of mortality in the old age (Fries, 1980.). The studies from West show fast decline in the mortality in the old population which is creating a nightmare with high incidence of morbidity. The changing pattern of morbidity puts elderly to a situation of risk in the old age where they are in a condition of lacking capacity to cope up with the risk. The changing patterns of morbidity in the late life have created challenges and burden to the existing health care system with higher incidence of social cost to provide extended access to health care to avoid the risk of morbidity.

Decline of mortality is always accompanied by high incidence of morbidity (Wilmut, 1993) among elderly in the later years of life. In poor and developing country, the health risk is not only measured in the outcome indicators on prevalence of the diseases (outcome indicator of risk as an indicator of vulnerability) but also addressed on the basis of access to health care. The process of ageing has resulted in the emergence of a new epidemiological scenario in the developing countries with high prevalence of degenerative diseases that act as a major cause of death and disability (Zwi, 1999). There are evidence of unhealthy ageing from almost all the developing countries of Asia, Africa, and Latin America. There is long run health degeneration in the ageing societies of Caribbean and Latin America with changing disease pattern. Studies from Africa also look into epidemiological shift among aged population. Various studies show that the health risk of the elderly is mainly confined to access to health care which results in an unhealthy ageing. The health risk of an aged person in a household can result in catastrophic shock in the family that can make households more exposed to poverty.

Various studies across the globe show that poverty and deprivation is one of the common phenomena in almost all-ageing society. Cross-country experience shows that despite major progress that has been made over the past 40 years, in most of the countries poverty remain among the elderly. With high incidence of social security system, poverty is a chronic phenomenon in the developed countries of Europe and America. Study among American ethnic minority shows that they are in a state of poverty and stress. Wolfe and Smeeding (1999) provided that poverty among aged in the United States remains to be increasing despite growth-induced development. Information provided by US household census in 2000 highlights the economic stress among elderly households. World Bank study in 1994 provides a detailed scaling of social and economic insecurity in the wake of dismantling social security in Europe. There are studies in Canada and other European countries where poverty among elderly is mainly attributed to health care shocks and after discounting subsidies on this expenditure. In short, most of the countries give a clear-cut picture of poverty among elderly and give signs of poverty despite the virtue of affluence that resulted in increased life expectancy.

The elderly in the developing countries are also suffering from chronic deprivation and thus in poverty as the socio-economic relation changes. Studies on the livelihood pattern of aged in Africa show that poverty among the elderly is one of the challenges in the new millennium. In Africa, poverty among the elderly is more acute in the areas where the younger population is affected by the spreading of AIDS that creates the intergenerational balance within the population and thus results in the chronic poverty among the elderly that highlights issue of missing generation. Empirical studies in South Africa and Nigeria highlight a large incidence of such families with missing generation or skipped generation that breaks intergenerational balance (Schwarz, 2003).

Though the household data do not provide a clear-cut picture of standard poverty estimation among elderly as it is subjected to intra-household dynamics. Various studies by HelpAge International (HAI) provide traces of poverty in the old age in the developing countries. Studies by HAI show that in Asian countries, such as Malaysia and Indonesia, poor elderly are burden to family due to changing family relationship. Offshoot of medical expenditure pushes aged in most of the Asian countries under poverty trap. Sri Lanka with a faster pace of ageing witnessed a general decline in the living condition of aged. Studies in Malaysia have found that cosmopolitan lifestyles have put elderly to a stage of physical stress that reflected in the living condition. With the onset of new economic and social set-up, poor in the Asia and Latin America are not covered by social security and are in a position of deprivation. In short, the aged in the developing countries is in a state of food and economic insecurity as the formal and informal mechanism fails to provide proper security for the aged (World Bank, 1994).

In a country like India where the majority of the population is suffering from the chronic poverty, it is found interesting to study the chronic poverty and vulnerability in the aged. Here poverty is looking into issues of hunger and vulnerability, a larger issue of the socio-economic insecurity among the elderly that acts as a determinant of the poverty among the aged. And poverty is addressed in terms of denial of livelihood to the aged where they are denied of adequate flow of food, cash, and assets to attain minimum basic needs (Project OASIS 1999). In a country like India that lacks proper social security system and majority of the population is in the hands of the chronic poverty, the condition of the elderly is in a mystery. The aged does not have adequate income to meet the basic needs. The socio-economic condition of the elderly in India is in a bad shape. The majority of the elderly are deprived of the basic necessity and thus in chronic poverty. The majority of the elderly are dependent and are even compelled to work when they are old to earn a living. The work participation of the elderly is mainly determined by the societal wealth and is implied with higher work participation among the elderly. In general, poor country will have much labour participation among the elderly since aged wanted to avoid poverty. The 55th round of the National Sample Survey Organization (NSSO) shows that nearly 55 per cent of the 60 plus are working to earn a livelihood for themselves. The work participation of the elderly is more visible in the urban areas where the deprivation is more acute in the case of elderly due to changing family and social relations.

Here, we intend to measure the income poverty among the elderly in India across the Indian states.

Income poverty: Income measure of poverty is the most widely used measure of poverty. Here, we fix the measure of income as an indicator of welfare and populations are divided based on minimum income requirement, to be poor or not. Income as such here takes as a measure of welfare function that determines the end outcome. Those with lack of income for minimum calorie intake is considered to be poor in terms of income poverty concept (Gordon and Spicker, 1999). Then fix the poverty band based on income to fix intensity of the poverty (UNDP, 2000). The measures of USD 1 per day in Purchasing Power Parities is the standard used to monitor poverty trends at the global level but for country-level monitoring, national authorities are encouraged to use indicators based on national poverty lines to measure the income poverty. There exist different bands to measure the income poverty in various countries as per the country-specific factors. One of the major limitations of measuring income poverty is that of likeliness of underreporting of income in the developing countries. The ability to transfer income to well-being is another serious issue raised. So, in general, income poverty is often attributed based on proxy of income.

The income proxy method is a behaviourist approach based on people's consumption patterns. Data on household expenditure are used as an income proxy to measure poverty. The theory is based on the fact that the consumption patterns of various family compositions are the results of the relative competition between need and choice. Whether need or choice prevails depends on the amount of income earned by the families. In practical terms, low-income families usually spend a greater proportion of expenditure on necessities, while better off families will purchase more quality goods and non-necessities. Therefore, from the data on household expenditure, poverty threshold can be worked out by identifying a proper proportion of expenditure on necessities against the total expenditure. This provides an income proxy for poverty, based on the proportion of total expenditure spent on the purchase of necessities. However, the cut-off point needs not be 30 per cent, and the measure needs not be restricted to expenditure on food. As societies are going through rapid changes, any standard devised in the past is difficult to be justified in new circumstances. Hence, these standards have to be recurrently checked in order to tie in with the development of social trends. However, the measures of ever-updating the standards would be costly and time consuming. The concrete definitions of necessities are always controversial (Rainwater and Smeeding, 1995).

Methods

There is no secondary data source for tracing the trend in income inequality in India and its state regions. Any study on poverty and inequality, therefore, depends upon NSSO quinquennial series of household consumption expenditure surveys to study trends in inequality in per capita expenditure (proxy for income) generally by estimating rural and urban poverty. These surveys started in 1972–73 (27th round) give detailed consumer expenditure data for 1983 (38th round), 1987–88 (43rd round), 1993–94 (50th round), 1999–2000 (55th round), and 2004–05 (61st round). In this case, consumption level of a household is compared with specific poverty line to get head count ratio (HCR).

Estimation of Poverty among Aged in India

Like most developing countries, India has been experiencing population ageing, attributable to the decline in both fertility and mortality over the past five decades or so. This phenomenon has important implications for the poverty reduction strategies in the country. Although demographic and other socio-economic and health (Jai Prakash, 1999; Rajan et al., 1999) aspects of ageing in India have been examined by various social scientists, there are no official measures of old-age poverty in India (as in many other developing countries, e.g., Barrientos et al., 2003). With the exception of Deaton and Paxson (1995), who provide estimates of old-age poverty in six large Indian states for 1987–1988, there has been a general lack of research into an understanding of the extent, magnitude, and nature of old-age poverty in the Indian states. Here, we estimate the poverty based on household expenditure. We try to adjust the size and composition of the households in the estimation of poverty as they directly imply on the welfare distribution of the households. Here, it is done by calculating dependency-adjusted poverty, sensitive to the composition of the household with old-age dependency.

Old Dependency-adjusted Poverty

In most practical work that documents levels of living and poverty, researchers make a look at differences in household size by working with income or consumption per capita. Such measures effectively assume that household resources are allocated according to need of a member within the household. We propose a simple method for examining the sensitivity of welfare comparisons to assumptions based on welfare distribution within the households. We try to look at two important issues. One is the question of how resources are allocated within the household with higher levels of dependency and their implications on overall welfare functions. Deflating total household resources by an equivalence scale, defined as a function of the size of the household and its demographic composition, measures individual living standards. The second issue that we do not consider is the traditional estimation of equivalence scales. There is a large and long-standing literature on the measurement of equivalence scales (see the 'Discussion' in Deaton and Paxson, 1998). Our approach here follows Buhmann et al. (1988) and Banks and Johnson (1994) in assuming a parametric form for the equivalence scale and examining the consequence of changing the parameters.

Methodology of Old Dependency-adjusted Poverty

We assume that an elderly costs a fraction of what a non-elderly costs, and that the elasticity of costs with respect to adjusted household size through following the redefining of N through a dependency-adjusted approach.

Here, scaling is done by adjusting N to capture effects on per capita consumption. N is calculated as follows:

$$N = (A + \alpha B)^{\theta}$$

where A is non-elderly population and B is elderly population in a household. The parameter α is obtained by adding up old-age dependency to unity (1 + ODR) to scale down welfare loss in the household due to old-age dependency. It controls the costs of elderly relative to total population. θ captures economies of scale that reflects in a family due to consumption of indivisibilities. Value of θ always takes the value between 0 and 1. Larger the value of θ, greater is the levels of economies of scale within the household consumption (see Deaton and Paxson, 1998). If θ is 1, there are no economies of scale within the household and thus average per capita expenditure (APCE) is the original per capita distribution and vice versa.

Adjustment in Poverty Line

After adjusting the per capita welfare to a revised APCE after adjusting the composition, size, and economies of scale, we revise the poverty line given by the planning commission for the Indian states for different levels of economies of scale. Following Drèze and Srinivasan (1997), we consider the following formula to adjust the different levels of economies of scale to given poverty line to calculate HCR at different levels of economies of scale:

$$Z_n(\theta) = Z(h)1 - \theta$$

where Z_n is new poverty line, Z is the old poverty line, and h denotes average family size of the states adjusted for ODR (αn). Here, we make adjustments of old poverty line in confirmation with different values of economies of scale value of θ, then there is a decline in the overall distributive justice of the welfare within the household. So here HCR will be calculated based on the newly adjusted APCE and the adjusted poverty line for each values of θ.

Results and Discussions

Here, we borrow from the estimates of Deaton's (1995) economies scale of 0.6, which is ideal for India, and estimates dependency-adjusted poverty within the Indian states. This is done for different combinations of the households that are possible in the Indian society say, the distribution of the population in such a way that there is occurrence of the households with elderly, without elderly, with single or multiple elderly (2 or 3 or more), and with elderly and children, elderly households without children.

Table 1

Poverty Line with Scale Adjustment

States	*Rural*		*Urban*	
	Original	*Scale = 0.6*	*Original*	*Scale = 0.6*
Andhra Pradesh	251.94	587.23	466.89	1079.91
Assam	333.37	858.82	325.8	761.82
Bihar	304.75	825.52	374.1	972.78
Chhattisgarh	277.27	724.49	481.6	1167.84
Gujarat	304.38	768.16	465.4	1132.65
Haryana	356.69	946.83	433.86	1076.79
Himachal Pradesh	339.08	842.75	433.86	960.37
Jammu and Kashmir	336.48	898.47	476.24	1181.04
Jharkhand	315.24	834.83	388.07	975.97
Karnataka	278.79	689.5	515.71	1210.41
Kerala	369.9	880.98	481.08	1149.94
Madhya Pradesh	281.89	750.26	490.33	1253.75
Maharashtra	311.54	779.89	572.67	1379.87
Orissa	280.18	704.95	454.5	1095.9
Punjab	352.93	917.3	400.9	987.44
Rajasthan	322.13	876.53	481.28	1220.49
Tamil Nadu	302.6	685.62	470.78	1047.18
Uttar Pradesh	314.62	879.96	415.6	1101.26
Uttaranchal	411.1	1074.35	548.4	1326.27
West Bengal	329.23	823.63	386.42	891.03

Table 1 gives the poverty line across different states of India with varying economic of scale in the households. It is clear that urban poverty line is higher than that of rural in all the states. As per our adjustments, we consider that poverty line with no economies of scale of distribution is when $E_s = 1$. When $E_s = 1$, the adjustment with newly defined dependency adjustment, we are getting newly adjusted poverty line which is having only slight deviation from the original estimates because of the revision in the welfare distribution within the population. As the economies of scales moves higher with revised N, there occurs a drastic change in the welfare function in terms of APCE and levels of APCE moves closer to Y. Thus, poverty lines will be revised. We get the poverty lines given in the table and shows that there is a relative increase in the levels of poverty line with an upward shift in the economies of scale component θ tends to zero.

The poverty line of Indian states after adjustment shows interstate disparity. The levels of urban poverty lines are higher than that of rural levels. It is because of relative increase in the levels of income to attain minimum calorie needs. States such as Uttaranchal and Kerala have the highest poverty line in the rural areas, whereas Andhra Pradesh, Chhattisgarh, Madhya and Pradesh report low levels of poverty line. Karnataka records highest poverty line in urban India and low levels of poverty bands are reported in the states of Assam, Bihar, and Jharkhand.

Table 2

Dependency-adjusted Poverty Estimates with Scale Adjustment of 0.6 for Rural India

Rural	*Non-elderly*	*Elderly*	*1 elderly*	*2 elderly*	*With 3 or more*	*Elderly HH children*	*Elderly HH without children*
Andhra Pradesh	31.49	41.58	38.87	41.98	49.48	52.16	35.13
Assam	9.66	13.76	12.87	13.9	16.39	17.28	11.64
Bihar	34.25	41.8	39.08	42.21	49.75	52.44	35.33
Chhattisgarh	34.46	47.96	44.85	48.43	57.08	60.17	40.53
Gujarat	20.18	31.13	29.11	31.44	37.05	39.06	26.31
Haryana	10.08	15.09	14.11	15.24	17.96	18.93	12.76
Himachal Pradesh	4.36	26.57	24.85	26.83	31.62	33.33	22.45
Jammu and Kashmir	17.78	23.74	22.2	23.97	28.24	29.78	20.06
Jharkhand	24.59	23.64	22.11	23.87	28.14	29.66	19.98
Karnataka	32.87	41.09	38.42	41.5	48.9	51.56	34.73
Kerala	16.48	34.97	32.69	35.32	41.61	43.88	29.55
Madhya Pradesh	41.32	49.33	46.13	49.82	58.72	61.89	41.69
Maharashtra	31.52	40.15	37.53	40.54	47.77	50.37	33.93
Orissa	39.01	53.78	50.29	54.31	64.01	67.48	45.45
Punjab	13.82	17.82	16.66	17.99	21.21	22.36	15.06
Rajasthan	34.21	48.07	44.94	48.54	57.2	60.31	40.62
Tamil Nadu	27.64	35.74	33.42	36.09	42.53	44.84	30.2
Uttar Pradesh	32.3	45.94	42.94	46.39	54.66	57.63	38.82
Uttaranchal	33.93	51.15	47.83	51.66	60.87	64.17	43.22
West Bengal	18.41	22.92	21.42	23.14	27.26	28.74	19.36

Table 3

Dependency-adjusted Poverty Estimates with Scale Adjustment of 0.6 for Urban India

Rural	*Non-elderly*	*Elderly*	*1 elderly*	*2 elderly*	*With 3 or more*	*Elderly HH children*	*Elderly HH without children*
Andhra Pradesh	26.25	34.2	31.98	34.54	40.7	42.91	28.9
Assam	46.59	52.29	48.9	52.81	62.23	65.61	44.19
Bihar	62.8	68.27	63.84	68.94	81.24	85.65	57.68
Chhattisgarh	56.25	69.36	64.85	70.03	82.52	87	58.61
Gujarat	34.01	39.5	36.93	39.89	47.01	49.55	33.37
Haryana	30.93	33.36	31.2	33.69	39.7	41.86	28.2
Himachal Pradesh	23.5	37.37	34.96	37.74	44.48	46.9	31.59
Jammu and Kashmir	18.79	29.93	27.98	30.2	35.61	37.55	25.28
Jharkhand	60.25	70.81	66.2	71.51	84.26	88.84	59.83
Karnataka	35.12	49.88	46.64	50.36	59.35	62.58	42.15
Kerala	20.28	32.69	30.56	33.01	38.91	41.02	27.63
Madhya Pradesh	52.67	63.18	59.08	63.8	75.18	79.27	53.39
Maharashtra	41.03	55.62	52.01	56.16	66.19	69.79	47
Orissa	58.47	66.09	61.8	66.73	78.65	82.92	55.85
Punjab	29.15	30.42	28.45	30.73	36.21	38.17	25.71
Rajasthan	6.65	6.95	6.51	7.03	8.28	8.72	5.87
Tamil Nadu	36.44	50.28	47.01	50.77	59.82	63.08	42.48
Uttar Pradesh	52.34	58.99	55.15	59.56	70.19	74	49.85
Uttaranchal	51.44	66.68	62.35	67.34	79.36	83.66	56.35
West Bengal	47.58	51.28	47.95	51.78	61.02	64.33	43.33

Tables 2 and 3 give the levels of poverty across Indian states for different combinations of households based on composition within the households. This is done for different combinations of the households that are possible in the Indian society say, the distribution of the population in such a way that there is occurrence of the households with elderly, without elderly, with single or multiple elderly (2 or 3 or more), and with elderly and children, elderly households without children. It is given across sector with economies of scale of 0.6.

In both urban and rural areas, the rates of poverty are higher in the elderly households in comparison to non-elderly households. As there is an increase in the number of elderly, there are high levels of poverty.

The elderly households without children in general report less HCR poverty on an average to that of elderly households. In the rural areas, states of Uttaranchal, Rajasthan, Chhattisgarh, and Madhya Pradesh record relatively high rates of poverty among elderly, while it is low in the states such as Assam, Punjab, and Haryana. In the urban areas, states of Uttaranchal, Chhattisgarh Orissa, Uttar Pradesh, and Madhya Pradesh show high incidence of poverty. It is lowest in Rajasthan. The gap between HCR in elderly and non-elderly is not uniform across the Indian states. It is relatively higher in the states of Himachal Pradesh and Kerala. And it is negative for Jharkhand for rural scenario. In urban India, the gap is higher in Uttaranchal, Madhya Pradesh, and Karnataka with the difference of more than 11 points. And it is minute in the case of Rajasthan, Punjab, and Haryana.

Determinants of Poverty among Elderly

There are studies that reveal that vulnerability of the aged is mainly caused by the changes in social relationship. Breaking down of family ties and formation of the small and nuclear family had led to a negligence of the aged (Achenbaum, 1978). As the family size cuts down as a result of demographic process, the belief that children will take care of the parents in old age is eroding in India (Dandelkar, 1996). The situation in the urban areas shows of a rejection of the older people by the next generation and such condition is spreading to rural areas (Desai, 1985). In the nuclear family regime, the position of the aged became more vulnerable and treated as a burden to the family. Changing social and economic relations with a change in the family and non-family relations within the society had resulted in the social exclusion among aged in India. This exclusion led to a state of deprivation and mystery among the elderly.

High levels of economic development in society are putting break on social relations. With increased modernization and migratory tendency, most of elderly are in a disarray. There also persist socio-cultural factors that can affect living condition of elderly.

Now in the logistic regression by taking poverty among the elderly as dependent variable, I assume that the economies of size of households are ideal to be 0.6. Here, I estimate odds of getting poor in comparison with non-poor in the elderly population.

We calculate odds of an elderly being poor in comparison with that of non-poor. From the logistic regression, it is found that the urban elderly is having less odds of being non-poor in comparison to a rural elderly with other things remaining the same. Like that, SC elderly is having high chance of poverty in comparison to ST. The elderly from

OBC and general population is with decreasing odds of being poor and it is lowest among the OBC population. In comparison to the Hindu elderly, Muslims are having larger odds of being poor and there exists less chance among the Christians to remain poor. It is clear that incidence of poverty goes high among the families with larger size and increasing number of children that can affect the welfare distribution. The rates of poverty among the aged is relatively lower in the states with high per capita net state domestic product (NSDP). With age, the likelihood of an elderly being poor also goes up.

Table 4

Logit of Determinants of Poverty among Aged (Poor Elderly vs. No Poor Elderly)

(N = 34831) Pseudo R2: 6578	*Coefficient*	*Standard error*	*P > z*
Rural (Ref)			
urban	–0.86	0.06	0.051
ST (Ref)			
SC	1.83	0.29	0
OBC	0.47	0.21	0.006
General	0.14	0.16	0.035
Hindu (Ref)			
Muslim	1.79	0.18	0.01
Christian	0.88	0.13	0.042
Per capita income of state	-0.69	1.35	0.01
Number of child	0.81	0.01	0.01
Household size	1.07	0.01	0.01
Age	1.47	0.00	0.01

Conclusions

This paper looks up on the economic well-being of the elderly by estimating poverty among the elderly. Here I adopted the income proxy measures. I adjusted size and composition of the household that influence the welfare of the individuals in the households by estimating dependency-adjusted levels of the poverty across the Indian states. This estimation is done with an assumption that the distribution of the income within the household makes economies of scale of 0.6. It is found that elderly households are poorer than the non-elderly households. The condition on poverty get worsens as the number of elderly goes up in the households. It is found that age, economic status of the households, relative economic status of the state, family size, and number of children in the household act as crucial differentials in the poor and non-poor elderly.

References

Achenbaum, W.A. (1978). *Old Age in the New Land: The American Experience since 1790* (Paper edition). Baltimore, MD: The Johns Hopkins University Press.

Banks, J., and Johnson, P. (1994). 'Equivalence scale relativities revisited', *Economic Journal*, 104, 883–890.

Barrientos, A., Gorman, M., and Heslop, A. (2003). 'Old age poverty in developing countries: Contributions and dependence in later life', *World Development*, 31(3), 555–570.

Buhmann, B., Rainwater, L., Schamus, G., and Smeeding, T.M. (1988). *Equivalence Scales, Well-Being, Inequality and Poverty: Sensitivity Estimates across Ten Countries Using the Luxembourg Income Study (LIS) Database*. Working Paper No. 17, LIS, Luxembourg.

Chambers, R. (1995). *Poverty and Livelihood Whose Reality Counts*. Brighton: Institute of Development Studies.

Dandekar, K. (1996). *Elderly in India*. New Delhi: Sage Publications.

Deaton, A., and Paxson, C. (1995). *Measuring Poverty among the Elderly*. NBER Working Paper No. 5296, Cambridge, MA.

Deaton, A., and Paxson, C. (1998). 'Economies of scale, household size and the demand for food', *Journal of Political Economy*, 106, 898–930.

Desai, K.G. (1985). 'Situation of the aged in India', *Journal of Indian Anthropological Society*, 20(3), 201–209.

Drèze, J., and Srinivasan, P.V. (1997). 'Widowhood and poverty in rural India: Some inferences from household survey data', *Journal of Development Economics*, 54, 217–234.

Fries, J.F. (1980). 'Aging, natural death, and the compression of morbidity', *New England Journal of Medicine*, 303(3), 130–135.

Gruenberg, E.M. (1977). 'The failures of success', *Milbank Memorial Fund Quarterly – Health and Society*, 55(1), 3–24.

Jai Prakash, I. (1999). *Ageing in India*. Prepared for WHO, Geneva. Available online at: http: //whqlibdoc.who.int/hq/1999/WHO_HSC_AHE_99.2.pdf

Kramer, M. (1980). 'The rising pandemic of mental disorders and associated chronic diseases and disabilities', *Acta Psychiatrica Scandinavica*, 62(285), 282–297.

Manton, K.G. (1982). 'Changing concepts of morbidity and mortality in the elderly population', *Milbank Memorial Fund Quarterly – Health and Society*, 60(2), 183–244.

Rajan, I.S. (2004). *Chronic Poverty among the Elderly*. Working Paper No. 17. Chronic Poverty Research Centre IIPA.

Registrar General of India (2004). Vital Statistics in India.

Registrar General of India (2003). Vital Statistics in India.

Schwarz, A. (2003). *Old Age Security and Social Pensions*. Washington, DC: World Bank, Human Development (Social Protection).

Serow, W. (2001). 'Economic and social implications of demographic patterns'. In Bienstock, R.K., and George, L.K. (eds.): *Handbook of Ageing and the Social Sciences* (pp. 86–102). New York: Academic Press.

The World Bank. (1994). *Averting the Old Age Crisis: Policies to Protect the Old and Promote Growth*. Washington, DC: Oxford.

Tout, K. (1993). *Ageing in Developing Countries*. London: Oxford University Press.

Zwi, B.A. (1999). *Lancing Imbalances: Facilitating Community Perspectives in Times of Adversity*. Available online at:www.practicinganthropology.org/napa.

11

Population, Poverty and Environment Dynamics in India

DEWARAM A. NAGDEVE

The United Nations Conference on the Human Environment held in Stockholm in 1972 (United Nations, 1973) stated that the growth of population in certain areas, through both net migration and national increase had the rates that could transfer all efforts to conquer poverty and underdevelopment and to maintain a safe and stable environment. The regions with high rate of population growth or excessive population concentration are likely to experience adverse effect on the environment and development. The United Nations Conference on Environment and Development (UNCED), held in Rio de Janeiro in 1992, discussed in particular the interrelationships between population and environment issues (United Nations, 1992). The poverty, environment, and population could no longer be dealt with, or even thought of, as separate issues and emphasized the integration of demographic trends and population factors into all aspects of sustainable development, planning, and environmental protection. Shortly after the Rio conference, the Fourth Asian and Pacific Population Conference was held in Bali, Indonesia, in 1992. Serious concern was expressed at the conference over population size and growth and the impact of those factors on resource loss and environmental degradation. It was noted that in many countries and areas, high population growth rates and density had caused various environmental problems, such as land degradation, deforestation, air and water pollution, and threats to biological diversity.

Poverty is among the consequences of population growth and lifestyle plays a major role in depleting the environment either due to fuel demands for cooking or for earning a livelihood. Poverty and the general lack of access to capital, resources, and technology contribute to deforestation. Poverty, apart from problems of its own, also supplements the impact of population on the environment. Poverty is found to lead to marginal agriculture, which result in many environmental problems such as deforestation, erosion, and desertification, as fulfilment of the basic needs remains the first priority of the poor people. The poor, in general, also do not have the means to undertake resource conservation measures, particularly soil conservation measures on which depends their long-term development (Gupta, 1997).

In India, the rapid increase of human numbers combines with desperate poverty to deplete and pollute local resource bases on which the livelihood of present and future generations depends. An increasing population requires additional land for farming, fuel wood, fodder, human settlements, roads, industrial and institutional establishments, etc. Thus, putting pressure on renewable and non-renewable resources, the additional population has to draw the means of sustenance as well as meet the growing demands from the ecosystem, which is finite. In addition, population growth is also found to inhibit economic growth, leading to poverty. Rapid population growth and poverty in a country deplete its natural resources and degrade the environment. India having 18 per cent of the world's population on 2.4 per cent of its land area has a great deal of pressure on all its natural resources. The growing population puts immense pressure on land extensification at the cost of forests and grazing lands because the demand for food could not increase substantially. The growing trends of population and the consequent demand for food, energy, and housing have also considerably altered land-use practices and severely degraded India's forest.

A rapidly increasing population, poverty, and degradation of environment has become the most critical problems faced by humanity in the country. However, the interrelationship between population, poverty, and environment is highly complex and not clearly understood. The exact nature of this relationship and to what extent population growth and its distribution creates a distinct impact on various environmental problems are still a matter of serious academic contention. Though the relationship is complex, population size and growth tend to expand and accelerate these human impacts on the environment. It is now well accepted that population, poverty, the economy, and environment are interconnected, be it direct or indirect, bearing on the availability as well as utilization of natural resources. The continuing need for family labour supports high fertility and rapid population growth. Continued deforestation will have grave consequences for the health of both humans and ecosystems. Rapid population growth in India has already adversely affected the environment, resources, and the quality of life (United Nations, 1997). How India deals with its population and poverty problem and protects natural resources in the coming years will determine the quality of life. In view of above, there is a need to determine the role of population and poverty and associated environmental changes so that necessary policy interventions can be made.

Objectives

This paper is an attempt to study the changes in population and poverty in India and its states over the four decades and to highlight the extent of environmental degradation in the states of India.

Sources of Data and Methodology

The analysis has been done by using data from various secondary sources. Bivariate analyses have been carried out to study the changes and trends from 1971 to 2001. To examine the interrelationship between population growth and poverty, and population growth and forests, bivariate relationship between these variables was analysed.

Results and Discussion

Population Growth in India

The growth of population in the states of India as recorded in various censuses from 1971 to 2001 is presented in Table 1. The population of India increased from 5482 lakhs in 1971 to 10,286 lakhs in 2001. The highest population of 1747 lakhs is found in Uttar Pradesh and lowest of 5 lakhs in Sikkim. The five states, namely, Bihar, Madhya Pradesh, Orissa, Rajasthan, and Uttar Pradesh constitute 44.6 per cent of the total population of India. The percentage annual growth rate during 1991–2001 has registered the sharpest decline from 2.23 per cent in 1971–1981 to 1.97 per cent in 1991–2001, i.e., a decrease of 0.26 per cent. The percentage annual exponential growth of population during 1971–1981 recorded a low of 1.63 per cent in Tamil Nadu, while the highest was in Sikkim (4.17%). During 1991–2001, the annual percentage growth varied from a low of 1.35 per cent in Kerala to 4.56 per cent in Nagaland followed by Mizoram (3.4%) registered very high growth rates. Kerala and two other major states in Southern India, i.e., Tamil Nadu and Andhra Pradesh reported low growth rates during 1991–2001.

Poverty in the States of India

India, with a high and increasing density of population relative to resources, faces developmental challenges in alleviating massive poverty and deprivation, and in raising the quality of life of poor people. The growth performance of the states has crucial implications in poverty reduction, which is an important objective of the economic policy. Most of India's poor are engaged in agriculture. India's efforts to reduce poverty through the anti-poverty and employment generation programmes along with overall economic growth-planning efforts have helped to reduce the poverty ratio in the country. The trends of state-wise percentage of population below poverty line and poverty growth in India are presented in Table 2. The people below the poverty line have declined from 55 per cent during 1973–74 to 26 per cent in 1999–2000 for India as a whole. Out of 25 states, 13 states have a lesser percentage of population below poverty line than the national average. There are wide interstate variations in the poverty ratios of different states. The poverty ratio in Orissa at 47.15 per cent is about eight times that in Punjab (6.16%). Almost half of the population in Orissa and Bihar are below the poverty line.

On the other hand, there are 10 states that have less than 20 per cent of population below the poverty line. The highest percentage of population below the poverty line is found in Orissa, Bihar, and Madhya Pradesh, whereas the lowest percentage of population below poverty line is found in Jammu and Kashmir, Goa, Punjab, Himachal Pradesh, and Haryana. States such as West Bengal and Kerala have seen tremendous improvements in poverty levels over the period. Haryana, Himachal Pradesh, and Punjab have also experienced significant gains in poverty reduction. The poverty ratios have fallen to less than 10 per cent in these states. The different levels of poverty in the states have, however, shown varying rates of decline. Noteworthy is the case of Kerala, which, from an initial position among the high poverty ratio states, has recorded a decline to be among the states with a very low percentage of population below poverty line.

An analysis of poverty data suggests that the percentage of average annual exponential growth rate of poverty dropped from 0.05 per cent during 1973–74 and 1983–84 to –3.4 per cent during 1993–94 and 1999–2000 in India. The highest average annual exponential growth rate is found in Sikkim and lowest in West Bengal. The decrease in average annual exponential growth rate in poverty across these six years was around -3.4 per cent for the country as a whole. During the same period, the percentage of average annual exponential growth rate dropped by -61.57 per cent in West Bengal and it increased by 2.1 per cent in Sikkim.

Identified/Estimated Slum Population in India

As urban areas expand, they take over agricultural land causing direct damage to the ecosystem and further deterioration of the environment.

Table 1

Population Growth in the States of India, 1971–2001

States	Population in lakhs				Per cent annual exponential growth rate		
	1971	1981	1991	2001	1971–81	1981–91	1991–2001
Andhra Pradesh	435	536	665	762	2.1	2.19	1.37
Arunachal Pradesh	5	6	9	11	3.05	3.19	2.41
Assam	146	180	224	267	2.12	2.19	1.75
Bihar	564	699	864	1099	2.18	2.14	2.44
Goa	8	10	12	13	2.4	1.5	1.43
Gujarat	267	341	413	507	2.47	1.94	2.06
Haryana	100	129	165	211	2.56	2.45	2.53
Himachal Pradesh	35	43	52	61	2.15	1.91	1.63
Jammu and Kashmir	46	60	77	101	2.63	2.57	2.77
Karnataka	293	371	450	529	2.4	1.93	1.63
Kerala	213	255	291	318	1.78	1.35	0.9
Madhya Pradesh	417	522	662	812	2.28	2.41	2.06
Maharashtra	504	628	789	969	2.22	2.32	2.07
Manipur	11	14	18	22	2.85	2.6	1.67
Meghalaya	10	13	18	23	2.82	2.88	2.71
Mizoram	3	5	7	9	4.05	3.4	2.57
Nagaland	5	8	12	20	4.15	4.56	5.1
Orissa	219	264	317	368	1.85	1.85	1.52
Punjab	136	168	203	244	2.17	1.91	1.85
Rajasthan	258	343	440	565	2.89	2.53	2.53
Sikkim	2	3	4	5	4.17	2.54	2.91
Tamil Nadu	412	484	559	624	1.63	1.44	1.11
Tripura	16	21	28	32	2.81	2.99	1.5
Uttar Pradesh	883	1109	1391	1747	2.3	2.3	2.3
West Bengal	443	546	681	802	2.11	2.23	1.65
India	5482	6833	8463	10286	2.23	2.16	1.97

Source: Census of India (1971–2001).

The existence of slums is essentially a manifestation of poverty, along with economic growth and with industrial development. In spite of the efforts to contain the number of slum dwellers, it has been increasing fast, which is exerting tremendous pressure on urban basic services and infrastructure. The slum population in the country as on 1981 was 27.9 million out of the 159.5 million urban inhabitants constituting 17 per cent of the urban population (Table 3). It is estimated that in 1991 and

2001, the urban slum population totalled 21.3 per cent (46.26 million out of the 217.61 million urban inhabitants in 1991 and 61.82 million out of the 290.94 million urban inhabitants in 2001). More than 25 per cent of the estimated slum population is found in states such as Jammu and Kashmir, Himachal Pradesh, West Bengal, Sikkim, Maharashtra, and Meghalaya, whereas less than 15 per cent of the estimated slum population is found in Karnataka and Madhya Pradesh. Most of the slums in the country are located in the metropolitan cities. The sprouting of slums in urban areas is the direct outcome of better economic opportunities available in cities and towns. The slums are found on road sides, footpaths, playgrounds, park, on vacant government land, semi-government and private plots, railway stations, the sides of railway tracks, ditches, sewage canals, and embankments. All the slums have an extremely high population density, while offering poor shelter, inadequate water supplies, and poor drainage facilities.

Table 2

Poverty Ratio and Growth of Population Below Poverty Line in the States of India, 1973–1974 to 1999–2000

States	*Population below poverty line*				*Annual exponential growth rate (%)*		
	1973–74	*1983–84*	*1993–94*	*1999–2000*	*1973–74 to 1983–84*	*1983–84 to 1993–94*	*1993–94 to 1999–2000*
Andhra Pradesh	48.86	28.91	22.19	15.77	–3.11	–0.66	–4.2
Arunachal Pradesh	51.93	40.68	39.35	33.47	0.59	2.84	1.09
Assam	51.21	40.47	40.86	36.09	–0.52	2.18	–0.32
Bihar	61.91	62.22	54.96	42.6	2.23	0.66	–2.43
Goa	44.26	18.9	14.92	4.4	–6.04	–1.54	–15.41
Gujarat	48.15	32.79	24.21	14.07	–1.59	–1.14	–7.02
Haryana	35.36	21.37	25.05	8.74	–2.55	4.02	–14.34
Himachal Pradesh	26.39	16.4	28.44	7.63	–2.69	7.92	–17.19
Jammu and Kashmir	40.83	24.24	25.17	3.48	–2.69	2.98	–25.91
Karnataka	54.47	38.24	33.16	20.04	–1.3	0.44	–6.52
Kerala	59.79	40.42	25.43	12.72	–2.36	3.29	–9.71
Madhya Pradesh	61.78	49.78	42.52	37.43	0.06	0.72	0
Maharashtra	53.24	43.44	36.86	25.02	0.12	0.48	–4.75

Cont'd...

...Cont'd

Manipur	49.96	37.02	33.78	28.54	–0.36	1.87	0.93
Meghalaya	50.2	38.81	37.92	33.87	0.18	2.76	1.83
Mizoram	50.32	36	25.66	19.47	0.74	–0.1	–0.79
Nagaland	50.81	39.25	37.92	32.67	1.9	3.73	1.4
Orissa	66.18	65.29	48.56	47.15	1.61	–1.21	0.86
Punjab	28.15	16.18	11.77	6.16	–3.4	–1.31	–8.76
Rajasthan	46.14	34.46	27.41	15.28	–0.13	0.13	–7.25
Sikkim	50.86	39.71	41.43	36.55	1.27	2.98	2.1
Tamil Nadu	54.94	51.66	35.03	21.12	0.83	–2.49	–7.03
Tripura	51	40.03	39.01	34.44	0.47	2.79	–1.13
Uttar Pradesh	57.07	47.07	40.85	31.15	0.39	0.83	–15.92
West Bengal	63.43	54.85	35.66	27.02	0.63	–2.22	–61.57
India	54.88	44.48	35.97	26.1	0.05	–0.21	–3.4

Source: Ninth Five-Year Plan 1997–2002.

Notes: 1. Poverty ratio of Assam is used for Sikkim, Arunachal Pradesh, Meghalaya, Manipur, Nagaland, and Tripura.

2. Poverty line of Maharashtra and expenditure distribution of Goa is used to estimate poverty ratio of Goa.

3. Poverty line of Himachal Pradesh and expenditure distribution of Jammu and Kashmir is used to estimate poverty ratio of Jammu and Kashmir.

4. Poverty ratio of Tamil Nadu is used for Pondicherry and Andaman and Nicobar Islands.

5. Urban poverty ratio of Punjab used for both rural and urban Poverty of Chandigarh.

6. Poverty ratio of Goa is used for Daman and Diu.

7. Poverty ratio of Kerala is used for Lakshadweep.

8. Urban poverty ratio of Rajasthan for the year 1999–2000 may be treated as tentative.

9. Poverty ratio of Himachal Pradesh is used for Jammu and Kashmir for 1993–94.

The effects of population growth and poverty on environmental problems are associated with changing consumption pattern, rising demand for energy, pressure on land, and deforestation. Deforestation, decline in pastures and grazing lands, overgrazing, cultivation of marginal lands, and cultivation of agricultural lands, all contribute to a host of land-related environmental problems. These include soil erosion, desertification, salinization, waterlogging, depletion of ground water resources, ground and surface water pollution, and losses in soil nutrients. However, decline in forest cover and grazing lands are closely associated with many of these problems and can provide some indication of the magnitude of environmental degradation in India.

Table 3

State-wise Identified/Estimated Slum Population in India

(population in lakh)

States/UTs	*1981*			*1991*			*2001*		
	Urban population	*Identified slum population*	*Per cent*	*Urban population*	*Estimated slum population*	*Per cent*	*Urban population*	*Estimated slum population*	*Per cent*
States	1528.8	260.2	17	2078.8	436.46	21	2769.4	580.67	21
Andhra Pradesh	124.88	28.579	22.9	178.87	43.133	24.1	249.65	60.166	24
Arunachal Pradesh	0.414	Nil	Nil	1.106	0.221	20	1.879	0.375	20
Assam	17.824	1.236	6.9	24.878	4.483	18	32.367	5.826	18
Bihar	87.19	32.699	37.5	113.53	26.906	23.7	149.56	35.444	23.7
Goa	3.518	0.242	6.9	4.798	0.883	17.4	6.559	1.141	17.4
Gujarat	106.02	15.316	14.4	142.46	25.814	18.1	189.99	34.388	18.1
Haryana	28.274	2.742	9.7	40.547	6.843	16.9	59.572	10.067	16.9
Himachal Pradesh	3.26	0.761	23.3	4.492	1.258	28	5.765	1.614	28
Jammu and Kashmir	12.604	6.27	49.7	18.394	5.922	32.2	24.173	7.783	32.2
Karnataka	107.3	5.745	5.4	139.08	12.934	9.3	190.99	17.761	9.3
Kerala	47.713	4.101	8.6	76.803	12.218	15.9	103.47	16.452	15.9
Madhya Pradesh	105.87	10.749	10.2	153.39	21.029	13.7	204.05	27.954	13.7
Maharashtra	219.94	43.149	19.6	305.42	78.724	25.8	416.16	107.37	25.8
Manipur	3.755	0.165	4.4	5.056	0.853	16.9	6.702	1.132	16.9
Meghalaya	2.413	0.66	27.4	3.3	0.833	25.2	4.608	1.161	25.2
Mizoram	2.218	Nil	Nil	3.179	0.572	18	6.424	1.156	18
Nagaland	1.202	Nil	Nil	3.082	0.416	20	3.049	0.609	20
Orissa	31.103	2.82	9.1	42.35	8.432	19.9	56.32	11.207	19.9
Punjab	46.478	11.668	25.1	59.932	14.144	23.6	80.241	18.936	23.6
Rajasthan	72.105	10.252	14.2	100.67	24	23.8	137.19	32.651	23.8
Sikkim	0.511	0.024	4.7	0.37	0.095	25.7	0.479	0.123	25.7
Tamil Nadu	159.52	26.76	16.8	190.78	35.713	18.7	233.08	43.585	18.7
Tripura	2.256	0.184	8.2	4.217	0.744	17.6	5.078	0.893	17.6
Uttar Pradesh	198.99	25.8	13	276.06	58.391	21.1	365.4	77.098	21.1
West Bengal	144.47	30.28	21	187.08	51.949	27.8	236.62	65.78	27.8
India	1594.6	279.14	17.5	2176.1	462.61	21.3	2909.4	618.26	21.3

Source: Compendium of Environment Statistics (2002).

Pressure on Land

India faces an acute pressure on agricultural land. Over the last 40 years, while India's total population increased by about two times, the total area of land under cultivation increased marginally by 8 million hectares (5%) from 158 million hectares to 166 million hectares. Despite the past expansion of the area under cultivation, agricultural land available to feed each person decreased. A change in land utilization pattern implies either an increase or a decrease in the proportion of area under different land uses at two or more points of time. Table 4 describes the land utilization pattern in India from 1971 to 2001. It shows variations in land use with a narrow range of fluctuations in the proportion of net sown area to total land in the country from 1971 to 2001. Out of total geographical area of 329 million hectares, only 306 million hectares is the reporting area (the rest being unadministered for various reasons). The land for non-agricultural uses (housing, industry, and others) has increased from 16.48 million hectares in 1971 to 23.57 million hectares in 2001. About 19 million hectares are snow bound and remote, leaving only 264 million hectare for agriculture, forestry, pasture, and other biomass production. The net sown area under cultivation has increased marginally from 140 million hectares in 1971 to 141 million hectares in 2001, indicating that the private efforts have peaked and the intervention of the government is required for further land reclamation. The extent of agricultural intensification and extensification is characterized by the increase in the cropping and irrigation intensity and by the higher use of chemical fertilizers, pesticides, and insecticides. The processes of agricultural extensification and intensification are leading to land degradation, overexploitation of underground water resources, and increased use of chemical fertilizers leading to eutrophication and water pollution. Agricultural intensification due to increasing cropping intensity, irrigation intensity, and excessive use of chemical fertilizers results in reducing the biodiversity by causing water logging, salinization and alkalinization of croplands, and eutrophication of water bodies and ill health of oceans.

Pressure on Forests

The category forest includes all areas actually under forests whether state owned or private and administered as forests under any legal enactment dealing with forests. The forest area and percentage of forest area in the states of India from 1971 to 2001 are given in Table 5. India has a forest cover of 69,407 thousand hectares. This accounts for 23 per cent of total geographical area against the 33 per cent recommended by the National Forest Policy of 1988 to maintain the ecological balance. Thus, there is scope to extensify land under forest. The forest cover in India increased from 65,757 thousand hectares in 1971 to 69,407 thousand hectares in 2001, an increase of 3650 thousand hectares. The percentage of forest area in India increased from 22 per cent in 1971 to 23 per cent in 2001. Yet there were variations at the state levels, the states of Gujarat, Haryana, Punjab,

Table 4

Land Use Patterns in India, 1971–2001

(million hectares)

Classification	*1970–1971*	*1980–1981*	*1990–1991*	*2000–2001*
I. Geographical area	328.73	328.73	328.73	328.73
II. Reporting area for land utilization statistics (1–5)	303.76	304.15	304.86	306.25
1. Forests	63.91	67.47	67.8	69.41
2. Not available for cultivation (a + b)	44.64	39.62	40.48	42.83
(a) Non-agricultural uses	16.48	19.66	21.09	23.57
(b) Barren and unculturable land	28.16	19.96	19.39	19.26
3. Other uncultivated land (excluding fallow land) (a + b + c)	35.06	32.31	30.22	28.47
(a) Permanent pasture and other grazing land	13.26	11.97	11.4	10.9
(b) Land under miscellaneous tree crops and grooves not included in net area sown	4.3	3.6	3.82	3.37
(c) Culturable wasteland	17.5	16.74	15	13.66
4. Fallow land (a + b)	19.88	24.75	23.36	24.91
(a) Fallow land other than current fallows	8.76	9.92	9.66	10.19
(b) Current fallows	11.12	14.83	13.7	14.8
5. Net area sown	140.27	140	143	141.1
6. Gross cropped area	165.79	172.63	185.74	187.01
7. Area sown more than once	25.52	32.63	42.74	45.91
8. Cropping intensity*	118.2	123.3	129.9	132.54
III. Net irrigated area	31.1	38.72	47.78	54.68
IV. Gross irrigated area	38.19	49.78	62.47	75.14

*Cropping intensity is obtained by gross cropped area by net area sown.

Sources: Compendium of Environment Statistics, 2000.
Statistical Abstract of India (2002).

Rajasthan, and West Bengal were found to have less than 15 per cent of forests. The states of Andhra Pradesh, Assam, Bihar, Himachal Pradesh, Karnataka, Kerala, Maharashtra, Manipur, Tamil Nadu, and Uttar Pradesh were found to have 16–30 per cent of forests. The states of Himachal Pradesh, Madhya Pradesh, Orissa and Sikkim were found to have 31–45 per cent of forest land. Highest percentage was recorded in Arunachal Pradesh, Mizoram, and Jammu and Kashmir, followed by the states of Tripura, Nagaland, and Madhya Pradesh that had more than 48 per cent of forest land during 2001.

The changes and growth in forest area of the states in India are presented in Table 6. The states of Bihar, Goa, Gujarat, Haryana, Karnataka, Kerala, Madhya Pradesh, Meghalaya, Mizoram, Nagaland, Orissa, Punjab, Rajasthan, Tamil Nadu, Uttar Pradesh, and West Bengal experienced an increase in the forest area from 1971 to 2001, whereas the other states experienced a decline in forest area. The average annual exponential growth rate of forest area decline from 0.25 per cent in 1971 to 0.21 per cent in 2001. The highest average annual exponential growth rate is found 3 per cent in Orissa and lowest -4 per cent in Haryana during 1991 to 2001. The states which have shown decline in average annual exponential growth rate of forest area are Andhra Pradesh, Arunachal Pradesh, Assam, Goa, Gujarat, Jammu and Kashmir, Madhya Pradesh, Sikkim, and Uttar Pradesh, whereas other states experienced an increase in average annual exponential growth rate of forest area during 1991 to 2001. The increase in the forest area may be attributed to the forest and social forestry programmes and to the afforestation of privately owned land. The decrease in the forest area may be due to deforestation, forest area coming under cultivation, and the demand for wood and the other forest products to satisfy the human wants of fuel, wooden implements, timber, and for other purposes. Forests are an important natural resource of India. They have moderate influence against floods and thus they protect the soil erosion. Forests also play an important role in enhancing the quality of environment by influencing the ecological balance and life support system (checking soil erosion, maintaining soil fertility, conserving water, regulating water cycles and floods, balancing carbon dioxide and oxygen content in atmosphere, etc.).

In 1981–1983, only 11.2 per cent of country's total land area comprises dense forest with a crown density of more than 40 per cent, thus reflecting a qualitative decline of forests in the country. The total forest area diverted for non-forestry purposes between 1950 and 1980 was 4.5 million hectares, i.e., at an annual rate of 0.15 million hectare. To regulate unabated diversion of forest land for non-forestry purposes, Forest (Conservation) Act, 1980, was enacted. It has resulted in reduction of diversion of forest area for non-forestry purposes considerably and the present rate of diversion is 16,000 hectare annually (Government of India, 1999). Continuing deforestation, therefore, has brought us face to face with a major ecological and socio-economic crisis.

Table 5

Forest Area in the States of India, 1971–2001

States	*Forest area (000 hectare)*				*Percentage of forest area*			
	1971	*1981*	*1991*	*2001*	*1971*	*1981*	*1991*	*2001*
Andhra Pradesh	6240	6213	6268	6199	22.74	22.64	22.84	22.59
Arunachal Pradesh	5154	5154	5200	5154	91.32	92.86	93.8	93.74
Assam	2080	1985	1984	1932	26.68	25.28	25.27	24.61
Bihar	2797	2826	2949	2949	16.14	16.31	17.02	17.02
Goa	105	105	105	125	28.38	28.3	29.09	34.63
Gujarat	1634	1966	1888	1865	8.8	10.45	10.03	9.91
Haryana	110	132	170	115	2.5	3	3.88	2.61
Himachal Pradesh	2783	807	1039	1094	54.83	27.04	30.85	24.06
Jammu and Kashmir	2776	2919	2747	2747	61.38	62.44	60.98	60.98
Karnataka	2895	3033	3074	3068	15.2	15.92	16.14	16.1
Kerala	1055	1081	1081	1082	27.34	27.82	27.82	27.85
Madhya Pradesh	14405	14044	14326	14958	32.56	31.77	32.31	48.64
Maharashtra	5417	5309	5410	5296	17.61	17.26	17.59	17.22
Manipur	602	602	602	602	27.23	27.23	27.23	27.23
Meghalaya	187	812	939	951	8.31	36.1	41.94	42.7
Mizoram	1298	1303	1303	1626	62.05	61.99	61.99	77.1
Nagaland	266	288	862	863	19.69	26.64	56.27	54.31
Orissa	4973	6640	5476	5813	32	42.73	35.24	37.33
Punjab	127	220	222	305	2.52	4.37	4.41	6.06
Rajasthan	1401	2088	2354	2606	4.09	6.1	6.87	7.61
Sikkim	NA	262	257	257	NA	36.44	36.2	36.2
Tamil Nadu	2007	2023	2155	2134	15.43	15.56	16.55	16.43
Tripura	630	578	606	606	60.11	55.15	57.77	57.77
Uttar Pradesh	4952	5129	5162	5155	16.6	17.25	17.33	17.32
West Bengal	1101	1184	1091	1190	12.44	13.38	12.33	13.7
India	65757	67421	67995	69407	21.52	22.17	22.29	22.66

Source: Statistical Abstract of India (1971–2001).

Table 6

Changes and Growth of Forests in the States of India, 1971–2001

States	*Changes during 1971–1981*	*Changes during 1981–1991*	*Changes during 1991–2001*	*Changes during 1971–2001*	*1971–1981*	*1981–1991*	*1991–2001*
Andhra Pradesh	–27	55	–69	–41	–0.04	0.09	–0.11
Arunachal Pradesh	0	46	–46	0	0	0.09	–0.09
Assam	–95	–1	–52	–148	–0.47	–0.01	–0.27
Bihar	29	123	0	152	0.1	0.43	0
Goa	0	0	20	20	0	0	1.76
Gujarat	332	–78	–23	231	1.87	–0.4	–0.12
Haryana	22	38	–55	5	1.84	2.56	–3.83
Himachal Pradesh	–1976	232	55	–1689	–11.64	2.56	0.52
Jammu and Kashmir	143	–172	0	–29	0.5	–0.61	0
Karnataka	138	41	–6	173	0.47	0.13	–0.02
Kerala	26	0	1	27	0.24	0	0.01
Madhya Pradesh	–361	282	632	553	–0.25	0.2	0.43
Maharashtra	–108	101	–114	–121	–0.2	0.19	–0.21
Manipur	0	0	0	0	0	0	0
Meghalaya	625	127	12	764	15.82	1.46	0.13
Mizoram	5	0	323	328	0.04	0	2.24
Nagaland	22	574	1	597	0.8	11.59	0.01
Orissa	1667	–1164	337	840	2.93	–1.91	0.6
Punjab	93	2	83	178	5.65	0.09	3.23
Rajasthan	687	266	252	1205	4.07	1.21	1.02
Sikkim	NA	–5	0	NA	NA	–0.19	0
Tamil Nadu	16	132	–21	127	0.08	0.63	–0.1
Tripura	–52	28	0	–24	–0.86	0.47	0
Uttar Pradesh	177	33	–7	203	0.35	0.06	–0.01
West Bengal	83	–93	99	89	0.73	–0.81	0.87
India	1664	574	1412	3650	0.25	0.08	0.21

Soil Erosion and Land Degradation in India

Direct impacts of agricultural development on the environment arise from farming activities, which contribute to soil erosion, land salination, and loss of nutrients. The spread of green revolution has been accompanied by overexploitation of land and water resources and use of fertilizers and pesticides has increased manyfolds. Shifting cultivation has also been an important cause of land degradation. Leaching from extensive use of pesticides and fertilizers is an important source of contamination of water bodies. Intensive agriculture and irrigation contribute to land degradation particularly salination, alkalization, and water logging. It is evident that most of the land in the country is degrading, thus affecting the productive resource base of the economy.

Land is degraded when it suffers a loss of intrinsic qualities, decline in its capabilities, or loss in its productive capacity. Land degradation may be due to natural causes or human causes or it may be due to combination of both. Soil erosion is the major cause of land degradation. Soil is the non-renewable natural resource, which supports life on earth. The estimated state-wise area affected by soil erosion and land degradation in India during 1984 is given in Table 7. The estimated area affected by soil erosion and land degradation in 1984 is considered to be 1731.1 lakh hectares. Land affected by soil erosion is the major contributor of 1266.2 lakh hectares and land degraded through the other problems is 465 lakh hectares. The highest estimated land affected by soil erosion and land degradation is 374 lakh hectares (21.6%) in Rajasthan, and land affected by soil erosion contributes to 199 lakh hectares and 175 lakh hectares through other problems. The estimated land affected by soil erosion and land degradation varies from 78 lakh hectares to 207 lakh hectares (4.5–12%) in Orissa, Karnataka, Andhra Pradesh, Gujarat, Uttar Pradesh, Maharashtra, and Madhya Pradesh. The estimated land affected by soil erosion was highest in Rajasthan (199 lakh hectares), followed by Madhya Pradesh (196.1 lakh hectares), Maharashtra (191.8 lakh hectares), Andhra Pradesh (115 lakh hectares), Karnataka (109.9 lakh hectares), Gujarat (99.5 lakh hectares), and Uttar Pradesh (71.1 lakh hectares). The estimated land degraded through other problems was highest in Rajasthan (174.9 lakh hectares), followed by Uttar Pradesh (60.1 lakh hectares), West Bengal (32.7 lakh hectares), Orissa (32.3 lakh hectares), Gujarat (26.4 lakh hectares), and Haryana (25.7 lakh hectares). The estimated area of land affected by soil erosion and land degradation in India varies from state to state and it varies 0.1 per cent in Goa to 21.6 per cent in Rajasthan. Soil erosion results in huge loss of nutrients in suspension or solution, which are removed away from one place to another, thus causing depletion or enrichment of nutrients. Besides the loss of nutrients from top soil, there is also degradation through the creation of gullies and ravines, which make the land unsuitable for agricultural production.

Relationship between Population Growth and Poverty

The association between changes in population growth in relation to poverty growth during the four decades from 1971 to 2001 is presented in Table 8. One would expect a positive association between population and poverty growth. But from the examination of Table 8, there is no such strong relationship between the growth of population and poverty. However, there are very wide interstate variations in relationship between the growth of population and poverty. In 1971–1981, it was seen that there was a positive association between population and poverty growth. Eight states recorded both high growth of population and poverty, while six states had low population and poverty growth.

Table 7

Estimates of Area Affected by Soil Erosion and Land Degradation in India, 1984

(lakh hectares)

States/UTs	*Land affected by soil erosion*	*Land degraded through other problems*	*Total problems area*	*Per cent to all India total*
Rajasthan	199	174.9	373.9	21.6
Madhya Pradesh	196.1	11.1	207.2	12
Maharashtra	191.8	6.7	198.5	11.5
Uttar Pradesh	71.1	60.1	131.2	7.6
Gujarat	99.5	26.4	125.9	7.3
Andhra Pradesh	115	7.3	122.3	7.1
Karnataka	109.9	4.1	114	6.6
Orissa	45.8	32.3	78.1	4.5
Bihar	42.6	22.9	65.5	3.8
West Bengal	10.3	32.7	43	2.5
Haryana	15.9	25.7	41.6	2.4
Tamil Nadu	36.4	1.8	38.2	2.2
Punjab	10.1	22.3	32.4	1.9
Assam	22.2	7.8	30	1.7
Arunachal Pradesh	24.4	2.1	26.5	1.5
Kerala	17.6	1.8	19.4	1.1
Himachal Pradesh	19.1	—	19.1	1.1
Meghalaya	8.4	2.7	11.1	0.6
Jammu and Kashmir	8.8	0.1	8.9	0.5
Manipur	3.7	3.6	7.3	0.4
Mizoram	4.2	1.9	6.1	0.4
Nagaland	4.1	0.8	4.9	0.3
Sikkim	3	—	3	0.2
Tripura	1.7	1.1	2.8	0.2
Goa	2	—	2	0.1
Union Territories	3.4	—	3.4	0.2
India	1266.2	464.9	1731.1	100

Source: The State of Forest Report (1999).

Gujarat, Haryana, Jammu and Kashmir, Karnataka, Manipur, and Rajasthan states had high rates of population growth and low growth rates of poverty. Bihar, Maharashtra, Orissa, Tamil Nadu, and West Bengal had low growth rates of population and high growth rates of poverty. In 1981–1991, also a positive association was witnessed between population and poverty growth. Thirteen states showed both high growth of population and poverty, five states had low rate of population growth and poverty, while five states had low rate of population growth with high poverty growth. Andhra Pradesh and West Bengal had high population growth with low poverty growth. In 1991–2001, seven states recorded both high growth of population and poverty, while eight states had low population and poverty growth. Gujarat, Haryana, Jammu and Kashmir, Maharashtra, Rajasthan, and Uttar Pradesh states had high rates of population growth and low growth rates of poverty. Assam, Manipur, Orissa, and Tripura had low growth rates of population and high growth rates of poverty. The average state figures of the corresponding variables are considered here to calculate the high and low value.

Relationship between the Growth of Population and Forests

The relationship between the growth of population and forests is presented in Table 9. One would expect a negative association between the growth of population and forests. The bivariate distribution showed interstate variations in relationships between the growth of population and forests. In the decade 1971–1981, Gujarat, Haryana, Meghalaya, and Rajasthan states recorded both high growth of population and forests, while eight states had low population growth and forests. Eight states had high rates of population and low growth rates of forests. In contrast, Karnataka, Orissa, Punjab, Uttar Pradesh, and West Bengal states had low rates of population and high growth rates of forests. During 1981–1991, an inconsistent relationship between the growth rate of population and forests is also observed in most of the states in the country. The high growth rate of both population and forest is found in nine states. In contrast, the low growth rate of both population and forests is observed in six states. Five states experienced high population growth with low forests and five states have low population growth with high forests. In the decade 1991–2001, Madhya Pradesh, Mizoram, and Rajasthan states registered both high population and forests growth. Eight states registered low population and forest growth, whereas 10 states registered high population growth and low forest growth. On the other hand, Goa, Himachal Pradesh, Punjab, and West Bengal had low population growth with high forest growth.

Table 8

Relationship between Population and Poverty in the States of India, 1971–2001

States	*1971–1981*	*1981–1991*	*1991–2001*
Andhra Pradesh	LL	HL	LL
Arunachal Pradesh	HH	HH	HH
Assam	LL	HH	LH
Bihar	LH	LH	HH
Goa	LL	LL	LL
Gujarat	HL	LL	HL
Haryana	HL	HH	HL
Himachal Pradesh	LL	LH	LL
Jammu and Kashmir	HL	HH	HL
Karnataka	HL	LH	LL
Kerala	LL	LH	LL
Madhya Pradesh	HH	HH	HH
Maharashtra	LH	HH	HL
Manipur	HL	LH	LH
Meghalaya	HH	HH	HH
Mizoram	HH	HH	HH
Nagaland	HH	HH	HH
Orissa	LH	LL	LH
Punjab	LL	LL	LL
Rajasthan	HL	HH	HL
Sikkim	HH	HH	HH
Tamil Nadu	LH	LL	LL
Tripura	HH	HH	LH
Uttar Pradesh	HH	HH	HL
West Bengal	LH	HL	LL

Notes: HH = High growth of population and high growth of poverty.
HL = High growth of population and low growth of poverty.
LH = Low growth of population and high growth of poverty.
LL = Low growth of population and low growth of poverty.
The average state figures of the corresponding variables are considered here as the crossing point of H and L cropped area.

Table 9

Relationship between Population and Forest in the States of India, 1971–2001

States	*1971–1981*	*1981–1991*	*1991–2001*
Andhra Pradesh	LL	HH	LL
Arunachal Pradesh	HL	HH	HL

Cont'd...

...Cont'd

Assam	LL	HL	LL
Bihar	LL	LH	HL
Goa	LL	LL	LH
Gujarat	HH	LL	HL
Haryana	HH	HH	HL
Himachal Pradesh	LL	LH	LH
Jammu and Kashmir	HL	HL	HL
Karnataka	LH	LH	LL
Kerala	LL	LL	LL
Madhya Pradesh	HL	HH	HH
Maharashtra	LL	HH	HL
Manipur	HL	LL	LL
Meghalaya	HH	HH	HL
Mizoram	HL	HL	HH
Nagaland	HL	HH	HL
Orissa	LH	LL	LL
Punjab	LH	LH	LH
Rajasthan	HH	HH	HH
Sikkim	HL	HL	HL
Tamil Nadu	LL	LH	LL
Tripura	HL	HH	LL
Uttar Pradesh	LH	LL	HL
West Bengal	LH	HL	LH

Notes: HH = High growth of population and high growth of forest.
HL = High growth of population and low growth of forest.
LH = Low growth of population and high growth of forest.
LL = Low growth of population and low growth of forest.
The average state figures of the corresponding variables are considered here as the crossing point of H and L cropped area.

Conclusions and Policy Implications

The analysis revealed that poverty and rapid population growth are found to coexist and seem to reinforce each other. There is no strong relationship between the growth of population and poverty, and growth of population and forests. However, there are very wide interstate variations in relationship between these variables. The country's population growth and poverty is imposing an increasing burden on the country's limited and continually degrading natural resource base. Population pressure on arable land contributes to the land degradation, thus affecting the productive resource base of the economy. It also contributes to environmental degradation through soil erosion and land degradation. From the effects of growth of population on poverty and environmental degradation, there is a need to give top priority to control population, poverty, and environmental degradation. The only viable long-term strategy for poverty eradication is increasing incomes of those engaged in agriculture. Such income growth will be gradual and only benefit the environment over the longer term. It should therefore be supplemented with targeted interventions that directly alleviate the risks faced by poor and secure their rights to natural resources. The creation of employment opportunities is essential in agricultural areas where high poverty, unemployment, and landlessness exist. In order to increase green cover and to preserve the existing forests, afforestation and social forestry programmes should be implemented at the local level.

References

Central Statistical Organisation (2000 and 2002). *Compendium of Environment Statistics*. New Delhi: Ministry of Statistics and Programme Implementation, Government of India.

Central Statistical Organisation (1971–2002). *Statistical Abstract of India*. New Delhi: Ministry of Statistics and Programme Implementation, Government of India.

Government of India (1999). "Economic Survey: 1998–99", Ministry of Finance, Economic Division, New Delhi.

Government of India (1999). *The State of Forest Report*. Dehradun: Ministry of Environment and Forests, Forest Survey of India.

Government of India (2000). *Ninth Five-Year Plan 1997–2002*, Volume-I. New Delhi: Ministry of Finance, Economic Division.

Gupta, K. (1997). 'Population growth, environmental degradation and its consequences for women's development in U.P.'. In Gupta, K., and Pandey, A. (eds.): *Population and Development in Uttar Pradesh* (pp. 415–416). Delhi: B.R. Publishing Corporation.

Registrar General and Census Commissioner of India (1971–1991). *Population Totals*. New Delhi: Census of India, Government of India.

Registrar General and Census Commissioner of India (2001). *Provisional Population Totals*. Paper 1 of 2001. New Delhi: Census of India.

United Nations (1973). Report of the United Nations Conference on the Human Environment, Stockholm, 5–16 June 1972.

United Nations (1992). *The United Nations Conference on the Environment and Development (UNCED)*, Rio de Janeiro.

United Nations (1997). *Population and Environment Dynamics, Poverty and Quality of Life in Countries of the ESCAP Region*. New York: United Nations.

Part III

Local Perspectives: Case Studies

12

Thinking about the Rural Poor

A Brief Appraisal of Rural Development Programmes in India with Special Reference to Ambedkar Gram Vikas Yojana

RAVI S. SINGH AND KAVITA JAIJAN

The word 'rural' continues to catch our attention (cf. Dev, 2004) as more than 70 per cent population of the India's national population and 79 per cent of Uttar Pradesh's population still live in rural areas. If academic engagements could be taken as some indicator of it, the frequency of articles dealing with 'rural' in a weekly academic magazine such as *Economic and Political Weekly* (EPW) is a good enough indicator. Any sensible society cannot afford to ignore such a large chunk of population. And, in the parliamentary democratic system, their neglect may cost the political parties heavily. One may state that if the development of these areas and people inhabiting them is ignored, it might bring disaster to both the local and national economies. Rural development means the development of rural economy as well as society. It is a part of a longer process of development of a national society of India such as developing countries of the Global South. The objectives of rural development are reduction of inequalities in income, employment, and the alleviation of poverty. World Bank defines rural development as a strategy designed to improve the income and social life of a specific group of people – the rural poor (World Bank, 1989). It involves extending the benefits of development to the poorest among those who seek a livelihood in the rural areas. It emphasizes that the overall goal of national development, growth, employment, equity, individual dignity, participation, and social competence will have to combat institutional forms which have the tendency to cause stagnation, concentration of social surplus in few hands, and alienation of a few sections in the society. Such sections include small-scale farmers, tenants, and the landless. In this backdrop, the objective of this paper is to present a brief appraisal of different rural development programmes implemented in India and a review of the Ambedkar Gram Vikas Yojana (AGVY) implemented by the Government of Uttar Pradesh.

Rural Change, Politics, and Development Agenda

Some like Dipankar Gupta may argue on the basis of own experience of rural India that with growing non-farm income in rural areas, perception regarding development and identity changes (Gupta, 2005). However, same sort of changes may not be the reality in all other parts where caste clutches are still steel-strong and bloody too. Uttar Pradesh is one such state where 'caste' has emerged as a very important factor in politics since the recent past. Pai et al. (2005), while attempting a critical appraisal of the Uttar Pradesh of the 1990s, referred to three facts – the phenomenon of 'majoritarianism' as the 'strategy under the hegemony of the upper castes', 'sandwiching' of the most backward castes between the emerging *dalit* assertion and dominant middle castes, and the rise of Bahujan Samaj Party (BSP) which has directly contributed to improving self-esteem among them together with long-term gains in terms self-confidence, political consciousness, local-level developmental leadership, and the strength to reckon with the power to challenge the political hegemony of the upper castes. Taking a critical view of the role played by media in projecting the BSP as 'party without an ideology and principle clamouring for power', it is argued by Kumar (2003) that emergence of this party has lead to change in the 'established social structure'. One may take the AGVY as a programme launched to co-ordinate as many as 36 rural development programmes but if seen critically, it was also an attempt to show that the BSP cares about the *dalits*. It is again believed that the BSP's emergence in Uttar Pradesh should be seen as the deconstruction and reconstruction of the new *dalit* identity. His understanding is not baseless rather it is logical in the sense that the BSP's model of *dalit* upliftment is based on political empowerment. The BSP government in Uttar Pradesh introduced many welfare measures for dalits including the AGVY. In 1995, such programmes received funds to the tune of 21.57 per cent of the total fund allocation and also distributed land to the landless *dalit* families (cf. Pai, 2004).

The development of infrastructure is very important if seen from the socio-economic development perspective. Rural electrification is one such infrastructure which can not only illuminate the 'dark houses' but also free them from 'smoky hearths' as reported by Mathur and

Mathur (2005) in their study apart from enlightening the process of education and strengthening health care indirectly. Through a wide gap between contemplated capacity and actually generated is found, on top of that the neglect of operation and maintenance is also apparent as reported by Reddy (2003) with respect to irrigation.

A survey reports that the word 'dalit' is neither popular nor commonly used by a member of this section of the society which refers to self as belonging to a particular *jati* or *harijan* or in a few limited cases even SC (Marriott, 2003). The issue of caste-based denial or violation of human rights in India has been visited by many revealing almost similar nature of problem. In a recent study of Thorat (2002), it is found that despite several constitutional provisions, this problem continues to persist ubiquitously perpetuating the exploitation of the dalits, of course in modified forms, especially in the rural areas where the underclass are yet to be fully politically mobilized against the dominant class (Chakravarti, 2001; Pai, 2004). Such a practice quite naturally results in the deprivation which is higher in the state where general development condition is quite poor (Srinivasan and Mohanty, 2004).

Development Programmes for the Rural Areas

To solve the problem of rural areas after independence, government introduced different developmental programmes. These developmental programmes are directly or indirectly affected by the concept of rural development which is changing in nature. Before 1980, the concept of rural development was mainly focused on the development of agriculture and allied activities. In response, quite naturally, the developmental programmes and schemes introduced in this time period are mainly related with the agriculture and allied sector. Package Programme (1960), District Intensive Agriculture Development Programme (1960), Tribal Development Programme (1968), Drought Prone Area Programme (1970), Command Area Development Programme (1974), Hill Area Development Programme (1974), Food for Work Programme (1977), Desert Development Programme (1977), Integrated Rural Development Programme (1978–1979), Training of Rural Youth for Self-Employment (1979), etc., are the major programmes introduced by the government before 1980 period. After 1980, the nature of developmental programmes changed. Development of infrastructure (physical and social), poverty alleviation, and employment generation in rural areas are the main issue for the government. Integrated Rural Energy Programme (1981), Development of Women and Children in Rural Areas (1983), Indira Awas Yojana (1985), Jawahar Rozgar Yojana (1989) restructured as Jawahar

Gram Samridhi Yojana, Operation Black Board (1990), Ambedkar Vishesh Rojgar Yojana (1991), AGVY (1991), Intensified Jawahar Rozgar Yojana (1993), Employment Assurance Scheme (1993), Ganga Kalyan Yojana (1997), Rural Housing Scheme (1998), Swarnajayanti Gram Swarozgar Yojana (1999), Pradhan Mantri Gram Sadak Yojana (2000), Pradhan Mantri Gramodaya Yojana (2000), Sampoorna Grameen Rozgar Yojana (2001), Accelerated Rural Water Supply Programme, National Drinking Water Mission, Rajiv Gandhi Drinking Water Mission, Rajiv Gandhi Grameen Vidyutikaran Yojana, National Rural Employment Guarantee Scheme (2006), etc., are major programmes introduced by the government in the post-1980 period.

Community Development Programme, or CDP (1952), was the first attempt towards the balance development, introduced by the government with the objective to build infrastructure in the rural areas with the participation of rural community. But the CDP was not successful in achieving the goals due the lack of coordination between the government bodies/agencies.

Tribal population mainly living in the forest area, hilly or rough surfaced regions, is socially and economically backward, mostly illiterate, very high death rate, and living below the poverty line. The Tribal Development Programme was introduced in 1968 with the objective to improve the living standard of tribal people. This programme has a great importance in the development of tribal people. This programme provides chance to the unknown and depressed section of the society, but due the corruption at different levels in the government bodies, this programme has been unable to achieve its aims and objectives.

To reduce the poverty and to generate the employment government introduced different programmes, food for work is one of them introduced in 1977. In this programme, the wages are given in the form of both food grains and cash. This programme was expected to play an important role in the employment generation in the rural areas. But, it was partly success due to the limited job days, wrong selection of participants (cf. Dogra, 2005).

IRDP, introduced in 1978, continues to be a major poverty alleviation programme in the process of rural development. The objectives of IRDP are to enable identified rural poor families to cross the poverty line by providing productive assets and inputs to the target groups in the form of subsidy. IRDP has a major role in the balanced development of rural society. However, due to the weak coordination between different government bodies, the programme was not successful in achieving its goals (cf. Marsden and Gillian, 2000).

To meet the shortage of housing in rural areas, the Indira Awas Yojana (IAY) was launched in May 1985, with specific aims to providing assistance to rural people below the poverty line belonging to SC/ST categories in construction of dwelling units and upgradation of existing unserviceable kachcha houses by providing grants-in-aid. Under this programme, the allotment is done in the name of female member and minimum of 60 per cent of fund is to be utilized for the construction of houses of the SCs/STs. Around 129 lakh houses have been constructed/upgraded during 1985–1986 to 2004–2005 onward under the scheme with an expenditure of ₹ 23,149.16 crore. IAY plays a very important role in the development of rural infrastructure, but selection of wrong beneficiaries and corruption in local government body badly affected the achievement of the IAY.

The objective of introducing Jawahar Rozgar Yojana (JRY) was to generate the additional gainful employment for the unemployed and under-employed men and women in the rural areas and creation of sustainable employment by strengthening the rural economic infrastructure.

Operation Blackboard was introduced by the government to promote the education in the rural areas. Universalization of primary education is the basic input for acquisition of functional skills which are absolutely essential for promoting self-reliance of the rural poor and their children. Sixty per cent of funds for the scheme are met by additional JRY grant and 40 per cent from state school and mass education department. Through this programme, the level of education got increased in rural areas. Still, the quality and quantity of the education is not up to the mark due the unwillingness of the concerned officers and unawareness of the target group.

The government started Swarnajayanti Gram Swarozgar Yojana (SGSY) in 1999 with the objective to bring the assisted poor families (*swarozgaris*) above the poverty line by organizing them into self-help groups (SHGs) through the process of social mobilization, their capacity building, and provision of income-generating assets through a mix of bank credit and government subsidy. The programme aims at establishing a larger number of micro-enterprises in the rural areas, building upon the potential of the rural poor. Emphasis under the programme is on group approach and developing activity clusters. SGSY is one of the major ongoing schemes and it plays a very important role in the development of rural areas, but badly affected by the corruption, unawareness of target group, and weak coordination between the local government bodies as had been the experience with the other programmes and schemes, as noted above.

The former Prime Minister, Shri Atal Bihari Vajpayee, announced a centrally sponsored scheme, called the Pradhan Mantri Gram Sadak Yojana (PMGSY) on 15 August 2000 and the scheme was launched by the Government of India same year on 25 December. This programme had the objectives of connecting all habitations with the population of over 1000 persons by 2003 and those with a population of 500 and above by the year 2007 (end of the 10th five-year plan) through a good all-weather road. The primary focus of the programme is on the construction of new roads and upgrading the existing roads. This programme has been able to connect many villages by the all-weather roads.

The Sampoorna Grameen Rozgar Yojana (SGRY) was launched on 25 September 2001 by merging two ongoing schemes of EAS and JGSY with the defined objective of providing additional wage employment in the rural areas as also food security, alongside the creation of durable community assets in the rural areas. The emphasis was mainly on women, SCs/STs, and parents of children withdrawn from hazardous occupation. The programme is implemented by all the three tiers of Panchayati Raj Institutions (PRIs). The programme is quite significant in terms of food security, but has not been able to fulfil its objectives due the corruption and intermediators.

In 2006, National Rural Employment Guarantee Scheme (NREGS) was launched in Anantapur district. Renamed as MNREGS, this Scheme guarantees a minimum of 100 days' employment every year to each rural household on demand for one member of the family. Though it plays important role in the generation of employment in rural areas today, but the 100 days' work for the one member of the family is not sufficient, joint families face a lot of problems; delay in grain and finance, less participation of women, and use of contractors are badly affecting the scheme as has been reported by studies (Kumar, 2003; Aiyar and Samji, 2006).

The success of any developmental programme is mainly depending upon the people's participation, maximum utilization of available resources, strong political willpower, and the coordination between different governmental bodies. The earlier developmental programmes in India were partly successful in there aims. Some socio-cultural, economic, historical, and political reasons badly affect the progress of these programmes.

The administrative machinery through which the rural development programmes are implemented remains the same, so are the crippling limitations. In recent times, there has been the spirited advocacy for people's participation. Unfortunately, the mechanism of ensuring people's participation has again failed to meet the people's aspiration(s) as it is yet to get free from the shackles of age-old prejudices and discriminations. As a whole, many reasons could be attributed for the failure of the rural development programmes identified by scholars. A few of the main reasons among them are as follows:

1. Less inclusiveness
2. Lack of awareness in the people and the related officers
3. High level of illiteracy among the rural society
4. Less participation of women in rural development programmes
5. Incorrect selection of beneficiaries
6. Weak coordination and corruption at different levels of government bodies
7. Polices of political parties, mainly they use the programmes as an election agenda
8. Inadequacy of funds for rural development programmes
9. Historical background of the development in rural area
10. Weak monitoring system
11. Power transformation.

The earlier developmental programmes laid emphasis on the sectoral development. Accordingly, they covered only one aspect of rural development and they are exclusive in nature. The correlation between the social dimension, economic dimension, and political dimension is found thus apparently very weak. The developmental programmes for rural areas are mainly related with the economic development of the rural society. Poverty, unemployment, unequal distribution of income and availability of resources, low agricultural production, depressed condition of women and lower castes peoples, illiteracy, poor sanitation and unhygienic environment, less availability of health care facilities, poor infrastructure facilities, etc., are problems having a historical root in our rural society which remained overlooked in majority of the early rural development programmes. They create gap between rural–urban areas and also between the developed and lesser developed regions; naturally, contributing towards heightening of the level of dissatisfaction among masses.

'Growth with social justice' has been the basic objective of planning in India. The Government of India views rural development as critical to India's economic and social development. The policy objective is to achieve '*Samagra Gramin Vikas*', addressing all the issues of basic needs of the people in the rural areas. In this direction, the Ministry of Rural Development plays a pivotal role, through a number of programmes, aimed at improving the life – both individual and community – of the rural people. But, the development needs of the SC/ST communities could not be taken care of especially in rural areas. Frankly speaking, in most of the settlements or hamlets of the SCs/STs, the ray of development did not reach at all. They had to depend on the mercy of others even for using the community resources and amenities. In many parts of the rural India, several instances of insults and conflicts on the issue of water and road/path use are known, thanks to the media reports. Ultimately, such incidents are related to the right to live a life with dignity and ultimately the larger issue of inclusive development.

Ambedkar Gram Vikas Yojana

In India, caste system largely determines the function, the status, the available opportunities as well as the handicaps for an individual. Caste differences even determine the differences in modes of domestic and social life, types of houses, and cultural patterns of the people which are found in the rural area and also it is the determinant of individual status and role. Many scholars are of the opinion that since Manu, the author of *Manusmriti*, caste system based upon the principle of labour, caste has been playing a prominent role in life and economy of Indian society. 'Higher' or 'upper' castes have ruled over the 'lower' castes for a considerably long period of time. The situation of the lower castes is very poor and a large number of them are below poverty line – mass poverty and hunger have traditional social and historical roots and the present picture shows gap between 'haves' and 'haves nots'. In India, the resource utilization is badly affected by the caste system in rural areas. The rural poor, in general, could be found facing the double-edged problem of rural–urban and rural rich–rural poor.

Economic development and social justice are the two major goals of rural development. Equal rights to different caste groups and equal distribution of resources and facilities are considered under social justice. Social injustices create tensions between different caste groups which is a big barrier on the path of development.

Equality in income and social status in rural–urban, rural rich–rural poor, different castes, and gender are the main aim of the rural development programmes, but one-fourth of the Indian (urban population) get more attention of planning commission and more facilities than the three-fourth population (rural population). In rural areas, the subsidy given on the agricultural equipments, fertilizers, HYV seeds, etc., is mostly utilized by the big farmers, whereas marginal and small farmers are unable to utilize these facilities (Murgi and Howes, 2003). In case of lower caste people and women, they still suffer since several centuries and have been dominated by the upper caste people. Still, a large number of SCs/STs are living below poverty line; also, the level of literacy and the percentage of these people living in the urban areas too are considerably low (Tripathi, 1999). Theoretically speaking, the women form half of the country's population; even then they are treated as the second person (Nakkeeran, 2003). Governments give reservation to the women in many programmes and also give priority to them in the PRIs; yet, the women village heads (*Gram Pradhan*) work only as the stamp, the actual power continues to lie in the hands of her husband or son(s), observed Narayana (2005).

Since independence, the Indian government launched different development programmes and schemes for rural areas with the objective of eradicating poverty. It means rural areas should have basic necessities of life, a good place to live, and clean environment where people can lead a dignified life which can give them satisfaction. These programmes and schemes are partly successful in their objectives or goals. The goal of social justice and equality has not been achieved and actually left behind, especially in the case of the marginal section comprised especially of lower income groups and lower caste people. The failure of different development programmes and schemes show that if these groups are ignored, the overall development will not be possible.

Various state governments introduced different programmes for the development of lower caste and poor people. AGVY is one of them. The scheme was launched in Uttar Pradesh during Ambedkar centenary year in 1990–91 when the BSP was in power. The aim of the scheme was to uplift the rural poor mainly those who belong to SC/ST communities, through the development of sound infrastructure in the Ambedkar *grams* (villages) – the name given to the villages covered under the AGVY.

The major objectives of the AGVY are to cover maximum population of SC under various development programmes, select villages having SC concentration and name them as 'Ambedkar villages' for the purpose of the scheme, saturate those villages under the earmarked different development programmes, and achieve integration of development programmes and schemes.

Hence, it is apparent that the redistribution of social justice is the main concern of the AGVY. Equal distribution of resources and equal social rights for all, especially for the SC/ST population, are the central focus of the AGVY.

The selection of Ambedkar villages directly depends upon the proportion of SC population. In principle, the concentration of SC population should be taken as a criterion for the selection of villages within an assembly constituency. In other words, villages having highest population of the SCs were to be selected for this programme, subject to the proportion of the population. When this programme was launched in 1990–1991, initially villages having highest SC/ST population concentration were selected followed by those with lower concentrations.

More than one-fifth (21.15%) of the total population of Uttar Pradesh belongs to the SC category. However, this average is not found ubiquitously distributed across the state. Considerable variation in the regional distribution pattern could be noticed at the district level. Baghpat district in the western part has only 10.98 per cent of its total population under the SC category. On the other hand, Sonbhadra district, in the south-eastern part with 41.92 per cent of its total population as SC, has the highest concentration.

As referred above, the AGVY was launched in 1990–1991. Initially, this scheme covered the villages with largest concentration of SCs. After 1990–1991, the numbers of Ambedkar villages increased as reflected by Table 1.

Table 1

Uttar Pradesh: Villages Covered under the Ambedkar Gram Vikas Yojana

Year	*Districts (No.)*	*Ambedkar villages*	
		No.	*Per cent of the total villages*
1990–91	63	3853	3.93
1997–98	71	3785	3.86
2002–03	71	11441	11.68
Total		19079	19.47

Source: Based on http: //www.censusindia.net/and http: //agvv.up.nic.in/.

In 1990–91, the AGVY was started in 63 districts – Meerut, Baghpat, Gautam Buddha Nagar, Bulandshahar, Hamirpur, Kheri, and Maharajganj districts were left uncovered. The total number of Ambedkar villages at the beginning was merely 3,853, i.e., less than even 5 per cent of the total villages of the state. In 1997–98, the scheme covered all 71 districts of the state, and number of the Ambedkar villages are 3,785. In 2002–03, the scheme covered 71 districts and number of Ambedkar villages increased to 11,441. The total number of Ambedkar villages in Uttar Pradesh has risen to 19,079 as per the latest data of 2002–03. One may infer that barely one-fifth of the rural settlements are officially receiving the AGVY benefits.

The distribution of Ambedkar villages in the entire state varies by districts. At one end, Gautam Buddha Nagar is having only 72 Ambedkar villages out of 392 villages (18.37%), and on the other hand, Sitapur district is having 746 Ambedkar villages out of its 2,321 villages (32.14%). Hence, it reflects considerable variation in the distribution of Ambedkar villages in different districts.

Challenges to AGVY

As mentioned earlier, based on the concept of redistribution of social justice and social equality, upliftment of economically and socially backward people, the aim of the AGVY, and various schemes under it was to develop infrastructure in SCs/STs concentrated villages. To become a successful programme, it needs to overcome political, social, and economic challenges. The major factors directly affecting the AGVY's effective implementation could be identified as the following:

1. Political parties use this programme as a political agenda, because it is introduced for the people who constitute a big vote bank and therefore political parties are making it as election rhetoric only.
2. Transference of power is one of biggest challenge confronting the AGVY. When the power gets transferred to a political party other than the last BSP, this programme is not paid proper attention rather gets neglected.
3. Poor implementation of the programmes and schemes is the one of the major challenge in the success of AGVY.
4. Corruption in different government offices and local government bodies badly affect the proper working of rural development programmes and their achievements; and the AGVY is no exception to it.
5. Officers do not have a clear concept about the AGVY and its schemes. The lack of knowledge about this in the local government body affects its progress.
6. The condition of lower caste people in many villages is socially and economically very bad and upper caste people dominate in routine intercourse in the society. In such a condition, the former group finds itself unable to get benefits of AGVY.
7. The main target of the AGVY was to bridge the gap between the upper caste people and lower caste people, but in many places it has created heightened tension between different groups and castes.
8. The literacy rate in SCs/STs population is very low. A big group of population does not know about the AGVY. People are unaware about their rights due to illiteracy.

9. Lesser participation of women in different schemes of the AGVY creates a gender gap in this respect.
10. In Uttar Pradesh, rural population live in 97,945 villages, but the AGVY scheme covers 19,079 villages only. The percentage of coverage area of the scheme is less than 20 per cent of the total area. It created a gap between Ambedkar villages and the non-Ambedkar villages.
11. Funds for the AGVY are not available sufficiently which are needed for the proper implementation of the AGVY schemes.

The AGVY has not been able to fulfil its aims and objective. The main reason of the failure is political. This programme was introduced by the BSP for the marginal sections of the society, especially the SCs/STs which was the main vote bank of the party. But when the BSP was dethroned, the progress of this programme came down almost to a halt. The changing nature of the party principles apparently have a direct bearing on the thrust as well as twists and turns in rural development programmes and schemes under implementation, often adversely than not. The distribution of the Ambedkar villages now depends upon the awareness of the village *Pradhan* ('headman'). There are many villages having zero per cent of SC population, but they are being considered under the AGVY. In fact, many such villages are already declared Ambedkar villages. Indirectly, it hints at the changing perspective of the BSP-like party which pragmatically aspires to be a national party and has thus adopted a new kind of social engineering technique in this process which has turned out to be a lottery for it in the context of its winning in the last assembly election as well as a sweeping win in the recently held State Council election. No wonder, the correlation between the distributions of SC population and the distribution of AGVY was very low (0.12). It again proves that the basic parameter for the selection of the programme has not been followed in the successive phases.

Conclusions

Realizing the fact that India, at least Bharat, lives mostly in the rural areas, the policymakers and planners have been formulating development programmes for such areas. Unfortunately, despite all good intentions, they have failed to be inclusive in nature. The marginal sections of the rural community have generally not been able to get benefits of the rural development programmes owing to a variety of traditional handicaps related to continuing exploitative nature of socio-cultural and economic relations in village society. Hence, an exclusive programme for the *dalits* was introduced by the BSP.

Implementation part in case of most of the programmes launched has been considerably poor. Rural development programmes particularly the AGVY are not exception to it rather in some cases it has been reportedly negative (cf. Pai, 2004). The AGVY also suffered due to a new kind of social engineering adopted by the BSP. Though the *dalits* still remain the main base of the BSP vote bank for political rhetoric, in the process of widening its social base, perhaps it is looking away from its focus on them and their welfare too.

References

Aiyar, Y., and Samji, S. (2006). 'Improving the effectiveness of National Rural Employment Guarantee Act', *Economic and Political Weekly*, 41(4), 320–326.

Chakravarti, A. (2001). 'Caste and agrarian class – A view from Bihar', *Economic and Political Weekly*, 36(17), 1449–1462.

Dev, S.M. (2004). 'How to make rural India shine?', *Economic and Political Weekly*, 39(44), 4415–4422.

Dogra, B. (2005). 'Rural Employment Scheme – Rhetoric and reality', *Economic and Political Weekly*, 40(18), 1809–1810.

Gupta, D. (2005). 'Whither the Indian Villages – Culture and agriculture in "Rural" India', *Economic and Political Weekly*, 40(8), 751–758.

Kumar, V. (2003). 'Uttar Pradesh: Politics of change', *Economic and Political Weekly*, 38(37), 3869–3871.

Marriott, A. (2003). 'Dalit or Harijan – Self-naming by scheduled caste interviewees', *Economic and Political Weekly*, 38(36), 3751–3752.

Mathur, J.K., and Mathur, D. (2005). 'Dark homes and smoky hearths – Rural electrification and women', *Economic and Political Weekly*, 40(7), 638–643.

Murgi, R., and Howes, S. (2003). 'Karnataka incidence of agricultural power subsidies: An estimate', *Economic and Political Weekly*, 38(16), 1533–1535.

Nakkeeran, M. (2003). 'Women's work, status and fertility – Land, caste and gender in a South Indian village', *Economic and Political Weekly*, 38(37), 3931–3939.

Narayana, D. (2005). 'Local governance without capacity building – Ten years of Panchayati Raj', *Economic and Political Weekly*, 40(26), 2822–2832.

Pai, S., Sharma, P., Kanungo, P., and Mukherji, R. (2005). 'Uttar Pradesh in 1990s – Critical perspectives on society, polity and economy', *Economic and Political Weekly*, 40(21), 2144–2147.

Pai, S. (2004). 'Dalit question and political response –Comparative study of U.P. and M.P.', *Economic and Political Weekly*, 39(11), 1141–1150.

Reddy, V.R. (2003). 'Irrigation: Development and reforms', *Economic and Political Weekly*, 38(10), 1179–1189.

Srinivasan, K., and Mohanty, S.K. (2004). 'Deprivation of basic amenities by caste and religion – Empirical study using NFHS data', *Economic and Political Weekly*, 39(7), 728–735.

Thorat, S. (2002). 'Oppression and denial – Dalit discrimination in the 1990s', *Economic and Political Weekly*, 37(6), 572–578.

Tripathi, R.M. (1999). 'Socio-economic profile of scheduled caste population in India', *Geographical Review of India*, 61(1), 47–59.

World Bank (1989). *India: Poverty, Employment and Social Services*. Washington, DC: World Bank.

Web Sources

http://www.sociologyguide.com/rural-sociology/caste-role-rural-society.php (accessed on 13 September 2009).

http://agvv.up.nic.in/(accessed on 15 May 2008).

http://nird.ap.nic.in/clic/uprural.html (accessed on 15 May 2008).

13

Poverty Alleviation Programmes in Tamil Nadu

S. GUNASEKARAN

In the year 2000, representatives of 189 nations including 147 heads of state and government gathered at the United Nations for a historic millennium summit. They adopted an ambitious set of goals, the Millennium Development Goals (MDGs) (UN, 2000). Achieving them by the target date of 2015 will transform the lives of the world's people, including reducing by half the number of people living in extreme poverty (UNFPA, 2003).

India is on fast track to economic growth with an annual growth rate of 8 per cent. Though growth has been seen viable, the trickle down theory of Simon Kuznet (1969) has not done any magic. When Mahbub Ul Haq (1976) wrote his 'poverty curtain', he advised the nations to take care of GNP, so that it will take care of everything. However, this could not happen. Around 300 million are living on less than a dollar a day. Inequalities between rural and urban areas are widening and the regional imbalances are deepening. The gap between men and women are also widening and one has to fear whether a big social divide is taking place. It is said that the scheduled caste and schedule tribes and women are further disadvantaged.

Although recent positive economic developments have helped the Indian middle class a lot, India still suffers from substantial poverty. The National Sample Survey Organization (NSSO) estimated that 22.15 per cent of the population was living below the poverty line in 2004–05, down from 51.3 per cent in 1977–78 and 25 per cent in 2002. As of 2006, India's Human Development Index is 0.611, higher than that of nearby countries such as Bangladesh (0.53) and Pakistan (0.539), but lower than Vietnam (0.709) or China (0.768) (UN, 2006).

Since the early 1950s, government has initiated, sustained, and refined various planning schemes to help the poor attain self-sufficiency in food production. These poverty alleviation programmes (PAPs) in India are of two types. The first one is the welfare programmes for the poor and the other is the programmes for economic and social justice. The welfare programmes are mostly concerned with transfer of income through transfer of payments, doles, and relief measures in either cash or kind. It is one thing to redistribute the generated income and another thing to redistribute the factors through institutional and structural changes which will raise the income-earning power, capability, and ultimately participation in decision making. Thus, people should be assured with economic freedom and to assure this, the anti-poverty programmes should be in the nature of improving their income-earning power, their capabilities, and their asset position, implementing participatory development programme and ultimately enabling them to participate in the process of decision making. In view of this fact, poverty removal and employment generation have become the two main pillars of planning in India. In correspondence to this thrust, a number of poverty alleviation and employment generation programmes have been initiated by the Government of India (GoI), through the Ministry of Rural Development (MoRD), keeping gainful rural employment and productive assets/infrastructure creation as the primary goals. As most of these direct PAPs are being implemented with minimum consideration on the human rights aspects, these programmes often failed and could not make any tangible impact on the living conditions of the poor, particularly women in rural areas. The human rights approach (HRA) to development demands: (a) participation and transparency in decision making (participation of all stakeholders); (b) non-discrimination (equity and equality); (c) empowerment; and (d) accountability of actors (United Nations, 2004). Hence, there is a need to assess the extent of HRA adopted in various anti-poverty programmes in India.

In this direction, this paper attempts to assess the extent of HRA adopted in the process of implementing various anti-poverty programmes in Tamil Nadu.

Objectives

The aim of this paper is to study the extent of HRA adopted in the implementation process of PAPs; to study the problems and bottlenecks in the adoption of HRA in the implementation of PAPs aimed to relieve women from poverty in rural areas; and to suggest suitable strategies to integrate a HRA to PAPs.

Methodology

This paper is based on the data collected for a UNESCO-sponsored research project on 'Integrating a HRA to poverty alleviation programmes in Tamil Nadu'. The data were collected during February to June 2006 from three districts of Tamil Nadu, viz., Villupuram, Vellore, and Tiruchirapalli representing high, moderate, and low level of development, respectively, as per the Tamil Nadu Human Development Report 2003.

The anti-poverty programmes considered in this study are: (i) Swarnajayanti Gram Swarozgar Yojana (SGSY), (ii) Sampoorna Grameen Rozgar Yojana (SGRY), (iii) Rural Housing – Indira Awas Yojana (IAY), and (iv) Public Distribution System (PDS).

Data were collected from 300 women beneficiaries of PAPs (PAPs) and 50 self-help group (SHG) leaders in each of the selected districts through personal interview. Thus, a total of 900 women beneficiaries of various PAPs and 150 SHG leaders were interviewed. Of the 900 women, 733 were beneficiaries of SGSY, 160 were beneficiaries of SGRY, 334 were beneficiaries of IAY, and all the 900 were beneficiaries of PDS.

Information was collected from the women SHG leaders and beneficiaries of various PAPs on the extent of HRA adopted in the implementation of PAPs. In this regard, a set of indicators on various aspects of HRA was developed for each of the PAPs and the beneficiaries were asked about the extent of the presence of the HRA on each of the selected indicators and the results are placed on a three-point scale as mostly, sometimes, and never. A score of 2 was given for mostly, 1 for sometimes, and 0 for never. Finally, the overall performance of each programme in adopting the HRA was assessed based on the total score obtained on each of the selected HRA indicators for each of the PAPs.

The human rights aspects considered in this study are: (a) dissemination and access to information; (b) transparency; (c) participation in decision making; (d) freedom of expression; (e) equality and non-discrimination; and (f) accountability.

Results

Swarna Jayanti Gram Swarozgar Yojana

The extent of the adoption of HRA in the implementation process of the SGSY programme was assessed based on the interview with the SHG leaders and beneficiaries of the SGSY programme. In the SGSY, the implementation process involves two stages, viz., (a) government to SHGs and (b) SHG to members. Hence, the leaders of the SHG were interviewed and their opinion was assessed on the adoption of rights approach in the programme implementation. Besides interviewing the leaders, the beneficiaries were also interviewed and their opinion on the adoption of HRA in the implementation of the programmes was assessed.

Opinion of SHG Leaders on the Rights Approach at Government Level

In order to assess the extent of HRA adopted in the implementation of economic assistance programme under SGSY by the government, the SHG leaders were briefed about the rights approach to development and asked about their opinion on the presence or absence of rights approach in the implementation of SGSY programme. The results presented in Table 1 reveal that dissemination of information about the programme details was mostly followed at all stages of the programme as reported by 78 per cent of leaders. Only 73 per cent of the leaders reported transparency being mostly followed. Participation in decision making was mostly present at all stages of the programme as reported by nearly three-fourth of the leaders (75%). Freedom of expression was mostly followed in the implementation of the programme as reported by about three-fourth of the leaders (73%). Just 7 per cent of respondents reported that discrimination was mostly present in the implementation process and only one-third of respondents (34 per cent) reported the presence of accountability most of the times in the implementation process. Majority of leaders felt that accountability of both government and banks was much needed.

Table 1

Per cent Distribution of SHG Leaders According to Their Opinion on the Extent of Human Rights Approach Adopted in SGSY Programme by the Government

Human rights issues	*N = 150*			*Score*		
	Mostly	*Sometimes*	*Never*	*E**	*O**	*P**
Dissemination	78	20	2	300	264	87.9
Transparency	72.7	26	1.3	300	267	89
Participation and decision-making	74.7	24.7	0.6	300	261	86.9
Freedom of expression	72.7	26	1.3	300	257	85.7
Discrimination	6.7	38.7	54.6	300	78	26.2
Accountability	34	61.4	4.6	300	235	78.3
Total				1,800	1,362	75.7

*E = Expected; O = Observed; P = Per cent.

The leaders are of the opinion that these agencies must come forward to empower the beneficiaries through skill training, advocacy, and counselling for undertaking independent economic activities, procuring raw materials, and marketing. The performance of the programme in adopting the HRA as perceived by the SHG leaders was scored and found that the overall performance was 76 per cent of the expected level. Thus, it is seen that the programme implementation is fairly better in adopting HRA. The accountability of the government has to be increased and the discrimination has to be minimized according to the SHG leaders.

Rights Approach at Group Level

The results of the analysis of data on the opinion of SHG leaders on the extent of HRA adopted by the SHG in the implementation of economic assistance programme at group level presented in Table 2 reveal that dissemination, access to information, and transparency in the programme implementation were followed mostly by the group as reported by most of the SHG leaders (93–97%). Participation in decision making and freedom of expression are reported to be mostly present according to 90 per cent of SHG leaders. Non-discrimination was mostly present in the implementation of the programme as reported by 80 per cent of leaders.

Only half of the group leaders have reported that the SGSY programme is mostly helpful to get employment opportunities and improve the economic status of the family. SGSY programme is mostly helpful to improve the status of women and improve their self-reliance according to 55 per cent of leaders. SGSY mostly facilitates women's access to credit facilities as reported by 82 per cent of leaders. Only 58 per cent of women leaders have reported that SGSY mostly helped women to get adequate standard of living. Accountability was mostly present in the implementation of the programme in the repayment of loan, as reported by 89 per cent of leaders. The overall performance was 89 per cent of the expected score, according to the group leaders. Thus, the group leaders opined that the HRA is mostly followed in the implementation of the PAPs at group level. The human rights components such as dissemination and access to information, participation, non-discrimination, and accountability are mostly present in the SGSY at group level. However, nearly one-third of the leaders reported that the SHGs were not always helpful to get employment, so as to improve the economic status and standard of living of the family.

Table 2

Per cent Distribution of SHG Leaders According to Their Opinion on the Extent of Human Rights Approach in the Implementation of SGSY Programme by the Groups

Human rights issues	*N*	*Presence*			*Score*		
		Mostly	*Sometimes*	*Never*	*E**	*O**	*P**
Dissemination of information	150	96.7	2	1.3	300	293	97.7
Access to information	150	96	4	—	300	294	97.9
Transparency	150	93.3	6	0.6	300	293	97.7
Participation	150	88.7	11.3	—	300	283	94.3
Freedom of expression	150	92	8	—	300	288	95.6
Equal opportunities to all members	150	82	17.4	0.6	300	272	90.7
Democratic way of selecting leaders	150	89.4	10.6	—	300	284	94.7
Equality and non-discrimination	150	80	20	—	300	270	90
Help to improve the economic status	150	53.4	46	0.6	300	229	76.3
Help to get employment opportunity	150	51.4	48	0.6	300	226	75.3
Help to improve the status of women	150	54.7	45.3	—	300	232	77.3
Help to improve the self-reliance of women	150	54.7	44.7	0.6	300	231	77
Easy access to credit facilities	150	82	18	—	300	273	90.9
Help to get adequate standard of living	150	58	42	—	300	237	79
Accountability	150	88.7	10.7	0.6	300	282	94
Total					4,500	3,987	88.6

*E = Expected; O = Observed; P = Per cent.

Opinion of the Beneficiaries of SGSY

In order to assess the opinion of the beneficiaries of PAPs on the adoption of HRA in the implementation of SGSY programme, a sample of 733 SGSY programme beneficiaries were interviewed. The results are presented in Table 3. It was observed that most of the respondents (more than 80%) reported that equality and non-discrimination (in the selection of beneficiaries for economic assistance and distribution of benefits) were mostly followed at all stages of implementation of the programme. Non-discrimination in the selection of beneficiaries for training was reported to be present for 56 per cent of beneficiaries. Only three-fifth of the respondents reported that dissemination of information about programme details and access to information were mostly present in the programme implementation. Only two-third of beneficiaries reported that freedom of expression was possible for most of the time in the implementation of the programme. Only 61 per cent of the beneficiaries reported that participation in decision making was mostly followed in the programme implementation.

Opportunity for self-employment/income-generating activities and adequate standard of living was reported to be mostly available for nearly half of the beneficiaries in the SGSY programme. Only half of the beneficiaries reported that transparency and accountability were present mostly in the SGSY programme. A little over half of the respondents (55%) felt that the benefits of the SGSY programmes availed through SHGs helped them to take decisions most of the times in the family. Nearly half of them felt that the status of women in the family increased due to the SGSY programme. However, a good number of the respondents did not agree to many of the human rights components related to self-reliance, group action, economic independence, participation in group activities and politics, and instilling confidence among women. According to the beneficiaries of the SGSY programme, the extent of HRA in the implementation process of various PAPs under SGSY was only 66 per cent of the total expected score.

Table 3

Per cent Distribution of Beneficiaries of PAPs According to Their Opinion on the Adoption of Human Rights Approach in the Implementation of SGSY

Human rights issues	*N*	*Presence*			*Score*		
		Mostly	*Some-times*	*Never*	*E**	*O**	*P**
Equality and non-discrimination in							
(a) Selection of beneficiaries for economic assistance	733	81.2	17.2	1.6	1466	1316	89.7
(b) Distribution of benefits	733	84.4	14.2	1.4	1466	1342	91.5
(c) Selection of beneficiaries for training	733	56.1	39.8	4.1	1466	1114	75.9
Inform the programme details	733	57.7	41.3	1	1466	1149	78.3
Access to information	733	59.8	39.4	0.8	1466	1165	79.5
Freedom to express views	733	66.9	31.1	2	1466	1210	82.5

Cont'd...

...Cont'd

Participation in decision-making	733	60.7	36.2	3.1	1466	1155	78.8
Opportunity for adequate standard of living	733	50.3	47.7	2	1466	1088	74.2
Opportunity for self-employment/ income-generating activities	733	46.8	51	2.2	1466	1060	72.3
Transparency in all stages	733	51.6	46.1	2.3	1466	1094	74.6
Accountability	733	51.5	46.5	2	1466	1095	74.7
Respect for members in the group	733	44.3	50.9	4.8	1466	1023	69.8
Improvement in self-respect	733	39.4	55.6	5	1466	984	67.1
Self-effort and self reliance among women	733	28.6	63.9	7.5	1466	887	60.5
Able to speak in public	733	19.8	50.6	29.6	1466	661	45.1
Fostering spirit of cooperation among women	733	20.9	69.6	9.5	1466	816	55.7
Promoting awareness	733	21.7	70.8	7.5	1466	837	57.1
Instilling confidence	733	19.5	74.4	6.1	1466	831	56.7
Decision-making in the family	733	55.1	42	2.9	1466	1116	76.1
Increase in women's status in the family	733	47.9	46	6.1	1466	1039	70.9
Free from economic dependence	733	33.7	58.8	7.5	1466	925	63.1
Providing opportunities to women in productive work	733	30.3	61.5	8.2	1466	895	61
Providing opportunities to acquire skills	733	28.4	59.6	12	1466	853	58.1
Came out of cultural taboos	733	33.9	54.9	11.2	1466	901	61.5
Opposing practices followed against women's interest	733	20.6	52.3	27.1	1466	685	46.7
Able to participate in political activities	733	19.8	32	48.2	1466	525	35.8
Group action	733	32.2	47.1	20.7	1466	817	55.7
Able to participate in Gram Sabha	733	35.3	49.3	15.4	1466	879	59.9
Contest election	733	14.6	31.2	54.2	1466	443	30.2
Total					42,514	27,905	65.6

*E = Expected; O = Observed; P = Per cent.

The results indicate that there is a need for a change in the implementation of SGSY programme with special focus on the HRA to development. The programme details are to be disseminated through various media and personal communication. Efforts should be made to make the programme more transparent in administration, monitoring, and evaluation. People's participation in decision making is very low and the accountability of the government is also very low. Most importantly, indicators related to women's self-respect, women's economic, and political independence are much to be improved.

Sampoorna Grameen Rozgar Yojana

In order to assess the opinion of the beneficiaries on the extent of HRA followed in the implementation of SGRY programme, a total of 160 beneficiaries of the SGRY scheme were interviewed. It was observed that only 44 per cent of beneficiaries had reported that equality and non-discrimination in the selection of beneficiaries were mostly followed in the programme. Discrimination in the allotment of work and payment of wages mostly exists as reported by a majority of beneficiaries. Nature of work is mostly acceptable only to 13 per cent of beneficiaries. It is a sad commentary to note that nearly four-fifth (79%) of beneficiaries reported that food grains have been never supplied to them. Most of the beneficiaries reported that they were neither given information nor had access to the details of the programme. Overall, the results on the opinion of the beneficiaries on the implementation of SGRY programme revealed that the programme did not follow any of the HRA and the procedures laid down for the implementation of the programme have not been strictly adhered.

Table 4

Per cent Distribution of Beneficiaries of SGRY According to Their Opinion on the Extent of Human Rights Approach Adopted in the Implementation of the Programme

Human rights issues	*N*	*Presence*			*Score*		
		Mostly	*Sometimes*	*Never*	*E**	*O**	*P**
Equality and non-discrimination in							
(a) Selection of beneficiaries	160	43.8	39.4	16.8	320	203	63.4
(b) Allotment of work (gender wise)	160	49.4	38	12.6	320	219	68.4
(c) Payment of wages	160	17.5	60.6	21.9	320	153	47.8
Nature of work is acceptable	160	13.1	53.8	33.1	320	128	40
Provision of food grains	160	3.1	17.5	79.4	320	38	11.9
Given details about programme	160	6.3	36.9	56.8	320	79	24.7
Inform the terms and conditions of the programme	160	6.3	25	68.7	320	60	18.8

Cont'd...

...Cont'd

Inform the allotment of food grains for the programme	160	15	17.5	67.5	320	76	23.8
Only BPL beneficiaries selected for the work	160	18.8	33.1	48.1	320	113	35.3
Beneficiaries are also members of the monitoring committee	160	8.1	37.5	54.4	320	86	26.9
Use of machineries for work.	160	21.9	55	23.1	320	162	50.6
Involvement of middle man/contractors	160	30.6	40	29.4	320	158	49.4
Getting regular employment	160	7.5	51.2	41.3	320	106	33.2
Increase in per capita income	160	5	61.3	33.7	320	114	35.6
Improvement in economic conditions	160	5	59.3	35.7	320	111	34.7
Help to avoid debt from money lenders	160	5	56.9	38.1	320	107	33.4
Creation of assets at							
(a) Community level	160	16.9	35.6	47.5	320	111	34.7
(b) Family level	160	5.6	54.4	40	320	105	32.8
Total					5,760	2,129	36.9

*E = Expected; O = Observed; P = Per cent.

The total performance on the adoption of HRA in the implementation of SGRY was just 37 per cent of the total expected score. As the adoption of HRA is very low in the implementation of SGRY programme, the programme has failed to achieve its objective of providing additional and supplementary wage employment to the needy people living below poverty line according to the opinion of the selected beneficiaries. Thus, the HRA makes the people to involve themselves in the implementation of the programme and lack of HRA takes the programme far away from the people.

Indira Awas Yojana

A total of 334 beneficiaries of IAY were interviewed on various aspects of human rights issues in the implementation of IAY programme. The results presented in Table 5 reveal that equality and non-discrimination was mostly followed in the selection of beneficiaries and allotment of house as reported by nearly two-third of beneficiaries. Equality and non-discrimination in the distribution of money and material was reported by only 59 per cent of beneficiaries which indicates the prevalence of discrimination in the distribution of money and material in the construction of house.

Only 27 per cent of beneficiaries reported that the dissemination of information/access to information was mostly followed in the programme. Thus, a majority of beneficiaries were neither given information nor were having access to information about the programme details. Just 12 per cent of beneficiaries reported that the implementation of the programme was mostly transparent, while the remaining 88 per cent reported either 'sometimes' or 'never'. Most of the beneficiaries (93%) reported that they had no right to express their views fully. Participation in decision making was mostly followed according to just 4 per cent of beneficiaries. Majority of the beneficiaries have not agreed fully for many of the human rights issues related to payment of money and materials for the construction of house. Overall, the extent of HRA followed in the implementation of IAY was

Table 5

Per cent Distribution of the Beneficiaries of IAY Programme According to Their Opinion on the Extent of Human Rights Approach in the Implementation of the Programme

Human rights issues	*N*	*Presence*			*Score*		
		Mostly	*Some-times*	*Never*	*E**	*O**	*P**
Equality and non-discrimination in							
(a) Selection of beneficiaries	334	64.7	31.7	3.6	668	538	80.5
(b) Allotment of house	334	66.2	31.7	2.1	668	548	82
(c) Provision of money and material	334	59.3	35.3	5.4	668	514	76.9
Dissemination of information	334	26.6	65.6	7.8	668	397	59.4
Access to information	334	27.2	66.8	6	668	405	60.6
Transparency	334	11.9	73.9	14.2	668	327	48.9
Right to express views freely	334	6.6	80.5	12.9	668	313	46.8
Adequacy of money for the construction of house	334	14.9	69.8	15.3	668	333	49.9
Satisfaction of housing design	334	55.4	33.5	11.1	668	482	72.2
Received full amount of money and material	334	29	54.8	16.2	668	377	56.4
Received money and material in time	334	30.8	55.4	13.8	668	391	58.5
Construction fully completed and satisfactory	334	43.7	46.1	10.2	668	446	66.8
Opportunity for creating assets	334	44.9	52.2	2.9	668	474	70.9
Opportunity to get adequate shelter (in terms of space)	334	62.9	35.6	1.5	668	539	80.7
Total					9,352	6,084	65.1

*E = Expected; O = Observed; P = Per cent.

only 65 per cent of the total expected score. The results indicate that though the IAY scheme provides shelter for the people living below poverty line, lack of dissemination of information, non-involvement of beneficiaries in decision making process, lack of transparency, and lack of accountability reduce the quality of the houses constructed under IAY. As a result, many of the houses constructed under IAY are not fully utilized by the beneficiaries and many of them are in depilated condition within a short period of time.

Public Distribution System

In the PDS, essential commodities are supplied through ration card to the beneficiaries and most of the people rely on the PDS to fulfil their basic requirement of food. They mostly fall below poverty line category. They do not have adequate income to buy commodities outside the PDS. The BPL people regularly buy the commodities from PDS. The prices of the commodities are comparatively very low and as per the directions of the government.

A total of 900 beneficiaries of PDS were interviewed to assess their opinion on the presence of rights approach in the implementation of PDS. The results presented in Table 6 reveal that access to information in PDS was very high as reported by 94 per cent of beneficiaries and 90 per cent reported that the commodities were mostly available for all time. More than 85 per cent of beneficiaries reported that stock availability is generally displayed, adequate stock available in all times, and they got commodities regularly. Most of the beneficiaries (98%) reported that the prices were as per the government direction and are also reasonable. Only two-third of beneficiaries had reported that the quality of commodities were mostly good. More than three-fourth of beneficiaries felt that the PDS is very much helpful to free them from hunger, save money, and improve their economic status.

Interestingly, the overall extent of HRA in the implementation of PDS was very high. The performance score was 93 per cent of the total expected score. Thus, the PDS is functioning well with the adoption of HRA and is a successful programme in removing hunger and improving the economic status of the poor families according to the beneficiaries.

Assuring adequate food is the basic fundamental right of any citizen and thus, the scheme safeguards the most important human rights, viz., right to live or right to existence. The results indicate that except in case of quality of goods, all basic human rights components are fully followed in the implementation of the programme. The most important human rights, viz., free from hunger is well implemented in this state and definitely any improvement in terms of quantity or quality or less price will definitely improve the living conditions of poor and will help in strengthening the basic fundamental rights, viz., the right to live.

Table 6

Per cent Distribution of Members of BPL Families According to Their Opinion on the Human Rights Approach Followed in the Public Distribution System

Human rights issues	*N*	*Presence*			*Score*		
		Mostly	*Some-times*	*Never*	*E**	*O**	*P**
Easy access to information	900	94	5.5	0.5	1800	1742	96.8
Always available	900	90.4	9.1	0.5	1800	1710	95
Stock availability displayed	900	85.8	13.6	0.6	1800	1667	92.6
Able to get the commodities regularly	900	88.4	10.7	0.9	1800	1688	93.8
Adequate stock in all times	900	85.6	12.3	2.1	1800	1651	91.7
Getting commodities regularly	900	87.9	10.3	1.8	1800	1675	93.1
Prices are as per government directions	900	98	1.8	0.2	1800	1780	98.9
Prices of commodities reasonable	900	98	1.9	0.1	1800	1781	98.9
The quality of commodities are good	900	65.3	32.6	2.1	1800	1469	81.6
Helps to free from hunger	900	77.2	22.2	0.6	1800	1590	88.3
Helps to save money	900	78.8	20.6	0.6	1800	1604	89.1
Helpful to improve the economic status	900	72	26.7	1.3	1800	1536	85.3
Discrimination in supply	900	0.7	7.7	91.6	1800	1717	95.4
Face any ill treatment in PDS	900	0.6	1.2	98.2	1800	1778	98.8
Total					25,200	23,388	92.8

*E = Expected; O = Observed; P = Per cent.

This subsidized programme has to continue without any flaw till the other basic human rights, viz., 'right to have gainful employment' is fully implemented so as to guarantee adequate income to all the marginalized people.

Summary and Conclusion

SGSY programme implemented through SHGs has involved the people both at the stage of planning and at the stage of execution. Every participant in the programme is aware of the salient features of the programme to a considerable extent and the end product of the programme is the empowerment of hitherto marginalized section of the population, viz., women. The two levels of analyses have revealed that at the government to SHG level, the accountability of government and the banks are very minimal and at the group level or at the beneficiaries level all the components are well implemented. Thus, a programme which has implemented with all the components of human rights has succeeded in spite of minor deviations and defects. The extent of HRA is observed to be 66 per cent of the expected level according to the beneficiaries. Hence, there is a need to strengthen the human rights components in the implementation process of SGSY programme at the first level, i.e., at government and bank level. The accountability of the government and the bank has to be ensured and a monitoring mechanism has to evolve to ensure the rights approach in the implementation process of the SGSY programme.

SGRY is a noble programme meant for supplementing the income of the marginalized people during agricultural off-seasons when there is no employment. The programme stipulates certain conditions such as (i) local workers should be employed, (ii) a part of wages should be paid in kind, (iii) labour-intensive methods should be adopted, and (iv) the work should result in community assets. Many conditions of human rights such as involvement of local people in decision making, empowerment of local people, and principle of non-discrimination and accountability have not been mostly followed at the time of implementation. On the other hand, the works were given to contractors preferred by the president, local people have not been involved in decision making, outsiders have been employed showing much discrimination to the local people, and wages have been paid only in terms of money. It is true that community assets have been created through SGRY; but the major goals of the programme which will go with human rights have not been followed and hence the programme has failed to enlist the cooperation and participation of the people at any stage of the implementation. The performance of the programme in terms of adoption of HRA is only 37 per cent of the total expected score.

Information through mass media and pamphlets in local languages should be given to the workers to make them aware that they are entitled for jobs and to receive a part of wage in kind. Contract work should be completely avoided. The officials should be made accountable in adhering to the conditions stipulated in the scheme. The decision of selecting the work and implementation process should be decided in Gram Sabha. Alternatively, after having decided at the Gram Sabha, the implementation work can be given to the SHGs. The distribution of wage in kind may be entrusted to the public distribution system with proper entries.

IAY programme has not succeeded much according to respondents because they have not fully achieved their objectives. It is so because, the basic components of human rights such as involvement of people in designing and executing the project, awareness about the project, and principle of non-discrimination have not been fully followed, though the programmes ultimately result in asset creation. The principle of accountability is not found anywhere in the programme. The overall performance in terms adoption of HRA was 65 per cent of the total expected score. The information system pertaining to the programme should be made available to the poor. Participatory approach should be implemented. The panchayat president should be made accountable for the implementation of the programme. The issues such as selection of beneficiaries and the quantum of assistance are to be discussed and decided at Gram Sabha meeting.

The PDS has succeeded in spite of minor deficiencies because it guarantees the basic human rights, viz., the 'right to exist' and follows the principles of non-discrimination, perfect awareness and information about price, availability of products, quantum of supply, and accountability in the process of implementation. Performance of the programme in terms of the adoption of HRA was 93 per cent of the total expected score. Therefore, the programme has succeeded among the people. However, there are still a number of poor families in remote rural villages who are inaccessible to the commodities under the PDS and this deprived section should also be covered under the PDS.

Overall, the results indicate that the components of human rights have been mostly followed in the process of implementation of PDS which results in achieving the aims of the programme. The working of SGSY and IAY has succeeded to a considerable extent and still there is a need to strengthen the programme with the adoption of HRA. The functions of SGRY performed very badly as the adoption of HRA is very low in the programme.

The results suggest the need to revise the implementation process of the PAPs with the incorporation of rights approach at every stages of implementation. There is a lack of commitment on the part of both government officials and the elected bodies in allowing the beneficiaries to participate in the decision-making process. The programme planners and the implementing authorities are to be sensitized about the need to adopt the rights approach for the successful implementation of various PAPs in India. Sensitization of the components of rights approach to development is very much essential to change the attitude of the programme implementers for the adoption of rights approach to development.

The study has clearly brought forth an important finding, viz., the anti-poverty programmes have succeeded wherever the HRA has been observed. The lack of accountability on the part of government agencies such as block development officials and bank officials happened to be most important lacuna and hence these officials have to be sensitized on HRA to anti-poverty programmes.

The stakeholders, viz., the existing SHGs and the beneficiaries of various PAPs have to be organized so as to enable them to insist on their rights, right to work, right to express, right to information and ultimately, and right to live as other human beings.

Thus, the information system has to be developed for the poor and an awareness campaign has to be made to make them realize their rights and duties. Any type of government intervention can succeed only if people participate at every stages of the programme and hence participatory approach to development is more essential. A sizable section of marginalized poor are illiterates and hence education to every one is again most important in this direction.

Perfect information and awareness among the people are basic pre-conditions for the success of HRA. Therefore, every citizen irrespective of caste, creed, or sex should be made aware of everything about the government schemes. Of course, the Tamil Nadu government has come with a novel idea of distributing TVs to the TV less. However, the government should see that programmes on government policies and rules and regulations connected with such programmes are telecasted so that people can assert their right to information and fight for their rights wherever there is infringement of rights.

References

Kuznet, S. (1969). *Economic Growth and Structure*. New Delhi: Oxford/IBH Publishing Company.

The Tamil Nadu HDR (2003). *Tamil Nadu Human Development Report*.

Ul Haq, M. (1976). *The Poverty Curtain, Choices for the Third World*. New York: Columbia University Press.

UNFPA (2003). *Population, Reproductive Health and the Millennium Development Goals. How the ICPD Programme of Action Promotes Poverty Alleviation and Human Rights*. New York: United Nations Population Fund [UNFPA].

United Nations (2000). *Millennium Development Goals*. New York: UNDP.

United Nations (2004). *Human Rights and Poverty Reduction: A conceptual Framework*.

United Nations (2006). *Human Development Report*. New York: UNDP.

14

Gender Perspective on Economic Status of Women in Unorganized Sector

A Study in Tamil Nadu

S. THARAGESWARI

Discrimination between men and women is one of the most crucial disparities in many societies, particularly in India. Indian women have travelled a long way through the process of development experience of the country. They were the worst and the most silent sufferers in the colonial days when disease and malnutrition, epidemics, and famine took a toll of their lives in thousands and millions. A rigid and highly stratified male-dominated society left little scope for independence and autonomy of women who were subjected to many forms of discrimination, oppression, and exploitation.

Women's status is an indicator of the level of development of a particular society. Women's workforce participation rates are also related to women's status. The concept of feminization of the workforce globally has been challenged on several grounds. One needs to seriously question the underlying relations and the assumptions in the labour market and in the household decision-making processes that assign particular type of work to men and women. This is as true of paid work as of unpaid work. While looking at women and health issues, we need to consider the structural nature of women's work and the totality of this work in these multifarious roles, activities, the time spent as well as the intensity of this time. This relates to women's paid as well as unpaid work, whether work is recognized as such or not, whether the impact on health is physical or mental.

The presence of vast multitudes of women as workers and producers in the unorganized sector, where earnings are low, employment is seasonal and insecure, supportive services is inadequate or even non-existent, growth opportunities are few, and collective organisation is weak, has brought into sharp focus the failure of the mainstream to alleviate their predicament. While it is true that workers, irrespective of sex, are exploited in the unorganized sector, women suffer more by the fact of their gender. There is enough evidence to substantiate the view that developmental processes have only pushed women to states of survival. Until recently, their contribution to the economy through self-employed and home-based work has gone unnoticed. The national database pays little attention to their presence or contribution. It is only in the past decade and a half that there has been some recognition of the fact that self-employed and home-based workers are part of the labour force. The collectivization of the self-employed into voluntary organizations and the success of their grassroots initiatives have done much to bring about this awareness.

In the unorganized sector, whether in rural or in urban areas, the overwhelming presence and struggles of women are manifested. Recent attempts in national and international fora to bring to light the nature of their work and relations of production that influence it have set a debate in motion. Critical questions have been raised concerning the lifestyles of labouring women, their struggles, and their contribution to the economy, their participation in development, their state of consciousness, and even more importantly the impact of attempts motivating them in self-help. The phenomenal growth of women in the unorganized sector has been a critical issue of prevailing oppressive situations. The underlying concerns and demands of these women are security of employment and a decent livelihood. Therefore, building unity on the basis of a broader consensus and evolving a demand strategy to focus their issues nationally have become important. An improvement in the economic role of these unorganized women workers in terms of women and work is very often considered to be an essential pre-condition for improving their status and contribution to economic and social development.

About 370 million workers constituting 92 per cent of the total workforce in a country were employed in the unorganized sector as per NSS (2000) (National Sample Survey 1999–2000). It plays a vital role in terms of providing employment opportunity to large segment of the working force in the country and contributes to the national product significantly. The contribution of the unorganized sector to the NDP (net domestic product) and its share in the total NDP at current prices has been over 60 per cent. In the matter of savings the share of household sector in the TGDS (total gross domestic saving), unorganized sector's contribution is about three-fourth. Thus, unorganized sector has crucial role in our economy in terms of employment and its contribution to the NDP, savings, and capital formation. At present, there is a special need to take care of the interests of these women by providing them training and upgrading their skills and other measures to enable them to find new avenue of employment and improve their productivity in the existing employment, necessary to enhance the competitiveness of their product in terms of both quality and cost which would also help in improving their income and thereby raising their socio-economic status. It has been experienced that organized sector could not provide adequate opportunities to accommodate the workforce in the country and unorganized sector has been providing employment for their subsistence and survival. Keeping in view the existing economic scenario, the unorganized sector will expand further in the years to come. It needs to be strengthened and activated so that it could act as a vehicle of employment provider and social development.

Increasing the role of unorganized sector in the economy of greater Chennai emphasizes the need to undertake the study on this sector. Different studies (Gulati, 1993) focused attention towards the adverse working condition of women as well as relatively low wages in this sector. Women in unorganized sectors are casual, contractual, migrant, home-based, and own-account workers who attempt to earn a living from whatever meagre assets and skills they possess. Women in unorganized sectors are self-employed as hawkers, vendors, and micro-enterprises involved in a large number of assorted activities. The series of economic problems that confront women in unorganized sectors are low earnings, continued indebtedness, harsh, exploitative working conditions, etc. The study focused on these issues of women in order to solve their problems. Thereby, these women workers in the unorganized sectors will be able to get requisite level of protection and security to have decent working environment enabling them to express their skills fully and according to their capabilities necessary for enhancing the competitiveness of their outputs and raising their income and socio-economic status. Hence, this study focused on gender perspective on economic status of women in unorganized sector.

Research Design

The research design used in this study is exploratory-cum-descriptive. Chennai, Tamil Nadu, is chosen as the study area. The study points out that there are two types of employment available in the city's unorganized sector: casual or contract labour and self-employment. Both provide low and irregular income, lack of social security, little regulation in work, and absence of legal protection. Types of work include hawking and street vending and providing services and home-based work. In this study, the four-fold classification of women workers has been adopted. Women participants in the category of trade are chosen for detailed empirical study. Women involved in fruit, flower, and vegetable selling are included in the category of trade. These women workers involved under the category of trade can also be classified under the category of self-employed or worker-cum-owner also. Chennai city is divided into three divisions on the basis of parliamentary constituency, i.e., Chennai North, Chennai Central, and Chennai South. In three divisions of Chennai, five areas from each division were randomly selected. So, 15 areas were taken from Chennai city for the study purpose. In total 450 respondents were selected for the study and in each area 30 respondents were interviewed.

The tools used for the data collection was an interview schedule. The schedule had both close-ended and open-ended questions. But mostly the framework of the schedule was based on close-ended questions.

Objectives of the study are to understand the employment pattern and the problem of women in unorganized sector in respect of opportunities for continuous employment and socio-economic improvement and expansion; to identify the influence on the unorganized sector in the generation of income, consumption, savings, and investment; and to analyse the economic freedom and the empowerment of women in unorganized sector.

This paper presents the descriptive and inferential analysis of testing various hypotheses by using Chi-square test, ANOVA, and *t*-test to understand the employment pattern and the problem of women in unorganized sector in respect of opportunities for continuous employment, socio-economic improvement and expansion, characterization of unorganized sector's employment, income and well-being, the economic freedom, and the empowerment of women in unorganized sector as deduced from the field data.

Results

Nature of Job and Problems in Unorganized Sector

Women's involvement in the unorganized sector has high incidence of casual labour with women mostly doing intermittent jobs at extremely low wages or working on their own for very uneconomical returns. There is a total lack of job security and social security benefits. The areas of exploitation are high in long hours, unsatisfactory work conditions, and health hazards. Most of the activities in the unorganized sector did not require special skill or experience. All the respondents

reported that they had taken up their respective economic activities as a source of living or to supplement their household income. It is observed that 36 per cent of the respondents have adopted their traditional occupation and 64 per cent of them did not follow their traditional occupation. Studies show that by and large those involved in unorganized activities are not in the job or trade by their own choice. Lack of other opportunities, partly due to their deficiencies such as illiteracy and lack of skill and partly due to failure in other ventures for want of drive, diligence, and determination, has constrained many to enter into unorganized activities which have the least restriction and only the discipline 'self-employed'.

Figure 1

Distribution Showing the Reasons for Taking up the Profession (in %)

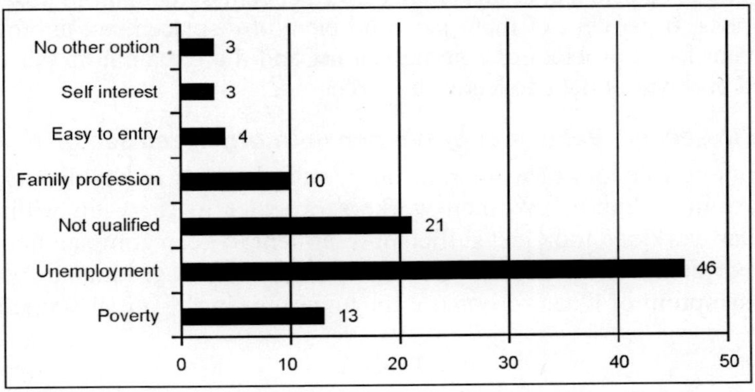

Majority of the respondents, i.e., 46 per cent of them entered this job because of unemployment, while 21 per cent of the respondents took this profession due to being less qualified, 13 per cent of them due to poverty, 10 per cent of them entered this profession because of it being the family profession, 7 per cent of them due to easy entry and self-interest, and the remaining 3 per cent of them had no other option (Figure 1).

Continuation in a particular job or economic activity over a time suggests two divergent reasons: One could be job satisfaction and increase in earnings in that job and the other reason may be there is no scope for another job and hence continuance in the same job becomes a necessity. Majority of the respondents, i.e., 49 per cent of the respondents have less than 10 years of experience, 25 per cent of the respondents have 11–15 years of experience, 14 per cent of them have 16–20 years of experience, 7 per cent of them have 20–25 years of experience, and 5 per cent of them have more than 25 years of experience. This indicates that they have a tendency to continue in the same profession either due to rise in income or because of their inability to move to other jobs. It was also observed that 62 per cent of the respondent's nature of job is stationary and the remaining 38 per cent of the respondent's nature of job is mobile. Hence, the study deals with both mobile and stationary nature of selling fruits, flowers and vegetables. Women in unorganized sector maintained rapport with the customers. For instance, 58 per cent of the respondents have regular customers' everyday, 27 per cent of them have regular customers every week and 15 per cent of them have occasional customers for their business. Sixty-five per cent of the respondents have no plan for expansion and the remaining 35 per cent of them have planned to expand the business. Half of the respondents reported harassment in their day to day business, 22 per cent of them faced problem of local notices, 12 per cent of them faced problem of bribes, 6 per cent of them faced problem of displacement, another 6 per cent faced problem of commercial tax and the remaining 5 per cent faced problem of debt collective by force.

Health-seeking Behaviour of Women in Unorganized Sector

Economic freedom of women in unorganized sector in health-seeking behaviour is limited. Women workers in order to carry on with the regular workload took just sufficient treatment to keep going and not to be bedridden. The process of treatment is very clearly graduated. When any symptom of illness crops up, they ignore it in the initial stage. If it

Table 1

Test for Significant Difference between Health Problems with Respect to Time on Economic Activity

Health problems	*Number of cases*	*Mean*	*SD*	*t-value*	*p-value*
Yes	407	7.88	2.43	2.1	0.037*
No	43	7.02	3.66		

*Significant at 5 per cent level.

Table 2

Freedom Enjoyed in Consulting Doctor by Women and Her Husband

Variable	*Number of Pairs*	*Mean*
Consulting doctor by women	248	3.06
Consulting doctor by husband		3.37

persists, they resort to self-medication with the help of the chemist or owner of a medical shop. If it is not cured, the third step is to consult the local doctor. Time is a major occupational variable that has a bearing on the income-generating activities and home-making activities. A major problem is also that the poor and the unorganized women have to resort to multiple and concurrent economic activities for their survival either because of the irregularities in the availability of work or because of low wage which leads to certain health problems.

The unorganized sector is characterized by a multiplicity of occupation in which women are involved in several ways. This multiplicity of work causes various health problems. Table 1 reveals that there is significant difference between health problems with respect to time allocation on economic activity of women in the unorganized sector.

From Table 2, it is highlighted that among the 248 pairs, 3.06 as mean value of enjoyed freedom by women, whereas 3.37 as mean value of husband in consulting doctor, if they fall in sick. This shows that less freedom is enjoyed by women in household decision making than men in the family.

Economic Status of the Women in Unorganized Sector

Household income is the most important variable in terms of which the economic status of the household is studied. Family income, family size, total expenditure, savings, assets, and indebtedness are the variables to determine the economic status of the unorganized women. Hence, in order to verify the degree of relationship among the above-said variables, the correlation coefficient technique has been adopted. It is evident from Table 3 that the degree of associates were quite high at 1 per cent level of significance for the variables Family size and family income (0.2060**), family size and savings (0.1697**), family size and indebtedness (0.2664**), family income and total expenditure (0.2364**), family income and savings (0.1491**), family income and indebtedness (0.1513**), total expenditure and savings (0.3381**), and total expenditure and indebtedness (0.4959**).

To conclude from the above data, the size of the household is positively correlated with family income, total expenditure, savings, and indebtedness: the family income, i.e., the household income also positively correlated with total expenditure, savings, and indebtedness; total expenditure of the family also positively correlated with savings and indebtedness.

Women in unorganized sector lead her family with own earnings. In order to make job profitable, the respondent invest sufficient amount in the vending business. Hence, to verify the degree of association

Table 3

Correlation Coefficients of Economic Status of Unorganized Women

Variables	*Family size*	*Family income*	*Expen-diture*	*Savings*	*Asset*	*Indebted-ness*
Family size	1	0.206**	0.53**	0.169**	0.042	0.266**
Family income	—	1	0.236**	0.149**	0.043	0.151**
Expenditure	—	—	1	0.338**	0.003	0.495**
Savings	—	—	—	1	–0.021	0.056
Asset	—	—	—	—	1	–0.004
Indebtedness	—	—	—	—	—	1

**Significant at 1 per cent level.

among the variables (age, number of years the business started, initial capital investment, daily investment, earnings per day, and loss of commodity), correlation coefficient technique has been adopted.

Table 4

Pair-wise Correlation Coefficients of Employment Pattern of Unorganized Women

Variables	*Coefficient of correlation*
Age and no. of years started the business	0.464**
Age and initial capital investment	0.165**
No. of years started the business and initial capital invest	0.178**
No. of years started the business and earnings per day	0.097**
Initial capital investment and daily investment	0.377**
Initial capital investment and loss of commodity	0.304**
Daily investment and earnings per day	0.144**
Daily investment and loss of commodity	0.337**

**Significant at 1 per cent level.

It is evident from Table 4 that the degree of associates is quite high (at 1% level of significance) for the above given variables. To conclude, age of the respondent is positively correlated with number of years of the business and initial capital investment, number of years of the business is positively correlated with initial capital investment and earnings per day, initial capital investment is positively correlated with daily investment and loss of commodity, and daily investment is positively correlated with earnings per day and loss of commodity.

Earnings per day of the respondent are one of the economic variables dependent on a number of socio-economic variables. Regression analysis reveals that time on household activity, traditional occupation, daily investment, purchase on credit, and shifting from one work to another are the significant determinants of earnings per day of the respondent in unorganized sector.

Inequality is a property of the distribution in a population of some (presumably valued) resource such as income or wealth. The distribution of such quantities is typically highly skewed, with a long tail to the right. Let us conceptualize inequality with the Lorenz curve. Table 5 presents the calculation of percentage of income share accruing to each category of the respondents from poorest to richest.

Table 5

Income Distribution of Women in Unorganized Sector

Income (Y)	*Mid-value*	*Cumulative frequency*	*Ratio*	*Percentage*
0–1500	750	750	0.062	6.25
1500–3000	2250	3000	0.25	25
3000–4500	3750	6750	0.562	56.25
4500–6000	5250	12,000	1	100
Respondents (X)	*Cumulative frequency*	*Ratio*	*Percentage*	
150	150	0.33	33.33	
125	275	0.61	61.11	
92	367	0.82	81.55	
83	450	1	100	

One common measure of inequality is the Gini coefficient. The Gini coefficient is a measure of inequality of a distribution, defined as the ratio of area between the Lorenz curve of the distribution and the curve of the uniform distribution.

The Gini coefficient (or 'Gini Index' or 'Gini Ratio') G is calculated from the Lorenz as the ratio:

$$G = 1 - \sum_{k=1}^{n} (X_k - X_{k-1})(Y_k + Y_{k=1})$$

The Gini coefficient for the analysis of income distribution of women in unorganized sector is 46 per cent.

Discussions

Thus, the gender perspective on economic status of women in unorganized sector is a study of hope and sustained efforts. The advancement of women and the achievement of equality between men and women are a matter of human rights and social justice. Women's involvement in the process of decision making and creating awareness are the most urgent requirements of modern society. Linkage between women's work and vulnerability clearly underlines the necessity of bringing the unorganized sector into the ambit of a national policy which recognizes their contribution to economic processes and protect their legal status. Steps to overcome these problems early especially since this sector is bound to demand the attention of the policymakers and planners as the pace of economic reforms gather further momentum. Particularly in the context of globalization, it is important to pay attention as to how women in this sector can benefit in the process of growth.

Women in unorganized sectors are performing well in the society. Most of the findings speak loudly and clearly in this tone. But there is always something better than the best in every sphere. In the light of such an inspired ambition, the study proposes to make the following suggestions. If the suggestions are well received and carried out, further improvements become easily possible. Based on the study of women in unorganized sectors, the following suggestions are listed to improve the rate.

Ensuring Equality for Unorganized Women

Urban economy with pronounced gender inequalities needs comprehensive programmes to take care of expectant mothers, immunization, awareness against female infanticide, educational attainment levels through higher literacy, educating parents about the benefits of schooling for girls, and increasing the female per capita income to reduce the wage differential between males and females. It is also necessary to draw up a gender policy of the state emphasizing equality for women that focus on the following:

1. Ensuring equal wages on par with women
2. Expanding income-generating activities for women by innovative schemes.
3. Empowering women through education and employment.
4. Gender equity in availing health services.
5. Highlighting gender-specific issues of vulnerable groups.
6. Drawing up a blueprint for the effective prevention of crimes against women.

SHGs for Unorganized Women

1. Development of strong, cohesive, self-help women groups, through inculcation of the spirit of mutual help, self-help, and team spirit.
2. Getting out of moneylender's clutches, the micro-credit should be arranged through banks or co-operative sector.

3. Increased asset base and income, through access to inexpensive and timely credit.
4. Improved access to vital credit for economic activities by making SHGs credit worthy.
5. Financial self-sufficiency and sustainability by building up of SHG corpus.

Social Security for Unorganized Women

Social security systems lead to greater organizing among the unorganized workers. System has to promote membership-based organizations which are controlled and managed by the women workers themselves. These can include trade union, producers' association, etc. Organizing the women in the unorganized sector and provision of social security are closely linked. The two processes need to go side by side and policies need to promote both.

Conclusions

One of the major problems in metropolitan city such as Chennai is urban poverty. Keeping this issue in mind, the government will have to frame suitable policies to enhance the economic status of urban poor, women in particular. Government should extend helping hand to the unorganized women through welfare boards. Study also highlights policy interventions that are require to correct the imbalances. Steps have to be taken to create a well-defined structure within which the diverse activities of this may be performed. The government should formally recognize the unorganized sector and should allocate sufficient funds in the government budget. The sub-sectors of the economy could be encouraged to form co-operatives among themselves for improving their operations. These co-operatives could also design programmes to train and develop the quality of the workers of the unorganized sector. Such measures would go a long way towards not only making the working population in this sector socially responsible but also in accelerating the nation-building process with the least undesirable after effects.

References

Census of India (2001). Government of India.

Gulati, L. (1993). 'Women in the unorganised sector with special reference to Kerala'. In Sharma, A.K., and Singh, S. (eds.): *Women and Work Changing Scenario in India* (pp. 253–266). New Delhi: Indian Society of Labour Economic.

15

A Tale of Two Villages of West Bengal

ASHIS SARKAR

Since independence, the issue of poverty in India has remained a prime concern. Basically, when a person finds it difficult to meet the minimum requirement of acceptable living standards, he or she is considered poor. According to government estimates, there were nearly 220.1 million people living below the poverty line in 2007, comprising nearly 21 per cent of the entire rural population and 15 per cent of the urban population. According to the World Bank estimates, the number of Indian poor constitutes about 33 per cent of the total global poor.

The rate of poverty decline in India was faster during 1981–1990 (59.8–51.3% or by 8.5 percentage points over 9 years) than during 1990–2005 (51.3–41.6% or by 9.7 percentage points over 15 years). Though the poverty rate declined very slowly (about 1 percentage point per annum), yet India has maintained steady progress in this regard. Such rates varied not only over the years but also across the states, being positively related to the average agricultural output per acre, illiteracy, high population growth rate, caste system, and other social evils. Over the years, agriculture in India has seen a steady decline in investment – a matter of great concern. Endowments of physical infrastructure and human resources appear to have played a major role in explaining the trends in poverty reduction; higher initial irrigation intensity, higher literacy, and lower initial infant mortality all contributed to higher long-term rates of poverty reduction in rural areas.

Resources, both natural and human, as well as wealth are very unevenly distributed in India. This disparity creates different poverty ratios for different states. Rural populations primarily depend on

agriculture, which is highly dependant on the spatio-temporal patterns of monsoon rain. Significantly, high variability of monsoon rain in terms of its time of incidence, duration and intensity, and total amount is certainly responsible for flood, draught, and crop failure. Furthermore, the average Indian family size unit is often very large that can amplify the effects of poverty. Also, the prevailing caste system is also a major reason for rural poverty – people from the lower casts are often deprived of a number of facilities and opportunities. The government has planned and implemented several poverty eradication programmes, but the fruits of economic benefits have failed to trickle down to the millions of India's poor. Wealth distribution in India is fairly uneven, with the top 10 per cent of income groups earning 33 per cent of the income. Income inequality in India (Gini coefficient: 32.5 in 1999–2000) is increasing. In addition, India has a higher rate of malnutrition among children under the age of 3 (46% in 2007) than any other country in the world.

Methodology

The interaction between man and his immediate environment produces a series of human and economic landscapes with, of course, various degrees of human control. Its geographical pattern is essentially a manifestation of the resource-based regional economics as controlled by the physical landscapes. The village landscape is usually rural with primary activities distinctively dominant. Agriculture forms the base of the economy, its land use pattern being controlled by the relative elevation of land, location of water body, distance from a river or water body, degree of soil fertility, and the lay out of the transport network. The physical landscape of a village located specially by a river is characterized by several features – first, the elevation of land increases from the channel bank to the village interior; second, the river forms the major source of irrigation; third, the highest part of the land, more precisely the levee is generally occupied by the settlements and roads; fourth, silt and clay often form the major component of soil texture and are most often suited to various forms of agriculture, and fifth, thus the village community always has traditional means of subsistence and often sustains its society and culture based on its physical resource base.

During the entire plan periods of India's economic development, several strategies have been formulated and executed for plugging the loopholes and gearing up the development process especially in the rural areas. But the degree of progress made for achieving better 'quality of life' has not been uniform. Some villages are really developed with better infrastructure for education, health, and transport connectivity, while some are not. Some villages contain better off high-caste community, while there are villages where majority of population is tribal. Thus, there remains a significant disparity of development at the community level in a village. This study is based on the postgraduate field study projects taken up in 2007–08 which focuses mainly on the geographical appraisal of the status of poverty and socio-economic development of two villages of West Bengal – Uttarasol and Barkala of the Paschim Medinipur district. Physical data have been extracted through ground surveying, while the socio-economic data have been collected by door-to-door household enumeration using well-laid questionnaire. Besides, interviewing the older people and some female persons has also been of significant help in identifying their status of living.

Location of the Study Area

Locationally, the study area lies on the *rarh* plain, i.e., the landscape fringing the eastern border of the Chota Nagpur plateau of India. Geologically and lithologically, the area is a little bit more complex one with a heterogeneous mix of the older and newer formations at places. The Dulung river flows across this landscape quite leisurely with some spectacular bends and fluvial features. It is a left bank tributary of the mighty Subarnarekha river and forms the lifeline of the villages situated on both of its banks.

The village of Uttarasol (86°52´54´´ E, 22°28´28´´ N) is situated on the left bank of the Dulung river in Jambani block of Paschim Medinipur district, West Bengal. The Dulung borders the village on its western edge, flowing for a while towards south–south-west and then turning towards south–south-east, with the land rising gently upslope from it towards the east. The cultivated lands are thus aligned in small plots in a west–east alignment, while the settlements though usually following the above alignment as well at time are aligned at right angles to the rivers flow, along either side of the narrow unmetalled roads that traverse the village.

The village of Barkala (86°55´25´´ E, 22°18´16´´ N) is located on the left bank of the Dulung river in Jhargram block, Paschim Medinipur district, West Bengal, downstream from the bridge over the Dulung at Pheko. Flowing towards south-east, the Dulung borders the village to the south-west and the village extends upslope from it towards the north-east, almost always perpendicular to the direction of the flow of the river. The agricultural fields are thus aligned in small plots in a south-west–north-east alignment, while the settlements though usually following the above alignment as well at time are aligned differently, along either side of the narrow unmetalled roads that traverse the village area.

Physical Characteristics

The study area belongs to the *rarh* plains with extensive undulating plains of both degradational and aggradational origin. Average elevation being of the order of 70–100 m, local relief is considerably low. Fluvial deposits are widespread within the flood plains as well as in the lower reaches of the Dulung river. Regionally, the land slopes from south–north as well as from north-west to south-east. Alluvium mixed with gravel occur near the higher grounds, while pure alluvium with different grades of sand, silt, and clay are predominant near the channel as well as near the lower elevation. The surface lithological cover is shallow to moderately deep, normally underlain by thick cover of black, gravelly sandy beds of Sijua formation.

The Dulung river exhibits marked entrenched meandering features upstream at and downstream of Uttarasol. The river winds its way through the landscape with alternate cliff slopes and slip-off slopes where the river is incident at the bank or bending away from it respectively. The river's flow in February was quite sluggish, and the channel had shrunk, not occupying the much wider valley that the river has carved out for itself in previous flood-level flows. The water level was only ankle deep. The velocity of flow in the stream is about 0.84 m/sec. The river exhibits neither proper laminar nor turbulent flow but seems to flow in swift narrow strands, at times gurgling over the stones, cobbles, and pebbles beneath. At this low flow level, a small shoal is seen in mid channel. Furthermore, a long sidebar has formed, attached onto the left bank of the stream, just downstream of the principal settled area of the village and the low bamboo bridge over the stream. The bar is composed of lateritic gravel of various particle sizes. Comparatively larger particle sizes are on top with the smaller gravel bits filling up the gaps within and forming the lower layers.

The river bank is quite steep at places, especially in the upstream portion of the village, where it is composed mostly of compacted sand layers. These sand layers, though apparently unconsolidated, are still quite hard to dislodge and thus form a bank that is steep and upstanding. However, in places, it is in danger of toppling over as the Dulung undercuts it at its base. The bank has a sparse growth of vegetation, mostly of the thorn and scrub type. The steep river bank has been gullied in a few places. Some of the small gullies that meet the Dulung are completely overgrown with these plants making access to them very difficult.

In the downstream direction, the bank height is relatively lesser. The soil too is more compacted and when moist, leaves a sticky film on the fingers. On the long side bar that has developed in the channel, small channels have developed that cut across the bar to meet the mainstream. The bank is quite exposed beneath the roots of the foliage growing on it. It is composed of lateritic beds interspersed with beds of conglomerate and gravel. The framework has attained a dull rust colouration, probably due to oxidization. The matrix having being eroded away in certain places, the bank seems to be pitted full of tiny openings. It is through these openings that water used to irrigate the fields on the higher bank surface above it seeps out and forms tiny channels to join the mainstream. As a result, the foot of the bank has been rendered very soft and squishy underfoot, with an abundance of mud and small puddles of standing water that have been colonized by reeds and algal matter. Where not cultivated, the bank top surface is grassy and has small undulations, all the time rising gently from the river. In keeping with this, all the land profiles measured and drawn show a similar alternating concavo–convex slope segments, which then fall away sharply on reaching the river bank towards the main channel. The gullies have much narrower cross-sections and twisted courses before they meet the main channel. The gully headwalls are quite marked, often devoid of any vegetation, with exposed soil profiles and it seems likely that they will be enlarged and extended even more by the next monsoonal rains.

The nature of the Dulung river at Barkala is markedly different from that at Uttarasol. Here, the river is quite broad and deep enough for small boats to ply on it, even in the dry season. However, the water flow is very sluggish; indeed, the river seems to have almost stagnated in certain parts of the reach bordering the village. The water has a murky grey colouration as compared to the faint blue tinge that characterizes its upstream where the water is much clearer as well. The broader river valley has steep slopes on its right bank, some of which have cascaded into the streams, leaving behind fresh, more lighter coloured, exposed sections of steeply overhanging bank.

Here, the exposed banks on either side are composed of the dull yellowish soil that characterizes the area, with hardly any sign of the rust-coloured banks and soils upstream that had formed due to lateritic influences. The soil is comparatively less friable and has greater clay content, causing it to compact readily and leave behind a stick film on the fingers when moistened. The river seems to have carved out two distinct flow levels for itself, the upper bank and the lower bank surfaces. During the dry season the river flows just below the lower bank surface which however gets submerged during the monsoon season. As a result, no human settlements have developed on the lower bank surface.

In the upstream part of the village, the lower bank surface abounds in reeds, grasses, and small groves of trees that are growing quite wildly. Access to the stream is only possible via a few gently sloping gullies that have been modified by human usage. In the middle of the stream, a small mid-channel island has developed due to local sedimentation. The flanks of this island have been converted into small plots on which paddy is cultivated.

The downstream section of the village area has steeper banks and shows more clearly the two different surfaces that have developed. In this downstream reach, the valley is markedly broader, with the river too seemingly rejuvenated and flowing briskly. The water is clearer and as such, a number of bathing ghats dot each bank. The lower bank surface has been converted into tilled plots, with paddy being the principal crop. The upper bank surface is covered by a dense bamboo thicket and a small mango plantation. The difference in elevation between the two surfaces varies between 6 m and 8 m with the bank wall demarcating it, and being gullied into. A number of gullies have developed, each with its own gently graded concavo–convex long profile and saucer-shaped cross profiles. As a result, the whole bank wall seems to be composed of alternating rises and slumps when viewed from the river and has a dense grass cover.

Table 1

Laboratory Results of the Analysis of Soil Samples

Sample no.	*Soil pH*	*Estimated nitrogen (N2) (lbs/acre)*	*Estimated available phosphate (P)*	*Estimated organic carbon*
S-1	7	45	Poor	below 0.5%
S-2	7	45	Poor	below 0.5%
S-3	6.5	45	Poor	below 0.5%
S-4	6.5	45	Poor	below 0.5%
S-5	6.5	45	Poor	below 0.5%
S-6	7	45	Poor	below 0.5%
S-7	7	45	Poor	below 0.5%
S-8	6.5	45	Poor	below 0.5%
S-9	6.5	45	Poor	below 0.5%

The study area enjoys the humid tropical monsoon climate with distinct wet season and dry season. The meteorological seasons are –

cold weather season (December – February), hot weather season (March – May), south-west monsoon season (June – September), and retreating monsoon season (October – November). January is the coldest month (2EC–5EC) and May is the hottest month (35EC–42EC) with annual range varying in between these extremes. Rain mostly falls during the months of July to September, occurring in the form of monsoon depressions. Annual rainfall lies between 80 and 120 cm and the intensity of rain is often very high. Average diurnal weather conditions during the field survey shows that temperature is high during day times and gradually decreases after sun set. Keeping parity with this, the humidity and pressure also changes. Soil samples have been collected from different locations in the Uttarasol and Barkala villages and their chemical characteristics have been analysed using soil kit.

Thus, it shows that the soil is slightly acidic to neutral. It is quite rich in nitrogen but organic carbon content as well as phosphate content is very low. The physical properties of the soil have been megascopically examined and the fact file is as follows:

Texture	–	fine to coarse
Structure	–	predominantly granular
Clay content	–	low
Porosity	–	high

Therefore, the water retaining capacity of the soil is poor. Considering all these, the fertility status of the soil is poor. However, crops are successfully cultivated during monsoon and using irrigation by either lifting water from the Dulung river or tapping underground water through shallow and deep tube wells (TWs) in favourable locations. Natural vegetation has been mostly cleared for agriculture. However, some still remains along the road side, meander bends at the very high grounds and at some other locations where people abstain from venturing. The species are of tropical deciduous type comprising *Sal, Haritaki, Bahera, thorny bushes*, varieties of *Babul, Mango, Jamun, Pineapple, Bamboo*, etc. Today, government has motivated the Gram Panchayats for afforestation through public awareness campaign in the Social Forestry Scheme and the fallows and unculturable waste lands are gradually being converted into green forest lands.

Thus, the village of Uttarasol has an upstream location, while Barkala lies about 20 km. downstream in the Jhargram block. The topographic character of the two villages is markedly different. Mean elevation of Uttarasol is about 75 m, while that of Barkala is 52m and average bank height in Uttarasol (6–12 m) is much more than in

Barkala (3–6 m). Therefore, the nature and pattern of relief is much more varied in the Uttarasol landscape than that of the Barkala landscape, i.e., spatial variation of relief is relatively more in the upstream location. The flood plain of the Dulung river is much more wide and flat near the Barkala village making irrigation from the river naturally easier. The bio-geographical composition of both the villages is broadly identical. Soils have medium to coarse texture, granular to crumb structure, neutral to acidic in reaction, and are poor in fertility. It requires application of fertilizers for a good harvest. Natural vegetation has been replaced by domesticated plants, although there are patches of *scrub jungles*, *kash ban*, *bamboo groves*, and even rows of *eucalyptus* and sonajhuris planted in an effort of social afforestation.

Economic Characteristics

Uttarasol is a village of Dubra Gram Panchayat (GP) of the Jamboni Panchayat Samiti (CDC) of the Paschim Medinipur Zilla Parishad (district). It covers a total area of about 40.15 ha. The land use/land cover of the village may be divided into seven different categories (Table 2). These are as follows – cultivated area, open scrub, fallow land, settlement, canal, roads, and mounds/higher grounds. The spatial extent of each of these categories is not the same, majority (about three-fourth) falls under the category of agricultural land and are cultivated. The second largest land cover category is the area occupied by natural vegetation of open scrubs that occupy about one-seventh of the total area. Only about 3 per cent of the total area is occupied by settlement holdings and about one-twentieth of the total area remains fallow throughout the year. The remaining categories together cover less than 3 per cent of the total area. Agriculture is the dominant and distinctive economic practice of this village.

The shape of the village is analogous to a wide arrow with its head pointing towards north-west. Morphologically, the arrow head is occupied by the bend of the Dulung river. The levee area and the high grounds are occupied by the settlement holdings. These are the areas free from the hazards of flooding or water logging. The village is connected by a metalled road with Jamboni and two unmetalled roads cutting across the village latitudinally and longitudinally joining the residential holdings and nearby settlements across the Dulung river. The canal and the river run approximately meridionally. About a dozen shallow tube wells (STW) are scattered over the agricultural fields providing irrigation for the crops.

Table 2

Land Use/Land Cover Categories of the Villages, 2007

Category	*Proportion of the Total Area of the Village (%)*	
	Uttarasol	*Barkala*
Cultivable land	74.9	67.9
Fallow land/mound/higher ground	05.3	08.1
Pond, canal, and nayanjuli	01.2	11.3
National highway and village road	00.7	02.5
Bamboo grove/open scrub	15.2	05.6
Settlement	02.7	04.6
Total	100%	100%

Barkala is a village of Chandri Gram Panchayat (GP) of the Jhargram Panchayat Samiti (CDC) of the Paschim Medinipur Zilla Parishad (district). It covers a total area of about 33.83 ha. The land use/land cover of the village may be divided into seven different categories (Table 2), viz., cultivated area, fallow land, nayanjuli, bamboo groves, settlement, canal, roads, ponds, and mounds. Thus, again the cultivated land occupies the largest area, i.e., about two-third of the total. Canal area is almost double and the road side ditches or nayanjulis, the man-made depressions for natural rain water harvesting further add to the order of about one-fourteenth of the total. Bamboo groves are widespread and the village is comparatively more settled with larger number of residential houses. National highway (NH-6) dissects the village through the northern half in a latitudinal fashion joining Kolkata and Mumbai. The Dulung and the canal are roughly parallel to one another's flow north–north-west to south–south-east.

The shape of the village is rectangular, oriented along the south-west–north-east fashion. The Dulung borders the south-east margin of the village. The levee area and the high grounds are occupied by the settlement holdings. These are the areas free from the hazards of flooding or water logging. Almost all the bamboo groves are found in this area. The village is well connected by a metalled road that originates from the NH-6 and goes through the village joining the residential holdings, village amenities, and nearby settlements along the left bank of the Dulung river. The canal and the river run approximately parallel to each other. It is a very old settlement inhabited by some well-off households/families and has a long tradition of agriculture. A very large pond with embankment bears a testimony to this. There is a primary school and also a health centre, both with concrete structure. Agricultural fields are spectacularly spread over the north-eastern part.

Table 3

Occupational Categories of the Villages, 2007

Category	*Proportion of the workers of the village (%)*	
	Uttarasol	*Barkala*
Cultivator + agricultural labourers	45	53
Landless labourer (including brick kiln workers)	23	13
Tutor + cultivator	08	—
Teacher	08	—
Driver + cultivator	08	—
Service holder + cultivator	08	—
Petty shopkeeper	—	07
Government service holder	—	07
Petty shopkeeper + cultivator	—	13
Petty shopkeeper + service holder	—	07
Total	100%	100%

Being a rural area, people are mostly engaged in agriculture. However, there are considerable variations in the functional category of workers. There are farmers, agricultural labourers, brick kiln workers, motor vehicle drivers, teachers, petty business, shop owners, and also service holders. In Uttarasol, about 45 per cent of the working population practice farming; about 15 per cent work as labourers in nearby brick kilns; and 8 per cent each find their employment as agricultural labourers, tuition plus farming, driving plus farming, teaching, and service plus farming (Table 3). The joint activities are remarkable because only farming cannot produce enough for sustenance. In Barkala, about 53 per cent of the working population practice farming; 13 per cent each work as agricultural labourers and farming plus petty business, and 7 per cent each find their employment as business man, government service, and service plus farming (Table 2). The joint functions are significantly high as farming alone cannot produce enough for sustenance.

Earning members vary in number from one family to another (Table 4). In Uttarasol, about 53 per cent of the families are run by only one earning member. There are two earning members in about 38 per cent of the families, three earning members in about 6 per cent of the families, and more than three earning members in 3 per cent of the households. As per capita income increases with higher number of earning members, about 9 per cent of the households of Uttarasol are comparatively rich, 38 per cent poor, and 53 per cent are very poor. In Barkala, about 65 per cent of the families are run by only one earning member. There are two earning members in about 23 per cent of the families, three earning members in about 8 per cent of the families, and more than three earning members in 4 per cent of the households. As per capita income increases with higher number of earning members, about 12 per cent of the households of Uttarasol are comparatively rich, 23 per cent poor, and 65 per cent are very poor.

Table 4

Distribution of Earning Members in the Villages, 2007

No. of earning member	*Proportion of the households of the village (%)*	
	Uttarasol	*Barkala*
1	53	65
2	38	23
3	6	8
More than 3	3	4

Thus, on an average, families are better off in Uttarasol than in Barkala. However, the figures hide an important fact that agricultural families in Barkala are really rich with larger amounts of land resources. However, variety of occupations is more in Uttarasol. This is restricted to the raring of domestic cattle and poultry fowls. The households of the villages also domesticate cattle and fowl to supplement their food as well income on subsistence scale, viz., hens, cows, ducks, and goats. The most notable feature is as follows: first, total number of domesticated animal in Barkala is more than twice than in Uttarasol; and second, the importance of animals as per decreasing order of choice is cow, hen, duck, and goat.

For transport or going places, the villagers mainly use their own feet as well as cheaper modes such as cycle and rickshaw van. Of these, bicycle is the most preferred and common one in both the villages (Uttarasol = 92.3%, Barkala = 62.5%). However, there are at least three households in Barkala, who own costly transports such as bike, jeep, and car. This is because the purchasing power of the Barkala households is relatively high than their Uttarasol counterparts. Besides, the condition of roads is better in Barkala and is suited for diesel- or petrol-driven modern vehicles. In both the villages, there are at least three to five households that do not have any mechanical means of transport as well.

Social Characteristics

In Barkala, about 81.25 per cent of the households are residing for more than 100 years, 12.50 per cent between 50 and 100 years, and only 6.25 per cent for less than 50 years. The corresponding figures for Uttarasol are respectively, 46.15 per cent, 15.38 per cent, and 38.46 per cent. Hence, Barkala is a very old settlement, while Uttarasol has experienced a lot of changes in the last 50 years. The village of Uttarasol has a total of 19 households containing a total population of 69 (male = 28, female = 25, and children = 16), while Barkala has a total of 29 households containing a total population of 117 (male = 45, female = 37, and children = 35).

Barkala has more proportion of population in the broad categories of children, working, old, and the aged, while Uttarasol has comparatively more in the young category (Table 5). About 52.14 per cent of population of Barkala are literate with 34.19 per cent male literate and 17.95 per cent female literate. In Uttarasol, the corresponding figures are 50.72 per cent, 34.78 per cent, and 14.49 per cent. The figures hide an important fact that most of the literate counts are from the children category, who go to school mainly on foot absolutely for mid-day meals.

Table 5

Age Distribution of Members in the Villages, 2007

Barkala		*Age groups (years)*	*Uttarasol*	
No.	*%*		*No.*	*%*
39	33.33	0–14	15	21.74
22	18.8	15–30	29	42.03
32	27.35	31–45	12	17.39
14	11.97	46–60	8	11.59
10	08.55	60+	5	07.25
117	100	Total	69	100

The single room dwelling establishment comprises about 23.08 per cent of households of Uttarasol, double-room about 53.85 per cent, and three-room about 23.07 per cent. In Barkala, the corresponding figures are 6.25 per cent, 43.75 per cent, and 18.75 per cent (remaining with 4–7 room establishments). There is no separate place for cooking in almost 76.93 per cent of the households of Uttarasol and in 50 per cent of the households of Barkala. Cooking is usually done in the courtyard adjoining the house. The poultry consisting of hens and ducks are generally kept in the pits carved in the basement of the house. For goat and cows, there are shed-like structures with open sides and thatched roof.

About 92.31 per cent of the houses of Uttarasol have clay and mud as wall material and only 7.69 per cent bricks. The corresponding figures are 75 per cent and 6.25 per cent (the remaining with concretes). About 75 per cent of the houses of Barkala have clay and mud as flooring material, the remaining brick and concretes. In Uttarasol, all houses have floor made of clay and mud. For roofing purpose, a variety of materials have been used, viz., hay, tiles, asbestos, concrete, thatch, etc. In Uttarasol, 7.69 per cent each of the houses have tiles and asbestos as roofing material; remaining (84.62%) have hay/straw/thatch. In Barkala, 12.5 per cent have asbestos and 25 per cent concrete roofs; remaining (62.5%) have hay/straw/thatch and tiles.

Findings and Discussion

From the perspective of geographical area, Uttarasol is a larger village than Barkala and is largely agricultural, containing a significantly large area under open scrub that provides the villagers the fuel they need. It has smaller household density and settlement frequency. Although it has comparatively more proportion under cultivable land, amount of gross cropped area is relatively less. It is because it lacks adequate facilities for irrigation; the Dulung river in this stretch does not have enough water throughout the year and water table being lower, hence cost of sinking DTWs for irrigation is too high. On the other hand, the proportion of water bodies is significantly high in Barkala, that enjoys better irrigation facility and as a consequence, gross cropped area is larger. This is why the proportion of cultivator is more in Barkala than in Uttarasol. The fertility status of soil is almost identical in both the villages; being poor the soil needs nutrients through fertilization, specially chemical fertilizer; then again it incurs considerable expenditure, the burden of which can be born by only a few. All these are responsible for poor agricultural productivity and smaller diversity.

From the perspective of occupational categories, Uttarasol and Barkala are roughly identical, both primarily in rural economy. However, labour force is relatively large in Uttarasol and unorganized sector is relatively more developed in Barkala. From the variety of occupational categories and their combinations, it is clear that no single occupation can satisfy their both ends meet. Problem of unemployment is huge. Everybody is trying to earn something for their sustenance in whatever ways they can. They live in abject poverty; about 30 per cent of the households can manage two meals a day throughout the year. There is only one tube well in Uttarasol; most of them draw water from Dulung and four wells of the village for domestic purposes. There is again absolutely no sanitation facility in Uttarasol and only a quarter of the households of Barkala have sanitation facility. During times of draught and flood, their condition worsens. Nobody cares for the infrastructure and amenities they should enjoy in their own soil, e.g., roads unmetalled and not maintained; schools and health centres few and far away; transport and communication less developed and costly to them; poor arrangements for STWs and DTWs; afforestation measures not worth mentioning; and electricity is there but very few is able to pay the tariff?

Thus, land use and land cover of both the villages are almost identical with cultivable land as the dominant category. In none of these villages, household industry has been found. However, because of better transport connectivity, early settlement, and cash-yielding bamboo groves, Barkala is more developed. Cost of irrigation is less in Barkala as there remains enough water in the Dulung in this stretch during the lean winter season that makes the cultivation of boro crops easier. Besides, some of the land owners were paid back a large amount of hard cash, when land was acquired by government for constructing and lay outing the national highway.

With deforestation, mainly for fuel wood, loss of top soil decreased the fertility status of soil. Average family size ranges between five and six members per household with poor agricultural productivity, high illiteracy, low income, lack of sanitation, and high dependency, and general status of nutrition has been very poor. Besides, the area is far from endowed with natural resources and poverty alleviation measures and their benefits are little perceptible. All these have given rise to very high BPL population and the prevailing status of poverty and hunger. Geography, both physical and economic, can be held responsible and symbiotically interrelated with the social geography and social issues. The area belongs to the *jangalmahals*, settled by mainly the tribals, where the so-called *Maoists* have been very active these days and are in the everyday news since 2008. Despite planning endeavours, areas mostly on the western fringe of *rarh* often suffer from aridity, deforestation, soil erosion, flash flood, poor economic opportunities, poverty, food inadequacy, and hunger.

The above discussion brings out the following points:

1. Cultivation in both the villages is restricted mostly to the monsoon season due to lack of irrigation facility.

2. Boro cultivation is restricted only to small pockets near the low lands close to the channel of Dulung.
3. Only some comparatively well-off households afford to have STWs for providing water in their fields.
4. Most of the lands remain barren and uncultivated for the remaining part of the year.
5. About 55–65 per cent of the households are run by only one earning member.
6. About 12–16 per cent of the households are comparatively well off in terms of monthly income.
7. More than 70–75 per cent of the households live in abject poverty far below the limit set by the national standard.

Conclusion

Judging from all perspectives, it is a grave situation. But why this is so, particularly in a state that has an experience with a well-functioning panchayat system since 1977? The panchayats implement programmes of poverty alleviation by measuring, targeting (the fraction of resources that were delivered to intended beneficiaries), observing changes in targeting over time within villages, and how these have been associated with changing patterns of inequality of land, literacy, and gender, and of political competition in gram panchayat elections (Bardhan and Mookherjee, 2005). Here poverty is greater, owing to lower wage rates and receive substantially fewer agricultural mini-kits, employment programme grants, and total grants. It is very much possible that, may be the panchayats have been 'captured' by local landed elites who diverted resources to their own benefits rather than the intended beneficiaries (Chattopadhyay, 2005). A major section of the BPL population fails to access the subsidized food meant for them. They are either too poor to lift their quota from the ration shops or some other kind of barrier exists.

It is not unusual that there is a close association between income poverty and under-nutrition. The former often results in food insecurity and low dietary intake due to poor purchasing capacity and poor access to food stuffs, poor environmental hygiene resulting in repeated infections, and low literacy hampering access to available services. Majority of the BPL population is unskilled labourers engaged in manual labour. Hence, under-nutrition has an adverse effect on work capacity and increased susceptibility to infections. Poor work output and absenteeism due to illness reduce their earning and purchasing power.

Now what is to be done! Poverty among the village households in this part of the Junglemahal mainly results from environmental conditions, such as soil erosion and water scarcity, resource constraints including small farms and lack of infrastructure, and institutional problems such as caste- and tribal-based divisions, corruptions, and missing markets (Edmonds et al., 2006). Agriculture needs to be diversified away from paddy to boost rural income. Schemes such as National Horticulture Mission (NHM) should be faithfully promoted by the District Horticulture Development Societies for the popularization and growth of horticulture covering fruits, vegetables, roots and tuber crops, mushroom, spices, flowers, aromatic plants, cashew, and cocoa in a well-planned manner. The Panchayats should be instructed to identify the real destitutes for providing food support, irrespective of caste, creed, religion, belief, and politics. It must also be kept in mind that only food support or cash dole cannot pull them out of the poverty trap; there is no alternative to universalizing elementary education if any long-term effect is sought for the programmes such as poverty alleviation. Besides, one more aspect should also be considered, i.e., the underutilization of government grants; the District Planning Office must take serious steps to eliminate the problem in sensitive areas such as Junglemahal (Srivastava et al., 2004).

References

Bardhan, P., and Mookherjee, D. (2005). *Panchayati Raj and Poverty Alleviation in West Bengal*. Available online at: http://policydialogue.org/tiles/events/bardhan-mookherjee-panchayati-raj-and-poverty-alleviation.pdf

Chattopadhyay, A.K. (2005). 'Distributive impact of agricultural growth in rural West Bengal', *Economic and Political Weekly*,40(53), 5601–5610.

Edmonds, C., Fuwa, N., and Banik, P. (2006). *Poverty Reduction in the Tribal Belt of Eastern India*. Asia Pacific No. 81. Honolulu, HI: East West Center.

Srivastava, S.K., Dutt, C.B.S., Nagaraja, R., Bandyopadhayay, S., Meena Rani, H.C., Hegde, V.S., et al. 2004. 'Strategies for rural poverty alleviation in India – A perspective based on remote sensing and GIS-based nationwide wasteland mapping', *Current Science*, 87(7), 954–959.

16

Case Study of Slum/Pavement Dwellers in Kolkata

ARUP RAY, GAUTAM KUMAR MALLIK AND
CHANDRIMA CHAKRABORTY

The definition of poverty could not be explained in simple way with wide accepted dimension. However, the new 'Encyclopaedia Britannica' has defined 'poverty is the condition that is said to exist when people lack the means to satisfy their basic needs' (1974: 935). In that context, the identification of basic needs is important, the basic needs are starvation or death and inadequate nutrition, housing, clothing, etc. The definition of poverty will not focus the versatile widespread canvas, thus the typology will elaborate the vast characteristic of the poverty. According to new 'Encyclopaedia Britannica', the types of poverty are as follows:

1. *Cyclical poverty:* This is a type of poverty, which is widespread within a population, but the occurrence itself is of limited duration.
2. *Collective poverty:* In contrast to cyclical poverty, it involves a relatively permanent insufficiency of means to secure basic needs.
3. *Concentrated collective poverty:* In many industrialized, relatively affluent countries, particular demographic groups are vulnerable to long-term poverty. The victims in a city, the region bypassed or abandoned by industry or insufficient agriculture, are termed as product of concentrated collective poverty.
4. *Case poverty:* While an individual or a family is incapable to secure basic needs even in social surroundings of general prosperity, this inability is generally related to the lack of some basic attributes that would permit the individual to maintain himself.

The problems in developing countries in regard to poverty are to some extent complicated. The parameters of requirements of basic needs in comparison to developed countries are different. Even the socio-cultural attributes are equally determinant factors in respect of problems related to poverty. However, the three major economic causes are important in respect of that problem, which are as follows:

1. The food supply is insufficient and distribution is not regulated properly.
2. The unequal possession of resources, which is related to gross national product.
3. The problem of financing agricultural industrial entrepreneurships.

The explanation of poverty is another important aspect. There are number of arguments encompassed by economic, social, and cultural reasons. In brief, these categorizations are as follows:

1. *Laissez-faire Theory:* This theory said economy is to be regulated only by the natural market process of supply and demand.
2. *Thomas Malthus' Essay on Principle of Population:* It emphasized and concentrated on population dynamics, which is regulated by war, disease, and famine – the major causes of poverty.
3. *Social Darwinism:* The justification of poverty was reinforced by the advent of 'Social Darwinism' theory, an application of the principles of biological evolution to the social sphere. English sociologist Herbert Spencer, who coined the phrase 'Survival of the fittest', explained the poverty as a phenomenon of unregulated competition among men that led to social and economic progress and the rise of the most able position of power and eminence.
4. *Social Structure of the Poor:* The more plausible approach may be in seeing that the social structure is the ultimate source of the bulk of poverty. This orientation allows one to encompass structural factors (for instance, technological change) that are implicated in poverty as well as to account for the ambiguous role of most of the personal and group attributes usually dealt with.
5. *Theory of Culture of Poverty:* The American anthropologist Oscar Lewis propounded this theory in 1959. He developed this concept from the fieldwork among the urban poor in Mexico. The reasoning is the distinct subculture of the poor with specific norms and values.
6. *The Perspective of Stratification:* Some sociologists have tried to explain the reasoning of poverty as the major cause of stratification, inequality, and conflict. These attributes are supplemented by the social implications of 'underdevelopment' in Third World countries due to malnutrition, poor health care, illiteracy, and lack of infrastructural development.

The above discussion is the outcome of academic discourse of many schools of thoughts. Apart from economic theories, the social theories are the facts of diversified segregated truth that covers a wide canvas without any interlinking. The historical preview may give rise to an insight of interlinking. The socio-cultural parameters are interlinked with the economic and political domain. The anthropological interpretation sometimes emphasizes the social or cultural reasoning without giving any due importance to economic and political situation. This paper is departure from this traditional orientation and likes to give a new kind of understanding on historical review on reasoning of poverty with special illustration to four case studies on pavement/slum dwellers of Kolkata.

Conceptualization of Perspectives

This paper intends to develop two propositions based on bipolar concepts – 'culture of abundance' and 'culture of scarcity', which are built on historical and ecological dictate. Poverty is not an individual occurrence without any socio-economic consequence. The economic theories and doctrines are well accepted and discussed in large spectrum. On the contrary, sociological and anthropological interpretations are not well accepted in this field. Even these theories are more concerned on the causes of social and historical facts, which are directly or indirectly dealt with poverty, but less concentration was given on sociological or cultural explanation on poverty. Amartya Sen gave the well-accepted explanation on eradication of poverty. The focus of his contention is a full-fledged effort on primary education, health and nutrition as well as employment generation.

The most discussed sociological theory on poverty is 'culture of poverty' propounded by Oscar Lewis. At the same time, this approach faced a wide criticism from the sociologists and social scientists. Challenging this approach, many other theses are developed, highlighting situational constrains, lifestyle, and stratification perspectives. Most of these theories are concerned with one aspect of ignoring other factors. Thus, one comprehensive social anthropological approach is required, which encompasses a large spectrum of dimensions, viz., socio-cultural, political, economy, and history. This paper intends to look at the poverty in respect of two social phenomena, 'culture of abundance' and 'culture of scarcity', which emphasize the interrelationship with the above proposition and political–historical truth that culminates the economic state resulting in origin of poverty.

At the onset of this formulation of this conception, there is a need to explain the above-mentioned two social phenomena. The 'culture of abundance' is a state of economic condition where the agricultural production is rich due to favourable ecological condition which entails rich mineral content in soil for good yield, a good irrigation facility along with high rainfall and appropriate temperature and humidity. The society of high productive zone develops a kind of culture that encourages expending and wasting food materials hastily without any thinking on savings. This cultural practice is inculcated historically. The leading role of political turmoil and movement of this region sometimes is a result of surplus food. Agony of majority of downtrodden people is the culmination of the outburst for inequality and the black storage of food material by a section of the society. This kind of social situation out broke into starvation, malnutrition, indebtedness, land alienation, and migration of a large section of people towards urban centres in search of employment. On the contrary, the contrasting social phenomenon 'culture of scarcity' is equally important. This is an economic state where agricultural productivity is low due to ecological constrain. Constrains are due to bad soil without sufficient irrigation and scarcity of rain, sometimes consecutive drought. This situation creates a bad agricultural yield and scarcity of food. The culture is outcome of this kind of adverse economy that encourages the people to develop an aptitude of savings and storage. The society is more susceptible towards protecting any wastage of food and control expenditure by adopting certain social norms and practices. This culture inculcates to form feudal mindset, which preaches royal system with accumulation of wealth or resources by virtue of food. As a result of the fact, a stratified class system develops where the lower strata is the victim of poverty.

These two propositions will help to explain the causes of poverty. We have dealt with the interpretation of the results of urban poverty with historicity of rural background story. By conceptualizing, the two propositions will enable us to interpret the same results of different social situations.

Case Study of Slum/Pavement Dwellers in Kolkata

Thousands of people under open sky with woeful life are a common scene in Kolkata and many other cities of the Third World countries. Kolkata is not only a metropolitan city but also a centre of international trade and market. This place is a melting spot of various sections of population from different parts of India. The geographical position of Kolkata created many problems such as congested housing, narrow roads, continuous traffic problem, and pollution. At the same time, another main problem is the incoming migrations from various parts of rural areas to the city in search of livelihood. In Kolkata, the encroachment of the pavements by the poor people can be considered as a socio-economic problem. However, apparently, it is evaluated as urban problem, though the root is inserted in the rural economic system. In spite of imposing laws and legislations, the authority is incapable of restricting the propensity of intensification of migrations to the major cities. The problem is analysed with proper emphasis on the socio-economic conditions of the slum/pavement dwellers to find out the real cause. Though the data are collected in 1989, but still these are relevant because the entire situation has not changed drastically.

We had selected four places – Narkeldanga, Chetla, Dattabad, and Behala in Kolkata where a large number of slum/pavement dwellers reside. The data are collected based on random sampling. This survey has given main emphasis on demographic aspects and very brief outline on their socio-economic condition traced. The structured schedule asks a set of predetermined questions to them. A total of 108 samples have been collected.

Results

Majority of the surveyed population is of the working age group. Birth places of the old-aged people are at the rural areas from where they had migrated, whereas the birth places of young and children are at Kolkata. The low income compels them to reside on segment manner and complete absence of landed property is the result of absence of large extended or joint families. The large frequency of middle-sized families is found due to high fertility rate. Low frequency of divorce signifies the stable societal bond. The large number of unmarried males and females are present due to limited space and housing. Majority of the people are illiterate or semi-literate. After migrating to urban areas, they have compelled to take varieties of occupations abandoning cultivation. They had come to Kolkata in search of employment for livelihood. These occupations have no security and they collect the salary on daily basis. They are not free from economic deprivation and indebtedness.

The Background Story

The above results are the outcome of certain socio-economic facts that require a thorough overview on the backdrop of their homelands. To understand the reasoning of the migration of the affected slum/pavement dwellers, the foremost task is to identify the regions, which were their homelands. If we look into their homelands, it is found that 24 Parganas and Bangladesh contribute the lion's share. Both regions are belonging to the same geographical territory comprising vast fisheries and water bodies. Thus, before going to discuss the original problem, the historical fact needs elaboration.

The vast tract of forest and swamp, forming the southernmost portion of the Gangetic delta or the Sundarban (the area of 24 Parganas and Bangladesh), extends along the sea face of Bay of Bengal. Its western part is bounded by the Hugli river and stretch up to the Meghna river to the east. It covers an area of 7,532 square miles. In the year 1765, after the Buxar Battle, the British rule started in undivided Bengal. That time the Sundarban occupied a great portion of the lower Bengal. In the year 1828, the British got the proprietary right of the Sundarban and in the year 1830, they started to give lease to the 'Zamindar' and 'Latdar' to reclaim the forest land area and to convert it into paddy land. In the year 1782, Mr Tilman Henckell, a judge and Magistrate of Jessore, first started systematic reclamation of Sundarban forest. Mr Henckell's first step was to clean the jungle of this area; the lands immediately around the clearings were gradually brought under cultivation. In the year 1784, Mr Henckell submitted a scheme for reclamation of the Sundarban, which was approved by the Board of Revenue. The principal proposal was that grants of jungle land should be made on favourable terms to people undertaking to reclaim them. At that time 7,000 acres of land was under cultivation (Omalley, 1941).

The tribes of Chota Nagpur region came in the south delta region and reclaimed the forest and converted that forest land into (paddy) cultivable land. In this reclaimed land, they worked as agricultural labourers and some of them acquired some patch of cultivable land and settled in some pockets of the Sundarban. In the middle of the 1970s, the demand of tiger prawn started in our country as well as in foreign countries. Many multinational companies were eager to export the tiger prawn to foreign countries. The growing demand of tiger prawn encouraged the local people to convert the paddy land into fisheries. The river belts of the deltaic region brackish water fisheries developed. The local Muslim as well as Hindu caste people first started fisheries in the associated lands of rivers where paddy were not growing well due to salinity. Further, due to the gradual growing demand of the tiger prawn in the foreign countries, the fishery owners started to convert the paddy land into brackish water fisheries. It is obvious that the vast paddy land was a mono cropland and the paddy land created the job opportunity for agricultural labourers. People cultivated their own small patch of land and during rainy season, they worked in other's lands as agricultural labourers. This process used to start in the month of June with the advent of rain and ended in the month of November–December. In 7 months of time, they engaged themselves as agricultural labourers for maintenance of their family. In the remaining five months, they worked in the vegetable garden of the local Muslim or Hindu caste people.

The vast tract of paddy field converted from forest in Sundarban helped 'zamindari' system to flourish with plenty in one hand and subsistence level of living in other hand. In spite of sharp class differentiation in a feudal society, it was capable to create job at a certain point of time. The induction of fisheries in that region developed a crisis in employment generation. This is one major cause of large tendency of migration from 24 Parganas and neighbouring Bangladesh. Few people had migrated from Bihar and Uttar Pradesh states. The reasons for this migration from 24 Parganas and Bangladesh are different from the causes of migration from Bihar and UP where main reason of migration from these places is the scarcity of employment in agriculture or any other non-agricultural occupational categories. Nevertheless, these regions are not desert lands and devoid of entrepreneurships. The crisis was due to scarcity of irrigation, control of resources by few people, and lack of effort of creating rural employment.

Discussion

The socio-economic condition of the slum/pavement dwellers and the background stories will help to understand the contention on poverty that is depicted in this paper. The above illustration is neither to consider as a unique situation nor to universalize the entire scenario of urban poverty. Before going to the elaborate discussion, it will be wise to concentrate on the theories and doctrine on poverty as a whole. According to International Encyclopedia of the Social Sciences (1968), poverty may be divided into three types, viz., 'social poverty', 'pauperism', and 'moral poverty'. 'Social poverty' involves, apart from economic inequality (property, income, living standard, etc.), the social inequality in terms of inferiority, dependence, or exploitation. 'Pauperism' is a special category where a certain section of population is conventionally regarded as maintaining minimal living standard without outside assistance. 'Moral poverty' defines a kind of poverty where a society is morally acceptable for the poverty and the people confer or prevent the poor men from enjoying.

Anthropology as a subject in the 19th century deals poverty as evolutionary categories, viz. 'primitive', 'savages', or 'barbarians'. These evolutionary categories were defined in the context of social or behavioural traits with a little emphasis on the occupational shift. Subsequently, the focus of anthropological research took a sharp turn away from poverty debate. Unfortunately, the analysis of power relationship between or within cultures is ignored and attention was given on cultural relativism linking social integrity of the people by virtue of symbolic and geographical boundaries by means of diffusion, borrowing of traits, etc., surprisingly avoiding the issue of poverty. On the contrary, few anthropologists in 1930s–1950s conducted ethnographic research among poor people of non-Western countries including Asia, examining the whole context in terms of ethnicity rather than poverty, class, or power relationship and the issue of poverty debate was disappeared from the anthropological parlance. Afterwards the cultural anthropological research transformed into above-mentioned focus area to analytical redefinition of the poor as 'marginal', 'underclass', etc. The strongest analysis, which is attributed, by Murray and Hernstein (1994) argued that the 'poor people in United States are both culturally and genetically stupid'. These kinds of analysis are termed as 'neo-Malthusian' by certain section. Contemporary cultural anthropologists studied the variegated poor people in the whole world where they are increasingly integrated into a single global economy.

Secluded and sporadic research attempted by certain social and cultural anthropologists by the influence of 'culture of poverty' theory was propounded by the American anthropologist Oscar Lewis in 1959. Despite the fact that serious attempts on the debate on poverty are still absent in cultural anthropological research where most of the studies are conducted on the population who are suffering from malnutrition, poor health, illiteracy, and devoid of opportunity of employment, etc., a comprehensive approach is required to supplement and testify the economic data on poverty. Many sociologists and social anthropologists give prominence of the stigma of caste system to explain the social inequality that according to them is one major cause of exploitation and poverty. This kind of approach is undoubtedly an analytical doctrine to explain the rural poverty in caste-ridden India. The serious setback of this kind of approach is that it ignores the fact of creamy layer within socially depressed caste groups as well as the other socio-economic facts. Thus, there is a need to elaborate what is the comprehensive approach indeed. Comprehensive approach is to explain any social fact considering all factors pertaining to the causes and consequences of this social fact, for instance, poverty in any particular area is to be explained in terms of socio-cultural, economic, demographic, political, ecological, and so on. Again, another bias is sometimes concentrated on the neighbourhood of the social background in a localized field and tries to universalize the parochial doctrine without considering the global scenario. Considering the above approach, the poverty of slum/pavement dwellers in some pockets in Kolkata is analysed and interprets on the backdrop of above illustration.

There are two phenomena, which are binary opposite, viz., 'abundance' and 'scarcity'. Literally both belong to opposite direction.

Naturally, on logical background, the 'abundance' will create affluence and 'scarcity' means attaining poverty. On the contrary, this is oversimplification of any logical conclusion and in the form of social anthropological dialect; this is not the real story. While interpreting the facts and phenomena of the poverty-ridden people of the slum/pavement dwellers of some pockets of Kolkata city, the overall situation is analysed with the help of ecological, demographical, and political background with a consideration of global scenario. The poverty of any urban area particularly in Indian situation is not a mere urban problem; its root has been penetrated into the rural economy. At present, even the rural economy is guided by global situation and the market demands are true exploitation of ecological advantage.

If the origin of the study people is looked into, the two major ecological or geographical territories are found, viz., Sundarban delta, a place of fertile land and plenty of agricultural products, and a plateau region of Uttar Pradesh and Bihar with scarcity of water and food as well as employment. In both cases, the rural people are the victims of poverty and have migrated to a city in search of livelihood and employment. The first case is the resultant of the demand of global market economy. This is a paradigm shift of paddy cultivation by constant conversion of agricultural lands into marine water hubs for prawn cultivation. The changing situation has a tremendous effect on gradual decrease of employment opportunity by means of daily agricultural labours. The situation in Uttar Pradesh and Bihar is not special where the ecology is not favourable to nurture. Obviously, the poverty in this area is a natural outcome and people of this region migrated to a metropolitan city.

Conclusion

The above facts reflect a typical version of poverty and probably challenge the doctrine of the development of localized poverty and urban offshoots. In India, there is a continuum of rural and urban areas. The common notion is that the effect of socio-cultural and economic phenomena of rural area percolates into urban fold. Another trend is to look entire urban problem from factors responsible solely on urban causes. The sole urban causes are also important. The origin of a major chunk of the population of slum/pavement dwellers is Kolkata and the factors of poverty of this section are certainly specific. However, without overlooking this aspect, the emphasis is given on the rural migration to urban centre. The global economy influences rural economy by converting agricultural lands into marine fisheries and because of such development the migration is observed. This analytical viewpoint is emerging from a comprehensive background story of urban poverty depicted by the help of the case study on slum/pavement dwellers of few pockets in Kolkata.

References

Omalley, L.S.S. (1941). *Bengal District Gazetteers 24 Parganas*. Calcutta: The Bengal Secretariat Book Depot.

The New Encyclopaedia Britannica (1974). Vol. 14, Chicago, IL. Available online at: http: //www.britannica.com/

17

Primary Schooling in a Tribal District of India

VIJAYA S. DURDHAWALE

The study is an exploratory analysis of primary education in some selected less developed, tribal villages of Nandurbar district of Maharashtra. According to official estimates as early as 1978, 93 per cent of the population in India was served by a tuition free primary school within 1 kilometre radius (NCERT, 1989). To understand why are so many children out of school, in spite of apparent access, is the basic aim of the study.

Nandurbar district has the maximum tribal population in Maharashtra, located near the hilly region of Satpura and at the southern part of the Narmada river basin. The main tribal communities in this district are *Bhil, Pawara*, and *Kokani*. Reasons for the selection of this district are many. Maharashtra as a whole and all districts, except Nandurbar, has added more literates than the net addition in population (as per District Census Handbook, Census 2001). Disparity in urban–rural literacy is one of the highest in Nandurbar district (28.87 percentage points). It ranked 27th out of 35 districts of Maharashtra in 1981 and over time its rank has been deteriorated as it stands the lowest among all the districts in 2001. During the last decade, the absolute number of illiterates of all the districts in Maharashtra except Nandurbar and Thane has come down. Nandurbar has added 8.1 lakh illiterates from 1991 to 2001 and majority of the illiterates are coming from the rural areas.

Only 23.59 per cent tribes are literate in Nandurbar district as per Census 2001. Gender disparity in Nandurbar district in literacy rate is also the highest in Maharashtra (rural: male literate 62.13% and female literate 40.5%; Census 2001). Thus, the problem of tribal illiteracy in this district is not solved. Hence, the study focuses on the situation of primary school attendance of six selected villages of Nandurbar district. The main objectives of the study are to assess the situation of non-attendance of schools among children aged 6–12 years as reported by their parents and to know the quality of schools of the selected villages.

Methodology

Nandurbar district of Maharashtra is predominantly a tribal district encompassing six tehsils. Out of these six *tehsils*, two are selected, namely, Dhargaon and Akkalkuwa based on the literacy rate (two lower most) and tribal population (two highest). Only 14 per cent population of Dhargaon and 26 per cent in Akkalkuwa are literate (Census 2001). Female literacy is abysmally low – only 8 per cent in Dhargaon and 17 per cent in Akkalkuwa. All the villages were listed of these selected *tehsils* and then six villages are randomly chosen, namely, Dhadgaon, Bijary, Molgi, Toranmal, Khuntamodi, and Khadki.

Total households interviewed were 183. Total children (6–12 years of age) out of 183 households were 245. Information of all eligible children as reported by either of the parents was gathered.

Results and Discussion

Majority of the parents are Hindus (96%), belonging to scheduled tribe category (78%). Fifty-one per cent fathers and 85 per cent mothers are illiterate. Majority of them are labourer. Thirty-three per cent households experience seasonal migration. Half of them have a poor standard of living. Eighty-seven per cent lives in Kachcha household. About four-fifths stay in a nuclear family, though the mean household size is seven.

Reasons for Non-attendance in Schools

Out of total 245 children, 60 per cent are going to primary schools, though proportion of boys is much higher than girls in terms of school attendance. When 70 per cent boys are attending schools, it is applicable only for half of the girls. Among those students who ever attended schools, about 44 per cent faced or are facing some problems in studying (Table 1). Majority of the students who are either dropped out or going to schools do not know how to read and write, as reported by the parents and also examined by the researchers. A large part of the dropped out students never understood what the teacher teaches. Almost 40 per cent parents complained that the teacher is not teaching properly. It is clear from the table that the maximum number of parents has complained about the teaching methods and the teachers instead of the infrastructural complaints.

Reasons for non-attendance to schools (Table 2) as opined by parents (whose child are either dropped out or never attended schools) are burden of household work, poor economic condition, and irregularity of teachers. A majority opined that until and unless their economic status is improving, they would not be sending their children to school as they could not afford both the school-related cost and the opportunity cost. To elucidate the reasons for non-attendance, two-thirds of those who never attended primary schools said that they are very poor and they cannot afford a single penny for sending their children to school. For them, child's schooling is a luxury. Little more than one-fourth of the parents complained about constraints in transportation as a reason for non-attendance in schools, irrespective of the sex of the child. To mention here, while doing the fieldwork researchers faced number of constraints in transportation as the areas are hilly with narrow roads and many a times they had to cross small rivers to reach the schools. Out of the dropped out children, a large proportion of the parents sighted the burden of household work (i.e., mainly taking care of the younger siblings and domestic animals as well as cooking), poverty, and inability of children to read and write as the other reasons for non-attendance.

Table 1

Problems Faced or are Facing by Children 6–12 Years in Studying, as Reported by Parents

(in %)

Problem in studying and in school	*Dropout (N=51)*	*Attending (N=148)*
Do not know how to read and write	49	42.3
No cloth	19.6	12.7
No book	7.8	7
No transport facility	13.7	10.5
No one to help in studying at home	45.1	26.8
Do not understand what teachers teaches	52.9	25.4
Teacher is not coming	15.7	21.8
School often remains closed	13.7	4.2
Teacher is not teaching	—	36
Faced at least one problem	45	43.4

Parents whose children are either not attending school or dropped out were further probed that under what condition they would like to send their children to school. A large proportion of the parents of the non-attendees said that only when their economic condition improves (74%) or the transportation facility is available (47%), they will allow their child to go to school.

Qualitative data reveal that the medium of instruction in these areas is Marathi, which is different from the tribal languages such as *Adivasi* and *Pauri*, and hence, it mostly results in one-way communication with no reciprocity, as reported by block development officer. Our observation reveals that locations of schools in hilly, inaccessible areas along with lack of transportation facility further reduce the school attendance. Forty per cent population of these villages migrates to Gujarat during the month of October to March, as indicated by *Sarva Shiksha Adhikari.* Children are absent in school for 5–6 months for such migratory movement.

Table 2

Reasons for Non-attendance and Dropouts in Schools among Children 6–12 Years, as Reported by Parents

(in %)

	Reasons	*Never attended (N = 47)*	*Dropouts (N = 51)*
1.	Problem related to teaching and school		
	Teacher irregular	31.91	31.37
	School not open	31.91	13.72
	Teacher not teaching/coming	65.95	52.94
	No ashram school	1.96	17.02
2.	HH-related factors		
	Doing household work	53.19	78.43
	Parent migration	14.89	19.6
	Working	57.44	58.82
	Caretaker for younger sibling	34.04	39.21
	No money, very poor	56.86	65.95
3.	Personal related to children		
	Do not know how to read and write	—	43.13
	Children not interested in school	14.89	31.37
	Illness of the child	31.91	23.52
4.	Village related		
	No transport facility	27.65	5.88

As reported by Block Education Officer,

> 'Schools remain closed for 5–10 days in a month (besides Sundays) as teacher visits Tehsil Office for collecting salary, attending teacher's meet, supplying School Statistics to Block Research Offices and attending educational training'. 'So, when will they teach?', added by Tehsildar.

Quality of Schools

Some of the indicators used by the researchers to capture school quality are student-teacher ratio, facilities available in schools, etc. In the selected villages, student-teacher ratio ranges from 24 to 30 students per teacher based on recorded statistics (collected from the schools by the researchers), though in actual terms (based on observation) it goes up to 65. Out of 11 surveyed public schools, fifth class is available only in two schools, though on paper, three schools are having classes up to seventh grade. As observed, seven schools are having only one class where students from first to fourth standard sit together. Out of these 11 schools, four are having single teacher and two teachers run another four schools. To add to inadequacy of space, even the rooms that exist are often used as offices and storerooms since most schools do not have

Table 3

Amenities in Surveyed Schools as Observed

Amenities	*Number of schools*
Electricity	1
At least one classroom	8
Free dress	1
Free books	9
Toilet facility	2
Drinking water	5
Mid day meal	8
Pucca building	2
Blackboard	11
Table–chair for students	5
Chair for teacher	10
Playground	3
Library	1
Hostel	1

Notes: Total number of schools observed is 11.
None of the teachers in the surveyed schools are female.

any space allotted for these purposes. It was common to see classes being held in verandahs and other open spaces. Classes held in open space are bound to be disrupted by monsoon and other extremes of weather, as reported by the teachers. In situation where there is no school building at all, the scope for disruption is enormous and the implications for school participation are obvious. Some statistics that are observed from the 11 schools are given in Table 3.

More than 70 per cent parents reported that free books and free dresses are provided, though toilet facility is lacking in most of the schools. More than half of the parents said that their children do not have the provision of mid-day meal or drinking water, which is a basic need. While more than four-fifth of the parents said that classroom is available, our observation does not support their saying. Observation in the field reveals that most of the schools do not have toilet facilities (for both students and teachers), electricity, and provision of free dress, enough classrooms and pucca building. Though about half of the schools do have the provision for mid-day meals, in most cases uncooked rice is distributed to students for lack of space for cooking, fuel, and also for low attendance of students. Provision for toilet facilities, drinking water, and sitting arrangements for students, and provision of basic books at schools are the bare minimal requirements for improvement of the quality of schools. The observation of schools in Dhargaon can give us a vivid picture about the standard of schools we have in tribal areas.

Excerpts of Observation of Schools in Dhargaon:

> Number of teachers in active service hardly ever crosses two in number and that too they attend school less than twice in a week. Generally majority of the schools have got one room which is also used as a store room for wood, rice grains, straw, etc. School timing is less than official hours. Although the average attendance ranges between 30–40 percent, the teacher records 100 per cent attendance for official statistics. Classes 1–4 are given the same instructions without any differentiation in syllabus or content. Even the medium of instruction (Marathi) is foreign to almost all the students. Instances of elder siblings accompanying their younger brothers and sisters to schools in the absence of proper caretaker at home are also recorded. Schools do not distribute mid-day meals but provide some uncooked rice per student per month on any particular day.

As reported by one of the teachers, they feel victimized for getting this assignment and they bide their time for the next transfer. Thus, majority of the teachers are dissatisfied with low motivation level.

Majority of the parents, when asked about what more they want in schools, demanded 'good quality schools', which means regularity of teachers, concrete school buildings, and provision of basic amenities. They have demanded the provision of drinking water and toilet facility in every school. Teachers have requested for storage facility of drinking water, electricity connection, and construction of more classrooms and renovation of school buildings. They have also suggested increasing the consciousness of parents regarding the need for education through folk media.

However, government is trying its best to universalize elementary education, as it is evident from BDO's comments:

> 'The S.S.A. scheme has a target of 100 per cent enrollment. We have reached very near to our target to enroll all children. But after enrollment, number of parents migrates to Gujarat or nearby cities during the month of October to March. The parents are apathetic in children's education. For these migrated children, we arrange "Sakhar Shala". The basic idea of "Sakhar Shala" is making of temporary arrangement for teaching the migrated children. Now 202 primary schools in Akrani (Dhadgaon) and 236 primary schools in Akkalkuwa are managed by Zela Parishad. We try to set up primary school in each and every village'.

> 'We provide "Wasti shala" for each Pada if it is demanded by parents. "Wasti Shala" is a scheme to bring each and every child to school. In this scheme we appoint a local educated person as a "Swayamsevi Shikshak" (volunteer teacher) and give an honorarium of ₹ 2000 per month. He teaches in local language.'

Policy Relevance and Suggestive Measures

Education still has to play a significant role in the overall development of the poor people and especially among the poor tribal population of India where there is high dropout and low participation rates which is again gender sensitive (Subrahmanian, 2003). The impact of education policy, as mentioned above, on tribal population is disappointing because education planning in India does not take into account the educational needs and aspirations of the poor people. Studies of Balagopalan and Subrahmanian (2003) highlight that children of tribals are pushed out of the schools because teachers feel that tribals are too slow in understanding, the parents are idle and disinterested in their children's studies. The above-mentioned authors also state that despite making elementary education a fundamental right, the sanctioning of one-room schools with less-qualified teachers under Alternate

Education Schemes points to their creating a parallel, second-rate system of schooling for marginalized children. The major strategy of tribal education in India is an assimilationist one of providing residential schools and scholarships for all scheduled tribe children to study away from their homes, without the distractions and contradictions of their homeworld (López and Hanemann, 2003). They study in a mainstream regional language and a curriculum divorced from their realities, transforming them, in most cases, into misfits in their own community by the end of their formal education. The Tenth Plan (2002–2007) in India has, for the first time, formally acknowledged the need to allow greater flexibility and initiate innovative programmes to meet the specific requirements of tribal pockets of the country (López and Hanemann, 2003).

The main reasons, as revealed in the study, for poor performance in literacy and in schools are the lack of information facilities especially in the interior areas along with very poor transport facility as well as pitiable quality of schools (see Ambasht, 2001). Teachers and students have to walk 5–6 kilometres daily to reach their school. These problems get more aggravated during rainy season. Majority of the schools do not provide residential facility for the teachers and student. Boys and girls from these interior villages prefer to go for work instead of attending school that are far away from their village. Second, the family size in many cases is very large (12–14 persons in each family) and for feeding these members, it becomes compulsory for them to go to work. Moreover, many of the parents are not interested to send their child to school because of their poor economic condition. The tribes have their own folk songs, myths, traditions, and stories. The tribal children would only feel a sense of oneness in their study and get interested in the school if their cultural aspects are embedded in the school curriculum. It is, therefore, necessary to keep these aspects in view while framing the syllabus.

Majority of the parents have demanded for good quality schools where the teacher will be present regularly along with the provision of drinking water and toilet facility at schools.

It is also evident from the study that the medium of instruction is the greatest disconnect in the education system. It makes sense to have teachers from the same community or at least people speaking the same language as instructors. In this connection, it is worthwhile to highlight the efficacy of the innovation of *Samaj Sevi Shikshak* which could be further developed. A fact that needs to be highlighted is the discordance of observed and recorded data regarding the quality of schools. In paper, all the schools have experienced regular inspection, a very favourable student-teacher ratio, and first-class school attendance, though in reality the scenario is utterly dull. So, poor school infrastructure, transportation bottleneck, unnecessary burden on teachers for clerical works, poor quality of teaching, insincerity of students, poor attendance, problem in language of instruction, and economic constraints at household are the main reasons of non-attendance.

The policy suggestions that can be based on this study are as follows:

We need to popularize the fundamental utility of education through campaigns, road shows, and door-to-door motivations by influential people of the locality; otherwise, children of the *adivasi* community would be failing to attend the basic education (see Jadhav, 2008).

Enhancing the power of women is necessary to make them understand the need for girl's education. A positive attitude for girls definitely helps girl's attendance to school, as revealed in the study (see Subrahmanian, 2003).

While to retain children in schools, some lucrative elements such as adding extra classes that they like and providing good quality mid-day meal are required. Compulsory vocational training along with regular study has to be included in the course curriculum. This training can augment future earning potential for these children who will benefit from dual utility of basic education along with an initiation into some basic vocational practices (see Chattopadhyay et al., 2005; Chattopadhyay and Durdhawale, 2009).

Economic uncertainty and financial hardship are the contributing factors for the age-old disinterest in education among the tribes of the less developed districts of Maharashtra. Thus, increasing the sources of income is the only way to encourage willing participation in basic education. In this connection, it is better to involve private sector's participation. Private–public partnership could be encouraged to actively promote income-generating schemes, such as contract farming on condition that government will extent tax holidays to the sponsoring companies if they provide financial and infrastructure support to take care of the educational requirement of the kiths and kins of the poor. As hunger is more dangerous than illiteracy, the policymakers need to sort out and prioritize area-specific problems. First and foremost, there is a need to implement programmes for a stable earning through land reform, extension of irrigation, small-scale industrialization, and provision of basic amenities for mere survival of the poor. Public–private partnership in innovative entrepreneurship is necessary to improve the demand as well as the supply side.

Teaching initiatives in local languages is a must for the tribal people, as our experience suggests (see Sinha, 2005). People must be taught and learn in everyday contexts and much learning must be centred on the activities of the cultural calendar and ceremonial events. Learning should be made integral to and relevant to life as it has been observed in many parts of South and Central America which are predominantly inhabited by indigenous people. Western-style education which is followed by the Indian system of education makes little effort to link numeracy to learners' prior knowledge and culture and hence fails to build on their understanding. Research proves that beginning schooling in the children's first language and using his language for continued learning and development is the best way for children to develop to their full potential (see López and Hanemann, 2003).

Provision of transportation and basic amenities in schools need to be guaranteed to attract and retain pupils. If Himachalis can make success in the midst of the mountain terrain, Maharashtra can also do the same. As transportation is one of the major bottlenecks for teachers to come to the schools regularly, teachers and trainers at elementary level must be selected by the community, for the community, and they will be monitored by the local governance.

Maintenance of registers and clerical jobs must be done by the para-teachers, while teachers must be trained for elementary-level teaching. Integrated culturally relevant thematic curriculum based upon cultural calendar should be developed by teachers and communities.

Indian education system has also declared in its policy plan that Universal Elementary Education (UEE) is contextual. The contextuality varies widely across the country. Therefore, the attempt would be to prepare district-specific and population-specific plans for UEE within the broad strategy frame of micro-planning through people's participation.

References

Ambasht, N.K. (2001). *Tribal Education, Problems and Issues*. Delhi: Venkatesh Prakashan.

Balagopalan, S. (2003). 'Neither suited for the home nor for the fields: Inclusion, formal schooling and the adivasi child, *IDS Bulletin*, 34(1), 55–62.

Balagopalan, S., and Subrahmanian, R. (2003). 'Dalit and Adivasi children in schools: Some preliminary research themes and findings', *IDS Bulletin*, 34(1), 43–54.

Census of India (2001). *Provisional Population Totals*, Series 28 Part II, India.

Chattopadhyay, A., Guha, P., and Durdhawale, V. (2005). 'Scenario of primary school attendance: A study of less developed states in India', *Journal of Education, Planning and Administration*, XIX(1), 111–130.

Chattopadhyay, A., and Durdhawale, V. (2009). 'Primary schooling in a tribal district of rural Maharashtra: Some policy relevance', *Journal of Education, Planning and Administration*, XXIII(4), 369–385.

Jadhav, N. (2008). *Empowerment of Dalits and Adivasis Role of Education in the Emerging Economy*, Keynote Address of the Dalit Studies Conference, Centre for the Advanced Study of India, University of Pennsylvania.

López, L.E., and Hanemann, U. (2003) *Adult Education for Indigenous Peoples and Minorities: A Thematic Review*. Report on the Workshop Held at the CONFINTEA V Mid-Term Review Conference, Bangkok, Thailand, September.

NCERT (1989). *Fifth All India Education Survey*. New Delhi: NCERT.

Subrahmanian, R. (2003). *Gender Equality in Education*. Background paper prepared for the Education for All Global Monitoring Report 2003/4 *Gender and Education for All: The Leap Equality*, UNESCO.

Wallace, B., and Eriksson, G. (2003). *Diversity in Gifted Education, International Perspective on Global Issues.* New York: Routledge.

18

Meta-organizational Issues Related to Public–Private Partnerships in Reproductive Health Care

Is Agenda for Access to Health for Poor Clients Clearly Set?

SANDIP ANAND AND R.K. SINHA

Globally, there is historical evolution of involvement of public and private sectors in health services provisioning including reproductive health services. Many a time, nature of relationship between the public and private sectors is seen on the dimension of four types of activities, namely, parallel activities, competitive activities, complementary activities, and collaborative activities. Parallel activities represent co-existence of public and private sectors with little contact between each other, and providing different sets of services to different sectors of the population. Competitive activities in the public and private sectors cater to the same population and compete with each other. Complementary activities from the public and private sectors complement each other either geographically and in terms of population coverage or in terms of range of services provided, e.g., primary care by the public sector and specialist care by the private sector. In collaborative activities, public and private sectors work together on the basis of shared objectives, strategies, and agreed monitoring and evaluation criteria, usually through the formation of a new joint entity for implementation. While these kinds of relationships between the public and private sectors in health care are not new, the 1990s witnessed the development of specific kinds of complementary and collaborative relationships between the two sectors, known as 'public–private partnership' (PPP) (Ravindran, 2003). In the 2000s, PPP seems to have matured further.

PPPs can be broadly defined as 'financial arrangements between governments' and the private sector where the private sector provides financial and other forms of capital to fund the construction and maintenance of government services, including schools, hospitals, water supplies, and road and rail networks (Blake, 2004).

Arguments for PPP

There are two major arguments given in the favour of PPP. The first argument is that it reduces the burden on tax payers by the introduction of private capital, private expertise, and competitive practices to the provision of public services such as family health care, reproductive health care (Grimsey and Lewis, 2002). The second argument is that the private sector is better able to provide services to a higher level of efficiency and effectiveness than the public sector. It is argued that the public sector is characterized by its bureaucratic, mechanistic, and politicized method of operation. So, the interaction of private sector ethos with public sector often helps in promoting managerial efficiency.

Further, on various platforms, it is argued that government alone cannot achieve the social welfare objectives. Many a time, words like state, nation, government, and public are used almost synonymously referring to one kind of 'entity'. Similarly, the term 'private' is also seen as homogeneous entity. However, none of these two can be seen in a monolithic fashion. There are cultural differences associated with these bodies which provide pluralism to it. Often it is quite hard to find a unique answer or the real direction. However, the recent past has given new direction to this. There have been attempts of deregulations in many sectors across the globe. In parallel, private sector has been engaged in enhancing its image in relation to corporate social responsibility and governance (Tapscott and Ticoll 2003; Willmott, 2003). Family health is one of the core sectors, which is being redefined by this. Concomitant impact is redefinition of reproductive health in terms of service providers. This redefinition has triggered many debates related to reproductive health services, its current providers, policy requirements, regulation versus deregulation, autonomy and its uses and misuses, active or passive role of government, control, lack of motivation, and integration of services and its level.

Health Systems and Role of State

The boundary between public and private sectors is blurred. It is observed that many countries have pluralistic health systems with a variety of providers of services and of health-related commodities, including drugs. These pluralistic health systems pose new challenges for government, markets, the organized professionals, and for a variety of organizations that have emerged to assist people in making choices in the new complex environment. It necessitates new approaches which could enable people in gaining access to appropriate health services in a highly pluralistic health system (Bloom and Standing, 2008).

In his description of pluralism, public choice, and the state in the emerging paradigm of health systems, Chernichovsky (2002) had given following classifications:

1. There are countries which provide health care directly through state owned and run facilities. The examples of this kind of system are former socialist states and Scandinavian countries.
2. There are countries with the presence of contract of state with free-standing partners, e.g., commonwealth systems of the United Kingdom, Australia, and Canada. In such countries, care is provided directly by these partners. This kind of system also includes public reimbursement system where consumers pay for care under public entitlement and subsequently get reimbursement by the state. This kind of reimbursement system is optional in Australia and France.
3. There are countries in which there is contract of state with health service providers indirectly through organization and management of care consumption (OMCC) institutions, e.g., in United States through sickness funds. In this system, there is sometimes contracting under compulsory insurance, e.g., in Germany.
4. There are countries where state supports health care consumers through 'vouchers' that they can use to contract directly with providers. In such a situation, citizens/households, usually in conjunction with employer, make tax-exempt contribution to a mandatory individualized account. Individualized account is a kind of medical saving account. Voucher system is present in Singapore (Hsiao, 1992; Massaro and Wong, 1996) and in China (Yip and Hsiao, 1997).

The above four points broadly indicate variations in the role of state in health care systems. These points are often seen in the context of following fundamental policy questions (Hsiao, 1992):

1. The first question focuses on availability of resources for health care in a state. How much resources for health care are present?
2. How and by whom resources are to be allocated among programmes, diseases, and regions?
3. How to maximize the utilization of the resources? There are two broad factors which govern this. The first factor is nature of ownership and organization, and management of health facilities. The second factor is incentive structure.

The study of PPP in reproductive health care primarily needs to address the issue of maximum utilization of the resources as stated by Hsiao (1992).

Method

Primary data collection work as part of qualitative research was undertaken during June to December 2007. In the first phase, the fieldwork was conducted in Patna and then during the second phase, in Ranchi. To conduct the fieldwork in Patna, Janani's staff was approached. Appointment was fixed on telephone and e-mail. Then, the researcher visited Janani's Patna office and interviewed the officers in the departments of MIS (Management Information System), Planning, Sales, Marketing, and Operations. Visits were also made to Titli[1] centre and Surya[2] clinic in Vaishali district of Bihar. Interviews were made of Titli centre owner, his partner, Surya clinic's (nursing home) owner, staff in ward of Surya clinic, staff at pharmacy shop in the campus of clinic, and Janani's NGO coordinator at Surya clinic. In Patna, Health Secretary, Government of Bihar, was approached on his public meeting day on Friday. With the help of his referral, Head (Population Bureau), Head (IEC – Information, Education and Communication), Director (Health and Family welfare), and one representative of health society were interviewed. Interviews of five poor clients were also conducted on the campus of Surya Clinic in Vaishali. The second phase of data collection was conducted in Ranchi (Jharkhand). In Ranchi, appointments were fixed with Constella Futures officials and XISS-Packard foundation representative, and in-depth interviews were conducted. In-depth interview of NGO coordinator of health society in Ranchi was also conducted. In addition, interviews of two representatives from World Bank Institute were also conducted. Primary data collection was aimed at exploring the issues related to PPPs. The following meta-organizational issues related to various stakeholders were explored in the interviews: functional goals, roles and responsibilities, incentives, conflicts, trust, work culture, reproductive health services, affordability, perspective towards poor clients, organizational change, communication, and aspirations.

The paper intends to analyse the meta-organizational issues related to the National Rural Health Mission (NRHM). NRHM aims to forge a partnership between the central, state, and the local governments, set up a platform for involving the Panchayati Raj Institutions (PRIs) and community in the management of primary health programmes and infrastructure, and develop a framework for promoting inter-sectoral convergence for promotive and preventive health care. It is very clear from NRHM goals that collaborations and convergence are the two key strategic issues. In NRHM's plan of action, 'public–private partnership for public health goals, including regulation of private sector' is highlighted as one of its key components (GoI, 2004a).

To empower the local government and PRIs, NRHM has envisaged certain roles. According to NRHM report (GoI, 2004a), the District Health Mission (DHM) has to be led by the *Zila Parishad*. The DHM has to control, guide, and manage all public health institutions in the district, sub-centres, primary health centres (PHCs), and community health centres (CHCs). PRIs have to be involved in the hospital management committees for good hospital management. It also aims at ensuring that health-related database is available to all stakeholders, including *panchayats* at all levels. NRHM report also elaborates on constitution of Hospital Management Society for district hospital, CHCs, and PHCs, after which maintenance grant of ₹ 1 lakh can be released by the Government of India. To ensure decentralization and empowerment of local bodies, there is facilitation of village health planning under the guidance of Village Health and Sanitation Committee (VHSC) of the Gram Panchayat. NRHM aims at exploring models of PPP to supplement with services in the district, such as contractual engagement of district paramedics, hiring services of district specialists on payment of remuneration, and contracting out services to NGOs/accredited private health facilities in the district (GoI, 2004b).

Analysis

First, qualitative data were analysed with the help of ATLAS.ti software package. After preliminary organization of the data and initial categorization, the content analysis was done. Content analysis was done on the categories of trust, conflicts, organizational change, communication, functional goals, roles and responsibilities, incentives, RH services, affordability, aspirations, work culture, and perspective towards poor clients.

Post-content analysis, the content or text was analysed with the help of tools of semiotic analysis. The most important component of semiotic analysis is the study of signs and sign systems. Sign operates on the basis of an agreement about what various images, words, sounds, gestures, and so on mean. Signs can be visual, linguistic, and aural. Understanding the signs requires appreciation of implied communication situation, textual structure (narrative structure or a set of rhetorical devices), and information structure. As well as looking at the form or structure of a piece of text, one has to look at its content. One has to notice what information is presented as new versus taken for granted, what is treated as the important point about the information versus what is treated as incidental. Semiotic analysis also requires understanding of communication codes. Codes are the sets of unspoken rules and conventions that structure sign systems and link signs to meanings. Because codes change over time, they are often talked about as being lapsed or residual (out of date), dominant (the main code or codes being used now), or emergent (new, on the way in) (Barley, 1999). In this study, the analysis covers only linguistic signs. Linguistic signs cover words and phrases, for example, 'Anti Retro Viral Therapy' as name is a linguistic sign – a metaphor – that evokes the curiosity. Curiosity is related to the knowledge of medical interventions. At the broad level, this signifies the complex medical technology and becomes a symbol of complex medical knowledge system.

Findings from Content and Semiotic Analysis

In this section, findings from content and semiotic analysis are presented. The content analysis has been done on the dimensions of trust, conflicts, organizational change, communication, functional goals, roles and responsibilities, incentives, RH services, affordability, aspirations, work culture, and perspective towards poor clients. From the verbatim, semiotic codes are inferred.

Trust

This refers to the verbatim related to trust or lack of trust among stakeholders. Content analysis shows that there is lack of trust among various stakeholders. It is reflected well in verbatim obtained from key stakeholders. Opinion of government is well reflected when a senior official, Ministry of Health, Government of Bihar says, 'NGOs are just interested in minting money'. It seems to be complete denial of the trust upon NGOs. From this, the semiotic code of 'unwillingness' is inferred. Representatives of funding agencies criticize the process followed by the government. In the words of senior representative of a funding agency, 'there has been problem in translating the things at the district level and then to the level of villages. It happens if the plan [NRHM plan] does not evolve from the grass root'. The representative adds to it by saying, 'thanks to our earlier health secretary who has also got education in USA. We avoided conflict between society and directorate. It was due to his vision only that it happened'. It is apparent that funding agencies do not have complete faith in the process followed in NRHM (a public partner), as in their opinion, currently this lacks professionalism. The second verbatim of funding agencies' representative clearly state that leadership in the health ministry is very critical and that only can create culture of mutual trust which is of critical importance for conflict management in partnerships. So, the semiotic code inferred is 'professionalism and leadership'. The lack of trust is further reflected when partner of a funding agency in Bihar says, 'They [funding agency/a large NGO] are doing just business and treat us like their agents'. This verbatim well reflects upon the power structure between funding agencies and their partners. The code of 'subjugation' is inferred here reflecting upon the feelings of partners. Probably, more egalitarian relationship is likely to strengthen the bond between funding agencies and their partners.

Conflicts

Conflicts refer to the work-related conflicts which may arise in the interactions among departments, organizations, or employees. These conflicts are mainly conflicts of interests. Content analysis for this dimension covers the verbatim related to these. Reflecting upon shift in the health care system due to NRHM, a government official in Health Ministry, Government of Bihar (GoB), says, 'People with no experience in [Bihar Health] society are writing BCC [behaviour change communication] reports for the state'. Another official in the same ministry shares the same opinion when he says, 'There was no need of this mission and restructuring, it is just to divide and rule'. These views clearly reflect upon the dissatisfaction of these officials and intra-system conflict within the government bodies. In the voice of government official, semiotic code of 'coercion' is inferred. It is apparent that a new system has been imposed upon them. A representative of a funding agency in Jharkhand shares the same opinion in following words: 'Definitely if we really need to create the convergence among various stakeholders we must have clarity upon the role of various agencies'. Conflict also exists between funding agencies and their partners. An MIS manager of a large NGO in Bihar (defined as part of funding agency) says, 'Even when they (franchise/partners) drop out they do not allow their sign board, etc., to be removed. They have got publicity because of us'. From the voice of funding agencies, the semiotic code of 'Heroism' is inferred. It is clear in their verbatim that they regard themselves as leader in the emerging meta-organization of PPPs. On other hand, partners of funding agencies look at these partnerships from different angle. Commenting upon the contract between funding agencies and its partners, one partner shares his personal experience as 'When they (large NGO) came to me for contract, they said that they had done the survey. As per findings of the survey, cost (including time cost) is 60 per cent for management and 40 per cent for medical component. They had said that they will take care of the 60 per cent. However, that has not happened. In many cases, doctors have not renewed their contracts. I think in the entire Bihar, only 10–11 franchise clinics will be active'.

Here, in the partner's experience, his tolerance towards his big partner is captured. It reflects upon the code of 'tolerance'.

Organizational Change

This dimension refers to the changes which these organizations are facing because of PPP policy. The analysis tries to capture the verbatim representing stakeholders' responses to these changes. It is apparent from the content analysis that like any other organizational change, changes infused through PPP may take longer period of time than the planned time frame of 2005–2012 in NRHM. Verbatim from these stakeholders reflect that. A government official sums it up aptly in following words: 'When the look of Secretariat cannot be changed, how difficult it is to change the PHC, CHC, you can imagine'. From this, the semiotic code of 'resistance' can be clearly inferred. Funding agencies are critical, but specific in their response, 'See, we have been talking about convergence of various stakeholders. But the role clarity is not clear. Even the basic things are not clear, e.g., who is going to handle finance, who HR, etc. There is lot of duplication of work. To give you an example of BCC. Before I came many people were doing the IEC activities. There was complete lack of coordination among those people. I spoke to Health secretary then and tried to streamline. Now I have given the work to an advertising agency and they are doing the things for the states'. From the above verbatim, semiotic code of 'proactivity' is inferred. They are responding more proactively to the process of organizational change. However, partners of these funding agencies are cautious in their approach: 'You have come here before time. Public–Private partnership shall happen but it will take years in Bihar …' Semiotic code of 'Wait and Watch' is inferred here.

Communication

This dimension mainly refers to the interactions (both formal and informal) among stakeholders. It focuses on the issues related to problems in communication. A government official puts these problems in straightforward manner: 'There is complete lack of interaction between us and society [NRHM]'. Semiotic code of 'complain' is inferred here. Complain is made that structure and policies do not facilitate the interactions between directorate and society. A representative of a funding agency in Jharkhand points out more specifically to the problems related to formal communication in heath system, 'Within the system, there has been problem in relation to the document. We got the document on Janani Suraksha Yojana one year before. It appears to me the document has not been understood completely by anyone. At least we need to have 8–10 people in the state who have thorough idea on the document'. From this verbatim, semiotic code of 'suggestion' is inferred here. Partners of funding agencies focus upon their relationship with funding agencies, 'After the contract they do not listen to us. In the beginning meeting and training programme were organized. Now, even that does not happen'. Here, semiotic code of 'complain' is inferred.

Functional Goals

Functional goals refer to the explicit objectives of three organizations, namely, government, funding agencies, and partner of funding agencies. This covers objectives as stated by the representatives of these organizations in the context of PPPs for reproductive health. The functional goals of the government in this context are very explicitly put forward in following words: 'Our objective is to create the common platform for all stakeholders. But prior to that, commitment is required'. It is quite clear that government officials want to take the lead role in governance of reproductive health services. Here, the semiotic code of 'regulation' is inferred. Funding agencies are following their own agenda. This is put directly in following verbatim, 'many a times these decisions are results of administrative simplicity. It may be that USAID was more welcomed in these states and we approached these states because of the needs of these states and finally started working'. From this verbatim, semiotic code of 'expansion' is inferred. It is very clear, that expansion, penetration, and influence are main organizational goals of funding agencies. For partners of funding agencies, this new context of partnerships is seen as an opportunity. It is put clearly by one of the partners, 'I have been associated with this clinic for the last few years. Rupees sixty thousand, I pay as annual fee for it ... I made a contract, with (a large NGO in Bihar) as they said that they will take care of my management issues'. Here, semiotic code of 'convenience' is inferred. This opportunity has come to them because of new policies, which they find very convenient to utilize for their own growth.

Roles and Responsibilities

This refers to the roles and responsibilities of the stakeholders in these organizations. In the content analysis, verbatim related to roles and responsibilities have been captured. Among their government officials, there is a feeling that their role and responsibilities are limited now due to various reasons. The following statement summarizes this, 'Ideally our department would like to handle all the services, but there has been fund crunch for the past several years'. This statement is clear sign or code of 'helplessness'. Stakeholders of funding agencies are more positive about their role and responsibilities. This is well described in following statement, 'I started my career in the Industry before joining Constella Futures, I worked with a market research firm known as Blackstone Market Facts with its New Delhi office. There I was working with social division. Blackstone was a multinational firm, after that I got an opportunity to work with an ad (advertising) agency. I also worked on communication with The Johns Hopkins project. I have been associated with Future group for the last two years and responsible for all its operations in Jharkhand'. From this, it can be clearly inferred that funding agencies are assigning responsibilities in quite liberal manner by giving opportunities to people from different backgrounds. From this, the code of 'openness' is inferred.

Incentives

Incentives refer to the work-related positive reinforcements or rewards as expected by stakeholders in these organizations. In the content analysis, verbatim related to roles and responsibilities have been captured. Work-related incentives are not strong enough for these stakeholders. Head of the Population Bureau in Bihar (part of Health Ministry) says, 'Forget about incentives, we are being discouraged from working. Our powers are being taken away'. An IEC official in the same ministry shares similar views. In his words, 'Things which we used to do earlier are being given to society'. These are the reasons of dissatisfaction in the Ministry of Health, Government of Bihar. From this, the semiotic code of 'helplessness' is inferred. Stakeholders in funding agencies or large NGOs share their views in corporate way. A marketing manager in a large NGO in Bihar says, 'The higher the sales or targets are better incentives we get. It is like a company'. From this, semiotic code of 'performance' is inferred. Partners of funding agencies have different views to share. A social marketing franchise of a large NGO in Bihar says, 'For one sterilization referral, I get only ₹ 50 as commission. Even ₹ 20 they take back as registration fee. Per month, I am able to do only 2–3 referrals'. From this, the semiotic code of 'injustice' is inferred.

RH Services

This refers specifically to stakeholders' views in relation to the delivery of reproductive health services. On the delivery of reproductive health services, a very senior official in Ministry of Health, Government of Bihar, says, 'We are here to ensure that people benefit from whatever action we are taking ...'. From this, semiotic code of 'control' is inferred. Funding agencies are critical on it, 'Grass root organizations have not been involved in the state. This is bound to happen if grass root organizations are not involved in the planning. If officials in Ranchi do not understand the document then how they will make district officials to understand it and finally how it will reach to the grass root workers. How is ANM going to understand it? To me, it appears that we have failed completely in meeting the objectives related to coordination between central government hospitals, state officials, district officials and local workers'. From this, semiotic code of 'criticism' is inferred. Partners of funding agencies claim that their services are superior to services at public health facilities. In the words of a partner, 'Emergency case, government hospitals cannot handle. Yesterday, one emergency case had come. They had gone to government hospitals. The government hospital could not handle it. Excessive bleeding was happening. Today, they came to my hospital. I got them operated here in my hospital, blood was given to her. Placenta was operated. Government doctors cannot handle pregnancy-related complications'. From this, the semiotic code of 'superiority' is inferred.

Affordability

This refers specifically to stakeholders' views in relation to the payment capacity by poor clients. Like on other dimensions discussed above, also on this, stakeholders have different views. A senior official in Government of Bihar says, 'We need scientific data on what people can pay for and what they cannot ...' From this, semiotic code of 'objectivity' is inferred. Funding agencies claim, 'We did the study and realized that most of the people can pay for basic services'. From this, semiotic code of 'Justification' is inferred. Partners of funding agencies share different perspective, 'People come to me because government hospitals are very dirty. There is no system. Nobody listens to them. There also they (poor clients) need to pay but in different form' and 'In my hospital, normal delivery charges are ₹ 1,000–1,200; for caesarean the charges are 6,000 to 7,000. The expenses include everything for a week at my hospital ... In Delhi, for similar facilities you will have to pay ₹ 30,000–40,000'. From this, the semiotic code of 'business' is inferred.

Aspirations

This refers to the motives related to the growth of the stakeholders in the organizations or their careers. The content analysis covers verbatim related to aspirations as expressed by the various stakeholders. In this, stakeholders are very clear about their career path and aspirations. The views are conservative and individualistic in nature. Their views are well represented in the words of a government official, 'It depends how close you are to power ...' From this, semiotic code of 'power' is inferred.

Representatives of funding agencies look at the growth of their organizations for their growth. In the words of a representative, 'It shall be great for us if that project on HIV/AIDS comes to us. That is huge. It will change the entire look of our organization'. From this, semiotic code of 'expansion' is inferred. Partners have different aspirations, 'We got associated with them because they were big organization but reality is that in local area people know them because of us, it is not that I am known because of them. It is Alok-Surya nursing home' and 'Alok-Surya nursing home is so popular that people know me as Dr Alok'. From this, the semiotic code of 'arrogance' is inferred.

Work Culture

Work culture in this analysis focuses upon the verbatim related to the process of decision making in these organizations. Work culture is well reflected in the words of senior government officials: 'We can do only those things which have been approved by seniors, irrespective of our opinions' and 'My seniors are not allowing me to go for a training programme abroad'. From this, very clearly, the semiotic code of 'red-tapism' is inferred. Funding agencies present different dimensions of work culture. In the words of a representative from a funding agency in Jharkhand, 'We do not go on our own to talk to any body in the health machinery unless and until secretaries tell me to do so. If secretary tell us to go to anybody then we shall be meeting those designates and shall be taking instructions from those people'. From this, semiotic code of 'professionalism' is inferred. On the contrary, a partner (franchise owner) of a large NGO says, 'All the decisions in my hospital I take'. That is a straightforward expression of semiotic code of 'entrepreneurial control'.

Perspective towards Poor clients

This dimension reflects upon stakeholders' views about policies and its impact on the poor clients. There are different opinions on this. In a widely established notion, the government officials or bureaucrats are regarded as generalist. But they think that they are experts as they are engaged in this profession over the years. They derive their expertise from their experience. This position of government is well captured in following verbatim, 'We have been doing this job since independence and know the best what should be done for people'. From this, semiotic code of 'expertise' is inferred. Funding agencies feel that they are providing alternatives for poor clients. In the words of one of their representatives, 'There has been complete failure of health system in Bihar ... we are providing alternatives for people. We are supporting government'. From this, semiotic code of 'plurality' is inferred. Partners of funding agencies look at it from poor clients' perspectives. In the words of one partner, 'Government is promoting its own system. In Janani Suraksha Yojna, the women are getting ₹ 1200 for delivery in government hospitals. So, they (poor clients) are going to those hospitals'. From this, semiotic code of 'demand' is inferred. Partner also hints upon the perception that though in policy, a woman is authorized to receive money even for delivery in private hospitals. However, there is perceptual barrier existing in the minds of poor clients that money claim is limited to public hospitals.

Views of Poor clients

This subsection is based on the opinion of only five poor clients. Two key verbatim have been used here to represent their opinions on this issue. One client says, 'These people [franchise/partner clinic of a large NGO in Bihar] are better than government hospitals; at least they listen to us'. Adding to it, 'In government hospitals, even if you spend money, nothing moves'. From these two verbatim, semiotic code of 'dignified treatment' is inferred.

Framework of Semiotic Analysis

Semiotic analysis identifies the codes of openness, performance, heroism, professionalism, criticism, justification, pluralism, proactivity, and suggestion (language of persuasion) in the verbatim from funding partners. It identifies the codes of regulation, helplessness, coercion, unwillingness, red-tapism, control, objectivity, expertise, resistance complain, and power in the verbatim from government and the codes of convenience, demand, injustice, tolerance, subjugation, control, superiority, business, wait and watch, complain, and arrogance in the verbatim from private partners. Code of demand for dignified treatment is deciphered in the responses of poor clients. This summary of semiotic analysis is presented in Figure 1.

From this framework, it can be inferred that funding agencies are the leaders in this emerging paradigm of PPP and seem to be playing a very proactive role. The role of government is being limited to the role of a facilitator. However, that seems to have led to dissatisfaction, helplessness, and resistance from the side of stakeholders in the government. For private partners, particularly in unorganized sector, PPP is an opportunity to make an impact. However, their focus seems to be only on profit and survival than anything else. In these interactions, there is a very positive sign from poor clients' point of view. There seems to be strengthening of poor clients' or customers' advocacy, resulting in voice assertion for dignified treatment.

Figure 1
Findings from Semiotic Analysis

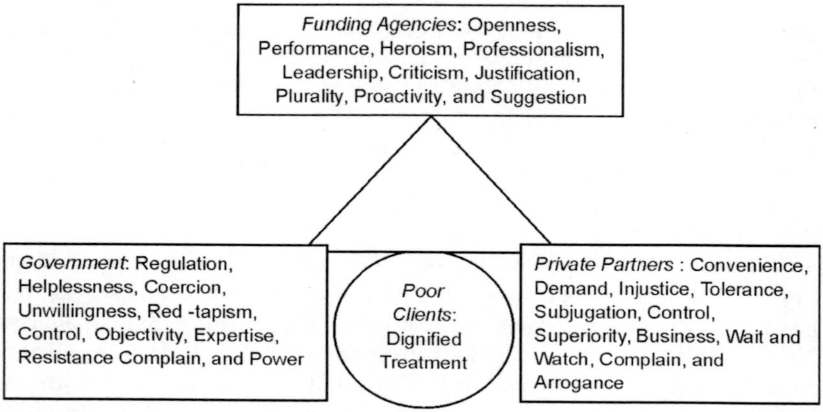

Meta-organizational Nature of PPPs

Findings seem to suggest that today it is not a PPP but it is rather public–private partnership(s). Janani, a reproductive health care organization, also collaborates with many other players apart from government. In such a scenario, the quality issues revolve around conflict of interests, care, and regulation. It is critical for PPPs to ensure that health care services are properly provided and poor clients are protected against negligence and exploitation. This requires efforts of regulation not only from the government, but self-regulation from other stakeholders as well. Partnership(s) also reflect upon the culture of organizations, e.g., in this case Janani, its associates, and policy of Janani. Therefore, the issue is not partnership per se, but collaboration among various stakeholders including the poor clients. Such an approach refers to multi-level partnership paradigm. It gets well reflected in the argument that such collaborations among organizations and communities are likely to provide the genesis for meta-organizations. The findings show that there are conflicts at various levels within Janani, among various departments of government, and partners. Due to lack of openness and trust, conflicts of interests prevail. There is clear lack of a policy which could integrate various players in this emerging meta-organization where organizations of Janani, Government of Bihar, NRHM, franchises of Janani, and poor clients are involved, but locus of control lies beyond any of these organizations. It is indicated that power play rules the decision making and does not allow any structure to emerge which does not fit into its power game. Philosophy is that power is limited and termed as 'zero sum game' cognition. The 'zero sum game' cognition not only promotes the culture of violence within meta-organization but also creates problem in delivery of quality for reproductive health services in India (Anand and Sinha, 2007). The belief that if one stakeholder gains in terms of acting its role towards PPP and other stakeholder gets weakened on that dimension has been referred as 'zero sum game' in the above sentence. It is detrimental for the delivery of reproductive health services as focus becomes on the vested interests and power politics than delivery of services for public. The following two subsections highlight upon the two main issues which have emerged in meta-organization of PPP. The first sub-section 'Meta-organizational Issues Related to Organizational Culture' focuses upon the issues related to organizational culture, while second subsection 'Conflicts of Interests among Stakeholders' discusses the issues of conflict of interests.

Meta-organizational Issues Related to Organizational Culture

Findings indicate that at Janani, employees have well-defined targets, rules, and regulation. They have clear targets in terms of sales, visits to the centres, etc. Office timings are very strict. If one reaches late in office for more than three days in a month, some amount is deducted from the employee's salary for that particular month. Though the exact compensation is not known, however employees feel that it is comparable with the private sector. There is a sense of pride in comparing the organization with private corporations. As per response of one official, 'We are getting more or less same salary as one gets in a good company. We are at par'. It can be inferred here that the reference group is 'corporations'. Corporations as reference group indicate certain set of values which are reflected in day-to-day activities of organization as well as in goals of organization. One of the desired values of organization is to expand its size. One official mentions that Janani also plans to enter into activities for HIV/AIDS in the state of Bihar. The official mentions that one big international donor agency is approaching them for it. The official feels if it happens, it shall be very good for them as they will get additional funds. The official feels that in this manner Janani will also become larger. Though Janani is an NGO, it aspires to become a large visible corporation in India. So, it is found that NGOs like Janani are making an attempt to become corporations.

Conflicts of Interests among Stakeholders

The findings indicate that in Bihar, there seems to be complete collapse of reproductive government/public health system. Even basic needs of employees such as proper compensation are not being met. According to Head, Population Bureau, Government of Bihar, there is minimum amount which a contractual employee is supposed to receive. He says that as per government rules, even for an employee working on contract basis, minimum salary needs to be protected. Even, they need to be given certain allowances. However, according to government official, in case where it has to be paid approximately around ₹ 7,800 per month, the actual payment given is around ₹ 3,900 per month. They feel that system is not ready for that. So, it is indicated that in multi-level partnership, the challenge is to manage the conflicting demands. Medical practitioners feel that it is too early to talk about PPPs in Bihar.

They also feel that the government needs to clearly decide what is good or what is not good for them. When they say that the government can think best in favour of public, it implies that the government is the best judge for collective good. They feel that it happens as government does not decide on ad-hoc basis, but decisions are institutional in nature. They feel that many a time decision-making in private sector is in hurry and takes lesser time than what is required for a wise decision. When asked if decision making takes longer time, then it is likely to result into a wise decision, they respond by saying that no it is not like that. They say that the process of decision making requires optimization of time. They feel that when they have decided to go for PPP, it becomes critical that decision-making process is optimized in its real sense. However, when public sector is compared with the private sector, in public sector delay may be there but the decisions are more going to be collective in nature and thereby meeting the requirements of larger good. This kind of logic as given by senior government officials/bureaucrats strengthens the argument in favour of state. By strengthening the power of state, these officials want to exercise control on the communities to which they serve through their role in health department. The attempt to exercise control is not unexpected. It has been associated with the process of corporatization of public sector's undertakings. The system faces the problems when 'stickiness of identity' is observed (Josserand et al., 2006). The process becomes further complicated in the context of meta-organization, where different kind of stakeholders at different levels are involved.

The above findings are indicative of the dynamics of prevalent conflict of interests. Conflicts are indicated between government (public sector) and NGO (private sector), NGO and its collaborators, and among various departments of these organizations. These conflicts necessitate the creation of a meta-structure. Meta-structure can handle the various conflicting demands emanating from various stakeholders (Anand and Parashar, 2006; Anand and Sinha, 2007). Semiotic analysis of this paper has clearly indicated that all these conflicts reflect upon the symbolism of power which is well grounded in culture of India.

Mechanism of PPP

It is observed in the qualitative study that currently outsourcing (contracting out) is being followed in PHC management particularly support services such as cleaning and maintenance are being contracted out. This kind of contracting out seems to be decentralized in nature. It is referred as decentralized PPPs, where contracting out is happening at the district/village level and decisions related to contracts are being made at that level only. There is second kind of contracting out in the PPPs which is referred as 'centrally decentralized PPPs'. Here, the contracting out is centralized, e.g., contract out of social marketing of contraceptives to Janani in Bihar of behavioural change communication (BCC) to Constella Futures. It is observed in the study that contracting norms are not fully evolved in practice. In NRHM, many committees such as VHSC and *Rogi Kalyan* at various levels of block and districts are planned and there are planned procedures to involve these committees in the monitoring (GoI, 2008). Planned community monitoring process flows from orientation of stakeholders and strengthening of district/block NGOs to mobilization of community to formation and strengthening of VFC/PHC/block/district committees to community-level enquiry to sharing of reports and planning. However, it seems that this kind of planned monitoring system shall require some time to evolve. Currently, government officials express the concerns for monitoring. Monitoring planning as put in NRHM document is not understood by all stakeholders in the state.

There are issues observed in the study related to contracting out. It is observed that there is dearth of 'RH contractors' in unorganized private sector. The term 'RH contractors' refers to contractors who are either trained or have some work experience in the field of reproductive health care. Currently, there are complaints from both the sides, from the side of government and from the side of contractors. Contractors/NGOs, in this case Janani, complain that payments are being not received by them. On the other hand, government officials are making charges of corruption to NGOs. Government officials are also saying that local contractors are mis-utilizing government resources for their personal gains. 'Centrally decentralized public–private partnerships' is found to be relatively better than 'decentralized public–private partnerships' in the study. Wider monitoring is possible in 'centrally decentralized public–private partnerships'. Triangulation in monitoring is possible in the system of 'centrally decentralized public–private partnerships'. There, monitoring could be done by mother NGO/funding agency, local government officials, and community. In 'decentralized public–private partnerships', monitoring is done by local government officials and community only.

Though government officials in Bihar appreciate the efforts of Janani in the area of social marketing and meeting targets on contraceptive, however, at the same time they are also apprehensive about the financial aspects of functioning of Janani. Blake (2004) argued that PPPs create the access to technology and management skills. Seemingly by increasing the plurality,[3] it could also facilitate the utilization of reproductive health services.

Summary and Conclusions

Semiotic analysis identifies the codes of openness, performance, heroism, professionalism, criticism, justification, pluralism, proactivity, and suggestion (language of persuasion) in the verbatim from funding partners. It identifies the codes of regulation, helplessness, coercion, unwillingness, red-tapism, control, objectivity, expertise, resistance complain, and power in the verbatim from government and the codes of convenience, demand, injustice, tolerance, subjugation, control, superiority, business, wait and watch, complain, and arrogance in the verbatim from private partners. Code of demand for dignified treatment is deciphered in the responses of poor clients. It has been inferred that funding agencies are the leaders in this emerging paradigm of PPP and seem to be playing a very proactive role. The role of government is being limited to the role of a facilitator. However, that seems to have led to dissatisfaction, helplessness, and resistance from the side of stakeholders in the government. For private partners, particularly in unorganized sector, PPP is an opportunity to make an impact. However, their focus seems to be only on profit and survival than anything else. In these interactions, there is a very positive sign from poor clients' point of view. There seems to be strengthening of poor clients' or customers' advocacy, resulting in voice assertion for dignified treatment. Findings seem to suggest that today it is not a PPP but public–private partnership(s). Janani, a reproductive health care organization, also collaborates with many other players apart from government. In such a scenario, the quality issues revolve around conflict of interests, care, and regulation. It is critical for PPPs to ensure that health care services are properly provided and poor clients are protected against negligence and exploitation. This requires efforts of regulation not only from the government, but self-regulation from other stakeholders as well. There are issues observed in the study related to contracting out. It is observed that there is dearth of 'RH contractors' in unorganized private sector. The term 'RH contractors' refers to contractors who are either trained or have some work experience in the field of reproductive health care. Currently, there are complaints from both the sides, from the side of government and from the side of contractors. Contractors/NGOs, in this case Janani, complain that payments are being not received by them. On the other hand, government officials are making charges of corruption to NGOs. Government officials are also saying that local contractors are mis-utilizing government resources for their personal gains. 'Centrally decentralized public–private partnerships' is found to be relatively better than 'decentralized public–private partnerships' in the study. Wider monitoring is possible in 'centrally decentralized public–private partnerships'. Triangulation in monitoring is possible in the system of 'centrally decentralized public–private partnerships'. There, monitoring could be done by mother NGO/funding agency, local government officials, and community. In 'decentralized public–private partnerships', monitoring is done by local government officials and community only.

Notes

1. Titli is a name given to franchise centres of Janani, which are responsible for social marketing of contraceptives.
2. Surya is a name of franchise clinics of Janani. These are basically private nursing homes, dispensaries, and clinics that have made contracts with Janani.
3. The term 'plurality' refers to utilization of health facilities in both public and private sector. The assumption is that availability and utilization of health facilities in two sectors enhance the choices or alternatives for public in reproductive health care.

References

Anand, S., and Parashar, V. (2006). 'Integrating local and global knowledge through ICT: Implications for rural business and development', *IIMB Management Review*, 18(18), 85–93.

Anand, S., and Sinha, R.K. (2007). 'Interplay of interests in a reproductive health meta-organization'. *APROS 12 Conference on challenges in Organizing and Managing in Rapidly Emerging Economies: Learning to Organize in the Global World.* Gurgaon: MDI.

Barley, S.R. (1983). 'The codes of the dead: The semiotics of funeral work'. *Journal of Contemporary Ethnography,* Vol. 12(1): 3.

Blake, N. (2004). 'Pros and cons of public private partnerships', *Australian Nursing Journal,* 11(8), 15.

Bloom, G., and Standing, H. (2008). 'Future health systems: Why future? Why now?', *Social Science and Medicine,* 66(10), 2067–2075.

Chernichovsky, D. (2002). 'Pluralism, public choice, and the state in the emerging paradigm in health systems', The Milbank Quarterly, Vol. 80(1): 5–40.

Government of India (GoI) (2004a). *National Rural Health Mission 2005–2012.* New Delhi: Ministry of Health and Family Welfare.

Government of India (2004b). *Report of the PPP Sub-Group on Social Sector*. New Delhi: Planning Commission.

Government of India. (2008). *Community-based Monitoring of Health Services under NRHM*. Available online at: www.nrhmcommunityaction.org (accessed on October 14, 2008).

Grimsey, D., and Lewis, M.K. (2002). 'Evaluating the risks of public private partnerships for infrastructure projects', *International Journal of Project Management*, 20, 107–118.

Hsiao, W.C. (1992). 'Comparing health care systems: What nations can learn from one another', *Journal of Health Politics, Policy and Law,* 17(4), 613–636.

Josserand, E., Teo, S., and Clegg, S. (2006). 'From bureaucratic to post-bureaucratic: The difficulties of transition', *Journal of Organizational Change Management*, 19(1), 54.

Massaro, T.A., and Wong, Y.N. (1996). *Medical Saving Accounts: The Singapore Experience*. NCPA Policy Report No. 203.

Ravindran, T.K.S. (2003). *Health Sector Reform and Public-Private Partnerships for Health in Asia: Implications for Sexual and Reproductive Health Services*. Johannesburg: The Initiative for Sexual and Reproductive Rights in Health Reforms (Women's Health Project).

Tapscott, D., and Ticoll, D. (2003). *The Naked Corporation How the Age of Transparency Will Revolutionize Business*. New York: Free Press.

Willmott, M. (2003). 'Citizen brands: Corporate citizenship, trust and branding', *Journal of Brand Management*, 10, 362–369.

Yip, W., and Hsiao, W. (1997). 'Medical savings accounts: Lessons from China', *Health Affairs*, November–December, 244–251.

19

Assessment of Cervical Cancer Prevention and Treatment Strategies in Low-Resource Countries

Challenges and Revelations

AGNIHOTRAM V. RAMANAKUMAR

In the past three decades, infections have been established as one of the leading aetiological causes of cancer. For example, the hepatitis B virus (HBV) is connected to liver cancer, *Schistosoma haematobium* for bladder cancer, human papillomavirus (HPV) for cervical cancer, and *Helicobacter pylori* for stomach cancer (Sankaranarayanan and Boffetta, 2010). Most of this infection-related cancer burden hails from low- or middle-income countries (LMIC) as epidemiologic observations relate a high prevalence of the virus with high incidence of cancers. These discoveries have resulted in major opportunities for primary prevention, including vaccination against HBV and HPV. At the same time, many developing countries are experiencing demographic and epidemiological transitions; these transitions coupled with aged populations, nutritional changes, and reproductive preferences increase the future cancer risk. Changing risk factors such as delaying the age of first pregnancy, a shorter period of breastfeeding, fewer numbers of pregnancies, increased numbers of overweight and obese individuals, low amounts of physical activity, and higher levels of alcohol intake and environmental pollutants are all strongly associated with an overall increase in cancer rates in the developing world.

Cervical cancer remains the second leading cause of mortality among women living in low-income regions of the world. It accounts for about half a million new incidences worldwide, and will kill about 200,000 women globally (Ferlay et al., 2008). Often cervical cancer-related deaths happen to be during middle age, between 35 and 54 years old, while women are still raising their families. In the past four decades, organized and government-supported cytological screening programmes using the Pap smear test have significantly reduced the rate of cervical cancer in many developed countries; conversely, the clinical burden of precancerous disease has increased significantly. These screening protocols require a minimum of three clinical visits: (a) for screening cytology, (b) for colposcopically guided biopsies for women with abnormal screening results, and (c) for the treatment of precancerous lesions. A single cytological screening test does not offer assurance that it will diagnose the cervical cancer at an early stage as a result of its poor sensitivity of detection. Effectiveness may be achieved only with repeated PAP tests, but such frequent testing is usually not possible in resource-limited counties, where four out of five cancer patients are present. Many countries do not support these preventive screenings or treatments, as they compete with many other communicable diseases or pandemics (Pendzich, n.d.). The key to this impediment is that these countries should not follow the established Western models. It is better to complete screening and treatment at one time for women with an abnormal cytology – which may potentially progress towards cervical cancer – making it more cost-effective for these countries (Schiffman and Castle, 2005). In some developing nations, Pap smear screening is available for only a fraction of the population, out of government services, and in low-risk populations such as maternal clinics. This approach may not help to diagnose cancer and it is not as cost-effective as organized screening programmes.

The Challenges in Resource-Poor Countries

The challenges and difficulties in implementing cytology screening in developing countries have stimulated the search for alternative low-cost methods of screening, such as visual inspection with acetic acid (VIA) or with Lugol's iodine (VILI) and HPV testing. A range of personnel including doctors, nurses, midwives, and paramedical health workers can be rapidly trained to provide visual screening in short-term courses (a week) and a wide range of teaching aids are readily available for training personnel in carrying out visual screening. However, these low-cost tests are subjective tests that have high false-positive rates and low specificity and reproducibility. Standardization and assuring consistent high performance are challenges in field conditions. Constant monitoring and frequent retraining of test providers are needed. In a randomized trail, a one-fourth reduction in cervical cancer incidences and a one-third reduction in cervical cancer mortality were found, following a single round of VIA screenings provided by trained nurses. This reduction is more evident in incidences and mortality rates were observed for the 30 to 39-year-old age group (Schiffman and Castle, 2005).

HPV is the necessary cause for cervical cancer (CCa), which is a common sexually transmitted disease (STD) that infects the cervical cells and slowly results in cellular changes that can ultimately progress towards cancer. These changes can be mild to aggressive and might often progress or regress naturally. Larger and deeper lesions (grade 2+) are more likely to progress towards cancer. In general, women are infected with HPV in their 20s or 30s, although the cancer can take up to two decades after HPV infection. Prevention strategies should identify women with these abnormal cervixes to treat them before they progress towards invasive cancers, continuing and enhanced knowledge is required on this natural history from HPV infection to the development of CCa. Most of the cervical cancer specimens (90%) contain of one of 13 oncogenic types of HPVs, predominantly HPV 16 and HPV 18. Because of this sole root cause of CCa, we can anticipate the primary prevention through vaccination against these two HPVs as the best alternative to preventing it in the future for women, and secondary preventive screening for middle age to older women (Schiffman and Castle, 2005).

Recent HPV DNA testing methods are more sensitive and the results are more easily reproducible than cytological screening for the detection of cervical lesions before they develop into cancer. HPV DNA testing for primary cervical cancer has several diagnostic tests (e.g., HPV high risk and HPV 16/18 DNA tests, and Hybrid Capture 2 HPV DNA test). However, HPV DNA testing is not recommended in women younger than 21 years (Schiffman et al., 2011). HPV DNA testing for high-risk virus types can also be used as a component of both primary screening and workup of abnormal cytology results; it is not useful to test for some low-risk virus types. Adopting these highly reliable HPV tests coupled with better understanding of the natural history of HPV types in relation to various phases of development of cervical cancer will help developing countries redesign or adjust screening algorithms according to their resources. Each country should adopt an optimal age to begin the screening, duration, and frequency of screening based on the most cost-effective strategies. Some mathematical modellers can devise various strategies if decisions are necessary based on hypothetical situations. HPV testing has clearly a higher sensitivity

(90%) but somewhat lower specificity (88%) than cytology. However, HPV tests are limited by its current costs, bulky procedure, and equipment. There are efforts to develop inexpensive and rapid, yet accurate HPV test formats and tests to improve specificity. We need affordable, safe, accurate, reliable, rapid, portable, and acceptable biochemical tests for use in low-resource settings. An important research question is to evaluate the accuracy of the quick HPV tests in routine screening settings. Other molecular markers such as serological testing and determination of viral load may not be cost-effective for low-resource settings (Schiffman et al., 2011).

Most developing countries are undergoing rapid political and economic changes. There is a severe shortage of health care professionals, disparities in health care access, and geographical gaps within countries, which make the cytology or overall screening and treatment very difficult. On other hand, lack of laboratory facilities, follow-up, and other cultural-related factors pose difficulties. In the past decade, several low-cost options have been proposed for cervical cancer screening and they were evaluated in sophisticated study designs (Partridge et al., 2010). Whenever we cannot implement these techniques in the general population, we can also restrict the screening to only high-risk women. High-risk women may be identified as those with a history of STDs, with history of multiple sex partners, and having had sex at a young age. Often countries assume that success of their screening programmes should be like a regular Western model that requires aggressive follow-up and treatment of women with moderate or mild dysplasia. The same goal of mortality reduction might be possible with other ways that better suit their resources. Cost-effective ways include targeting women over 35 years old and treating only women with advanced lesions as outpatient. To become absolutely certain about screen-and-treat strategies (Sankaranarayanan and Boffetta, 2010), we urgently need to validate a treatment that is low-cost, protective, dependably efficient, and similar in performance to cryotherapy, which is not widely available. Cryotherapy with carbon dioxide is an inexpensive treatment option and ever-present but is not reliable in terms of performance. Finding an alternative for this treatment in low-resource settings is a critical missing link that will translate improved screening into improved prevention (Denny et al., 2005). The screening and treatment methods discussed above that are being developed to identify and treat cervical cancer will only be of use to women in developing nations if they are given access to these resources. In recent years, new models have been proposed to maximize the participation of women in screening and treatment and to improve cost-effectiveness and efficiency. This means monitoring a woman once or twice in her life-time screening, between 30 and 50 years, using HPV testing as a primary screening test followed by cytology triage or VIA triage (in low-resource settings). This 'single-visit approach' entails treatment with a cryotherapy or loop electrosurgical excision procedure in the same sitting of screening following of VIA- or HPV-positive women, without diagnostic procedures such as colposcopy and biopsy. The cost-effectiveness of this approach has been confirmed using computer-based models of a variety of cervical cancer screening strategies in India, Kenya, Peru, South Africa, and Thailand, with a one-third lifetime cancer risk reduction for a cost of <500 US dollars (Agosti and Goldie, 2007).

Vaccines designed to prevent dominant HPV types 16 and 18 (which account for 70% of the risk) have been shown effective against new infections with these major carcinogenic types. Since these vaccines only prevent infection before sexual exposure, young women would need to be vaccinated to achieve the maximum effect. Initial data from these trials have established the protective effects and roles of HPV vaccination in cervical cancer prevention. Another advantage of the current vaccine includes cross-protection against other related oncogenic types 31, 33, 35, 45, 52, and 58 (Santos et al., 2004).

Despite advantages that have been seen with the vaccination, there are several disputes and doubts that need to be resolved before it can be widely implemented in developing countries. Current challenges include high cost, feasibility, acceptability, and lack of platforms for delivery systems to adolescent girls. Again, we need long-term follow-up to know their immunogenicity and cross-protection, besides a dose regime (single vs. multiple). These issues are critical and adequate for the global implementation and acceptance of these vaccines. In developing countries, vaccines take a long time (decades) to enter into the public health system; however, they are available on the market to those who can afford them. If we observe previous vaccinations such as Hepatitis B, it took decades to promote them and educate physicians, decision makers, and the public on the benefits of the newer vaccines. In particular, it is challenging to promote these vaccines where public health insurance systems are very week, and health care disparities are widespread.

The coverage of the WHO-recommended universal vaccinations is only about 50–70 per cent in many developing countries, despite the fact that they cost about 5 USD. HPV vaccine prices are currently labelled at about 100 USD, so it is clear that cost is the single most important factor for not reaching the public sector in these countries. Local production of the vaccine, WHO intervention to supply it under its treaties, and alterative technologies are needed for the critical introduction of these vaccines. The GAVI Alliance (formerly known as the Global Alliance for Vaccines and Immunisation) – a partnership of national governments, the World Health Organization, the World Bank, the Bill and Melinda Gates Foundation, the vaccine industry, public health institutions, and non-governmental organizations – provides technical assistance and financial support for vaccines in countries with a gross national income of less than $1,000 per capita, as well as in China, India, and Indonesia (Sankaranarayanan and Boffetta, 2010).

There are several cultural barriers surrounding vaccines. Routine HPV vaccinations are not easy like other mandatory childhood immunizations such as polio or measles, which are contagious in nature. Sex is a major route of transmission, so this may not be placed on the same priority level as other contagious diseases; hence, there are exemptions to vaccine requirements for parents who do not want their children vaccinated based on religious and philosophical grounds. There are still many unknowns for it to be considered as a credible extension to the abstinence-only campaign. Other unknowns include not knowing if and when boosters will be required and not knowing all the side effects and long-term effects of the vaccine including its effects on fertility and pregnancy. There is also fear in some societies that HPV vaccination will encourage premarital sex in adolescents and give them implicit permission to engage in risky sexual behaviours. In addition, adolescents may over-generalize its protection to include other sexually transmitted infections (STIs) such as HIV and therefore practice unsafe sex with devastating consequences. Adolescents are vulnerable to risky behaviour including experimenting with sex without full understanding of the consequences; traditional societies believe that they need to know emphatically that abstinence is the only perfect method of prevention against STIs and unwanted pregnancies. Moreover, some people might misunderstand that the vaccine might give full protection against cervical cancer and may therefore not participate in screening programmes. The HPV vaccine is also more likely to create health disparities between the 'haves' and 'have nots' and it is also not fair to be gender biased since HPV is an STI and therefore should be given to boys as well (Edwin, 2010).

Cancer control strategies should be evidence-based and attentively adapted based on country-specific disease requirements and a country's human and economic resources. If there is no efficient coordination among screening services, most likely new technologies will not be effective in reducing the disease burden. Primary screening with HPV testing is expected to be the future standard of care, but only if the screening is affordable and provides same-day results. New screening algorithms, with HPV testing as the initial screening test, followed by cytology of HPV positives, has been proposed, as this will permit flexible screening intervals. The use of HPV tests is mainly recommended for women 30 years of age and older, where specificity is highest. Women with an abnormal cytology would need to be re-screened with HPV testing at 6–12 months, and if persistently positive, referred for colposcopy (Edwin, 2010). These tests might result in the inappropriate screening of young women, with an important risk of overloading the screening programme (as 80 per cent HPV infections clear within 1 year), overtreating lesions that normally clear within the first few months, and of potential harm, as certain treatments increase the risk of complications in pregnancy. In addition, inadequate counselling and follow-up of women with a positive HPV test and negative cytology might also result in over treating and unnecessary psychological distress, including fear of cancer, anxiety, and being stigmatized. Developing the compliance of professional training programmes and regulatory procedures, and monitoring of health providers are of utmost importance.

In the third world, inequities in access to health care and deprived health care within countries are largely caused by the unequal distribution of power, income, goods, and services, resulting from a mixture of social policies, inequitable economic planning, and bad politics. It is the downstream effect of developmental factors such as nourishing food, clean water, sanitation, housing, health care, literacy, and employment that act in synergistic ways with genetics to determine the life expectancy of a population. With respect to the access to global finances, currently only 5 per cent of global spending on cancer is directed towards developing countries. There is a lack of information regarding health care disparity among gynaecologic cancers worldwide. Yet, one thing is clear, women in developing countries have access to fewer resources and are more likely to suffer serious morbidity and mortality from cancer than their counterparts in the developed world, partly due to the social stigma associated with cancers that primarily affect women. Only 5 per cent of the world's total resources for cancer control reach the developing world. Perhaps the most obvious difference may be found in simply comparing the data available to analyse the problem of different diagnosis and treatment throughout the world. To effect change, steps must be taken to ensure that the degree of the problem can be accurately documented. It is also clear that the health problems of developing countries ultimately become the health problems of developed countries. This was evident in the HIV/AIDS epidemic, which began in sub-Saharan Africa and has become a global disease. The converse is also true: smoking and obesity, which began as health concerns of the developed world, are now playing great roles in disease causality in developing countries. It is the responsibility and moral obligation of international health organizations, as well as resource-rich and developed countries, to provide capital resources, mentorship, and training to aid developing countries in control efforts. In this technologically connected world, mentoring and training colleagues who are thousands of miles away is no longer a frightening task. Many organizations have initiated programmes to help with cancer education and screening programmes in Asia, Africa, and Latin America. The goal of providing equal access to the prevention and treatment of cancers that primarily affect women is a clear issue of social justice (Arrossi et al., 2010).

Conclusions

In conclusion, the burden of cancer in low-income countries is expected to increase in the next few decades, largely because of ageing populations. While this future burden is unavoidable, it will pose an alarming burden on the health systems of these countries. The application of current knowledge from ongoing research in all key areas outlined above would contribute to managing this burden. This includes investigating specific exposures to known carcinogens and to agents, as well as interactions among carcinogens and between genetic and environmental factors. Early detection and down-staging both by screening and by early clinical diagnosis represents an important component of cancer control. All developing countries should support cancer prevention research and should give high priority to their public health agendas at the local and national levels.

References

Agosti, J.M., and Goldie, S.J. (2007). 'Introducing HPV vaccine in developing countries: Key challenges and issues', *New England J of Medicine*, 356(19), 1908–1910.

Arrossi, S., Paolino, M., and Sankaranarayanan, R. (2010). 'Challenges faced by cervical cancer prevention programs in developing countries: A situational analysis of program organization in Argentina', *Revista Panamericana de Salud Pública*, 28(4), 249–257.

Denny, L., Kuhn, L., De Souza, M., Pollack, A.E., Dupree, W., and Wright, T.C., Jr. (2005). 'Screen-and-treat approaches for cervical cancer prevention in low-resource settings: A randomized controlled trial', *JAMA*, 294(17), 2173–2181.

Edwin, A.K. (2010). 'Is routine human papillomavirus vaccination an option for Ghana?' *Ghana Medical Journal*, 44(2), 70–75.

Ferlay, J., Shin, H.R., Bray, F., Forman, D., Mathers, C., and Parkin, D.M.; GLOBOCAN (2008). *Cancer Incidence and Mortality Worldwide: IARC Cancer Base No. 10*. Lyon, France: International Agency for Research on Cancer; 2010. Available online at: http: //globocan.iarc.fr

Partridge, E.E., Abu-Rustum, N.R., and Campos, S.M. (2010). 'Cervical cancer screening', *Journal of National Comprehensive Cancer Network*, 8(12), 1358–1386.

Pendzich, M. (n.d.). 'Cervical cancer: The issue in developing nations'. *Serendip*. Available online at: http://serendip.brynmawr.edu/biology/b103/f01/web1/pendzich.html.

Schiffman, M., and Castle, P.E. (2005). 'The promise of global cervical-cancer prevention', *New England Journal of Medicine*, 353(20), 2101–2014.

Schiffman, M., Wentzensen, N., Wacholder, S., Kinney, W., Gage, J.C., and Castle, P.E. (2011). 'Human papillomavirus testing in the prevention of cervical cancer', *Journal of National Cancer Institute*, 103(5), 368–383.

Sankaranarayanan, R., and Boffetta, P. (2010). 'Research on cancer prevention, detection and management in low- and medium-income countries', *Annals of Oncology*, 21(10), 1935–1943.

Sankaranarayanan, R., Esmy, P.O., Rajkumar, R., Muwonge, R., Swaminathan, R., Shanthakumari, S. et al. (2007). 'Effect of visual screening on cervical cancer incidence and mortality in Tamil Nadu, India: A cluster-randomised trial', *Lancet*, 370(9585), 398–406.

Santos, C.L., Torres, J., Sanchez, J., Dasgupta, A., and Jeronimo, J. (2004). 'Lack of effectiveness of CO. cryotherapy for treatment of CIN', *International Journal of Gynaecology and Obstetrics*, 87(1), 44–45.

Index